P9-ARU-425

PAGES FROM MY LIFE

Zo⁷/
1921
2 short.

Photo by Nickolas Muray, New York

Feodor Chaliapin
1924

PAGES
FROM MY LIFE
AN AUTOBIOGRAPHY

BY

Feodor Ivanovitch Chaliapine

(AUTHORIZED TRANSLATION BY H. M. BUCK)

REVISED, ENLARGED AND EDITED BY

KATHARINE WRIGHT

NEW YORK and LONDON
HARPER & BROTHERS PUBLISHERS
MDCCCCXXVII

PAGES FROM MY LIFE
COPYRIGHT, 1927, BY KATHARINE WRIGHT
PRINTED IN THE U. S. A.
FIRST EDITION
I-B

CONTENTS

CHAPTER ONE

CHAPTER TWO

CHAPTER THREE

CHAPTER FOUR

CHAPTER FIVE

CHAPTER SIX

ILLUSTRATIONS

PAGES FROM MY LIFE

CHAPTER ONE

*Early Childhood—My Parents—I Learn to
Read—Yashka Mamonov, the Clown—I
Become a Choir Boy, Acquire a Violin and
Compose a Trio.*

I REMEMBER when I was five years old.
We lived in a village hut which cost one ruble and a
half a month.

On a dark autumn evening I was sitting in the house of
miller Tikon Karpovitch, in the village of Ometevo near
Kazan, beyond the Sukonnaya suburb. The miller's wife,
Kirilovna, with my mother and two or three neighbours, was
spinning yarn from flax in the semiobscurity of the room,
which was illumined by the flickering, uncertain light of a
torch of firwood called a *loutchina*. The rude torch was
thrust into an iron holder, and the expiring embers fell into
a tub of water, hissing and wheezing, while shadows crept
over the wall, as though some one unseen were hanging up
a black curtain. The rain could be heard pouring down
outside; the wind sighed in the chimney.

The women spun, telling one another in hushed tones
dreadful stories of how dead husbands come to visit their
young widows after dark. The dead man would come flying like a fiery serpent, changing into a sheaf of sparks over
the chimney of the *izba* (peasant hut) and suddenly appearing in the living room in the form of a sparrow, which
changed into the dear one for whose loss the widow was
grieving. She would kiss and caress him, but, should she wish
to put her arms about him, the dead man would ask her not
to touch his back.

"That, my dears," explained Kirilovna, "is because he has no back. There is green fire in the place where his back should be, and if one were to touch it, body and soul would be burned together."

A fiery serpent used to visit a widow in a neighbouring village for a long time, so that she began to wither up and grew very melancholy. The neighbours noticed the change in her and, discovering the cause of her trouble, told her to gather branches in the forest and place them crosswise over all the doors and windows of the hut and over all the cracks and openings. She followed the good people's advice. When the serpent came again he could not get into the hut. In a rage, he turned into a fiery horse and kicked the door so hard that he broke down a whole panel.

My mother also joined in the story-telling. One of her stories I remember to this day, and when I was called upon to sing Rubinstein's opera "The Demon," with the text by Lermontov, our famous Russian poet, my mother's description of the fallen archangel provided a foundation for my study of the rôle. It was about the Archangel Satanail, leader of the heavenly hosts in the service of God. This archangel became very proud and arrogant and tried to stir up the other angels to rebellion against the Most High. God found out about his treacherous plottings and banished Satanail from heaven. It was necessary to find some one to take his place. In heaven there also existed a certain Micha, very shaggy in appearance, with hair growing from his ears and nose and all over his body. This Micha was kind and in general not given to deceiving. Only, once he stole the earth from God. Thereupon God sent for him, shook his finger at him and commanded him to give back the earth. Micha began taking the earth from his ears and nostrils, but did not reveal what was hidden in his mouth. God com-

ROOM IN WHICH I WAS BORN AT KAZAN, 1873

ROOM IN THE HOUSE OF TIKHON KARPOVITCH, WHERE MY MOTHER WENT TO
SPIN WITH HER NEIGHBORS AND I LISTENED TO THEIR SONGS AND STORIES

manded him to open his mouth and spit. Micha did so and out of his mouth came mountains.

Having banished Satanail, God called Micha and said to him:

"Although you are not clever, I think it best for me to appoint you leader of the heavenly hosts. You will not stir up rebellion in heaven. Henceforth you shall be known as Michail. As for Satanail, he shall hereafter be called simply Satan."

Such were the stories the women used to relate. They excited me very much and, although they frightened me, I enjoyed listening to them.

"What wonderful things there are in the world!" I used to think. . . .

Later, the women would begin to sing, to the humming of their spinning wheels—mournful songs about white snowflakes, girlhood's sadness, and the dim light of the *loutchina*, the peasant's torch of firwood. And it really did burn dimly. To the doleful accompaniment of their songs I would begin to see visions of my own. Sometimes I imagined myself flying over the earth on a fiery horse, dashing swiftly past fields of snow. Or I pictured God in the early morning, letting the sun soar like a flaming bird out of a golden cage into the blue expanse of the skies.

"It is late; Ivan should come home soon!" I would hear my mother say through my dreams.

Ivan was my father. He used to come home about midnight, drink his tea at seven every morning, and go away to the Ouprava. The word "Ouprava" used to frighten me, as it reminded me of the court and magistrates, and I had heard much that was terrifying about magistrates. Afterwards I learned that the "Ouprava" was the rural county courthouse, where my father was a clerk.

The Ouprava was about four miles from our village. My

father went to his work at nine in the morning, and came home at four to dinner. At seven in the evening, after resting and drinking tea, he again disappeared to his work until twelve at night.

I noticed once that my father had not come home for two days and that my mother was worried. The third day he came home drunk, and my mother met him with tears and reproaches.

"What shall we do now? What are we going to live on?" she asked in fear and grief.

"Let me be. Go to the devil. Leave me alone! I am tired of hearing you. All I know is that I work, and I must amuse myself sometimes!"

Then I understood that my father went to the Ouprava to work, and that he had spent his month's salary of 30 rubles on drink, as many of the clerks did. I gathered also that our entire life was built up on father's earnings. It was with his money that my mother bought cucumbers and potatoes, made tasty dishes of crumbled stale bread with *kvass* (a drink), pickled cucumbers and onions. And it was with father's money that mother used to make once a month my favourite dish of meat dumplings, a treat I always impatiently waited for, though I knew we could eat it only once a month "after the 20th."

From that time on I took more notice of my father, either because I felt my dependence upon him or because the scene with my mother had upset and frightened me. And he began to drink more and more often, till in the end he used to have a bout every 20th of the month.

At first the date used to go by without quarrels, only mother would cry quietly somewhere in a corner, but after a time my father grew rougher in his way with her, and at last I saw him beat her. I howled, screamed, and tried to help her, but of course it was useless; I only caught some painful blows on my head and neck. I jumped out of reach of my father's blows and went head over heels on the floor; no resource was left me but cries and tears. Once he struck my mother such a blow that she lost consciousness, and I thought she was dead: she lay on a chest with her dress dishevelled and torn, motionless, her eyes closed. I howled with despair, and she opened her eyes, looked round, and then, caressing me, said quietly:

"Don't cry; it's all right!" And taking my head in her lap as she always did, she stroked my hair, saying sadly:

"Never mind what drunken fools do. Take no notice, sonny. Never mind, dear!"

After this scene our life took its usual course: father went punctually to the Ouprava every day; mother spun flax, sewed, mended our clothes, and did her washing. She always sang songs at her work, in a sad, thoughtful way, although she was very thorough in what she was doing.

She must have been a very healthy woman in her youth, for she would complain sometimes:

"I never thought that my back could ache or that it would tire me to clean the floors or do the washing! I used to do all sorts of work without feeling tired, but the work gets the better of me now!"

Father beat her often and sorely. When I was nine years old he had begun to drink not only on the 20th of the month, but on almost every date. I was sorry for her. She was the only person I altogether believed in and to whom I could tell everything that I felt or thought.

She taught me to obey my father and her, impressing on me that life was hard, that it was necessary to work incessantly, and that there was no easy path for the poor. She told me I must strictly obey my father's counsels and commands, that he was wiser—for her he was the undisputed lawgiver. Our home was always spotless, thanks to my mother's labors; a little lamp burned incessantly before the ikon, and I often saw my mother's sad, submissive grey eyes fixed upon the holy symbol, which the tiny spark of light faintly lit up.

Externally my mother was such a woman as you may see by thousands in Russia; she was small, with soft features and grey eyes, and her fair hair was always smoothly combed down. She was modest and unassuming to a degree.

In spite of the continual quarrels between my father and mother, I lived very happily. I had many friends in the village; they were all jolly boys. We used to turn cart-wheels, clambered on roofs and trees, made catapults, and manufactured "serpents" that floated in the wind. We ran about the kitchen gardens, shook the seeds out of the ripe poppies to eat them, stole turnips and cucumbers, wandered about the threshing floors up hill and down dale, finding something to interest us everywhere, and everywhere life showed me her little secrets, teaching me to love and understand living things.

I made a cave for myself behind the kitchen garden, into which I used to get and imagine that it was my house and that I lived alone in the world and free, without father or mother. I used to think how nice it would be for me to have my own cows and horses, imagining in a childish, indistinct way a life like that depicted in fairy tales. The choral dances were my especial delight, which used to be got up twice a year, on two of the great holidays. The girls came with bright-coloured ribands twisted in their long braids and dressed in gaudy gowns, with rouged and powdered faces. The young men also got themselves up especially; they all stood in a circle and, dancing a round dance, sang legendary songs. The action and dress and the holiday faces of the people all seemed to depict another sort of life, beautiful and dignified, free from brawls, disputes, and drunkenness.

My father went into the town with me once to the baths.

It was late in the autumn and there was a hard frost, but no snow. My father slipped, fell, and dislocated his foot. We got home again somehow or other. My mother was greatly upset.

"What will become of us?" she kept saying in a crushed way.

Next morning my father sent her to the Ouprava (Administration), to tell the secretary why he could not come to his work.

"Let him send some one to see that I really am laid up! Otherwise they may discharge me, the devils. . . ."

I understood already that if my father were discharged our position would be frightful; we should be on the street! I well remember the alarm with which my father and mother spoke of being discharged.

Mother called in village quacks, people with an important and intimidating air, who massaged my father's foot, rubbed it with some preparation with an extremely disagreeable smell, and even, I remember, singed it; but in spite of their efforts it was long before my father could get out of bed. The accident compelled my parents to leave the village, and in order to be nearer my father's employment we removed to the Ribnoriadskaya Street in the town, to the same house where my father and mother had lived before, and where I was born in 1873.

I did not like the change to the noisy, dirty life of the town. We all lived in one room, father, mother, myself, and my little brother and sister. I was already six or seven years old at that time.

Mother went out to work by the day, scrubbing floors and washing clothes, and shut me up with the babies in the room all day from morning till night. We lived in a wooden house, and if there had been a fire we should have been burned to death, shut up as we were. But I discovered how to remove part of the framework of the window, and we all three used to climb out and run about the street, not forgetting to return home by a certain time. I again put the window frame back in its place, and everything appeared as before.

It was rather dreadful at nightfall in the locked-up unlighted room; I used to feel particularly bad when I recollected Kirilovna's dreadful tales and gloomy stories; it used to seem as if an old witch or a spectre might appear at any moment. In spite of the heat we all snuggled down under the coverlet and lay silent, afraid to put out our heads and holding our breath. If one of us coughed or sighed we would say to each other:

"Don't breathe; keep quiet!"

There were indistinct noises in the courtyard and muffled rustlings in the corridor. . . . I was awfully glad when I heard my mother confidently and calmly turning the key in the lock.

The door opened on to a very dark corridor, which was the "back entry" to the flat occupied by a general's wife. Meeting me once in the corridor, she spoke kindly to me about something or other and then asked whether I knew how to read or write.

"No."

"Well, come to see me. My son will teach you your letters!"

I went to see her, and her son, a schoolboy of sixteen or so, at once began to teach me to read, as if he had long awaited the opportunity. I learned to read fairly quickly, which pleased the general's wife, and she used to make me read to her in the evenings. But for some inexplicable reason, after reading a page I could not imagine which way I ought to turn it. I turned it first this way and then the other, and again began to read what I had only just read through. The lady explained very circumstantially how one ought to turn over the leaves of a book, and I thought I had grasped the art, but when I came to the last lines, for some reason or other I again turned the left-hand page back over the right-hand one so that the side I had been reading again lay before my eyes. This oddity caused the general's wife to lose her temper on one occasion, and she called me a blockhead. But that did not help her; having read the page through, I still did not know which way to turn it, and burst into bitter tears. I don't think I have ever wept so bitterly before or since. Evidently my tears touched the lady, for she said to me:

"You have read enough!"

After that I did not go to her again.

But I finally managed somehow, with a little assistance, to learn how to turn over the pages.

Soon afterwards the story of Bova the Crown Prince fell into my hands. I was much astonished that Bova [1] could defeat and scatter an army of a hundred thousand men with nothing but a broom.

"That was a fine fellow!" I thought. "I should like to be like that!"

Aroused by the desire to perform feats of valour, I went into the courtyard, took a broom, and energetically chased some chickens, for which the owners beat me mercilessly.

I liked reading, and used to read any printed paper that came under my eyes.

Once on picking up the family register, I read:

"Living: Ieraksa, Ivan, Evdokia, Feodor, Nikolai, Evdokia." . . .

Ivan and Evdokia were my father and mother; Feodor was myself; Nikolai and Evdokia were my brother and sister. But who or what was Ieraksa?

---

[1] Hero of one of the most popular folk tales in Russia.

The unheard-of name seemed to me ominous; I imagined its bearer to be no ordinary creature, but probably a robber or a wizard, and perhaps even worse. . . .

I summoned up courage to ask my father:

"Papa, who is Ieraksa?"

My father told me briefly but impressively:

"Till I was eighteen years of age I worked in the country as a ploughman, and afterwards went to live in the town. I did all the work I could find. I was a water carrier, yard porter, got dirty at the candle factory; finally, I went to work for the rural police commissioner, Chirikov, at Kliutchistchi, where the sacristan at the church was named Ieraksa, and he taught me to read and write. I shall never forget the good deed he did me thereby! And don't you forget people who do good to you. There won't be many of them, and it will be easy to remember them!"

Soon afterwards the name of the sacristan Ieraksa was transferred by my father from the page "Of the living" to the page "Of God's servants laid to rest."

"There," said my father. "I will put his name at the head here, too!"

My father was an unusual man. Tall and flat-chested, his beard always neatly trimmed, he did not look like a peasant. His soft hair was always carefully brushed; I never saw anyone else with hair so beautifully arranged. I loved to smooth his hair when we were on good terms. He wore a soft shirt made by my mother, the collar of which was turned down and fastened with a riband instead of a necktie, but later on when fancy shirts came into use the riband was replaced by a little coloured cord. He had a short coat or jacket over his shirt, and wore blacked boots. Instead of socks he used *partianki,* pieces of linen wound around the feet and legs.

When sober he was taciturn, said only what was absolutely

necessary, and always very quietly, almost in a whisper. He was caressing in his manner with me, but in moments of vexation he would call me for some reason or other, "*Skvajina*" (Slit).

I don't remember him ever saying a coarse word or acting rudely when he was sober. If anything annoyed him he would grind his teeth and go away, but he only concealed his vexation until the next time he got drunk, and he only needed to drink two or three liqueur glasses to be that. Then I saw before me another man altogether—my father showed a sarcastic turn of character, was ready to quarrel about any trifle, and it was disagreeable to look at him.

I thoroughly disliked to come in contact with drunken people, whoever they were—and still more when it was my own father. I was very much ashamed about him before the boys I knew in the street, although in most cases their fathers were sad drunkards too. I wondered what the secret was. Once I tried a little vodka, but it seemed to me a bitter, evil-smelling fluid. I could understand the pleasure of drinking various kinds of kvass, but why drink such poison as that? I made up my mind that grown-up people drank to make themselves more courageous when they wanted to create a disturbance. It seemed to me quite natural and unavoidable that a drunken person should kick up a row. All drunkards made scenes.

When he was drunk my father would attack absolutely anybody who for any reason aroused his dislike. First of all he would politely bid the stranger good day and talk to him in an apparently good-humoured strain. For instance, some decently dressed gentleman, with a courteous inclination of the head, would listen to my father with a pleasant smile, and ask politely:

"What do you wish?"

Then suddenly my father would say:

"I want to know why you have such pig's eyes?"
or:

"Aren't you ashamed to take such a disagreeable mug about with you?"

The stranger would swear, and shout at my father that he was a madman and that he, too, had an inhumanly ugly face.

Usually this happened "after the 20th" of the month, a day I hated. On the 20th the men of the circle in which I lived got drunk to a man on vodka and held a wild debauch. Those were nightmare days; people lost all human semblance, howled senselessly, fought, wept, rolled in the dirt—life became horrible and frightful.

Afterwards my father would lie in bed for days and drink iced kvass.

"Kvass!"

He would say nothing else all day. His face was drawn; his eyes looked imbecile. I was astonished that he could drink so much, and boasted to my friends that my father could drink kvass as a horse drinks water—in pailfuls! They showed no surprise and appeared to believe me.

When sober my father did not often beat me, though he did do so sometimes, as it seemed to me, without any reason.

I remember letting fly a paper serpent which I had made very skilfully and decorated with paper rattles. The serpent caught on the top of a tall birch tree and I was afraid I should lose it. I climbed up the birch tree, got the serpent, and began to get down, but a branch broke under my weight. I fell head over heels, counting the branches, first on the roof and then on the fence, and finally on my back on the ground with such force that the breath was audibly driven out of my body. I lay for some time on the ground with the torn serpent in my hands. When I had rested I grieved over the serpent, then discovered other amusements and forgot all about the incident.

Next day in the evening my father ordered:

"Skvajina, get ready to go to the baths!"

Even now I adore going to the baths, but going to the baths in the country is delightful! Especially in autumn, when the air is clear and fresh, and smells a little of mushrooms and of those bunches of twigs which careful folk have made use of in the steam bath and which they are now taking home under their arms. On dark autumn evenings, in the dim light of the kerosene street lamps, it was pleasant to see freshly washed people going along the street and breathing forth steamy vapour, and to know that they would drink tea with jam when they got home. I loved going to the baths all the more because we always drank tea with jam afterwards, as a matter of course.

Well, so off I went with my father to the baths. He was in a splendidly good-humoured mood. We undressed. He jabbed me in the side with one finger and enquired in tones which boded ill:

"What's this?"

I discovered that my body was covered with blue and yellow marks, like the skin of a zebra.

"I fell down and hurt myself a bit."

"A bit? Why are you all covered with stripes? Where did you fall from?"

I told him all about it conscientiously. Then he pulled several thick twigs out of the bath switch and began to beat me, saying:

"Don't clamber up the birch tree; don't clamber about!"

I was not so much hurt as ashamed before all the people in the disrobing room. The spectators were hugely delighted at the unexpected diversion; they shouted and guffawed, though not ill-naturedly, and egged my father on:

"Give it him! Give it him! Whip him well! Don't spare leather, and he'll be all the better! Give it him good and hard!"

Usually I did not feel very much hurt when I got beaten; it seemed to me to be the way of the world. I knew that in the Sukonnaya suburb everybody got beaten, both big and little, morning and evening. Drubbings seemed to be lawful and inevitable. But a public punishment at the baths, before people in their birthday suits for whom it was an entertainment, wounded me very bitterly.

Later on when I was twelve years old I began to protest against my father's drunken debauches. I remember my protests once angered him so much that he picked up a good-sized stick and went for me. I feared he would kill me, and ran out just as I was, barefoot, in thin drawers and shirt, into the street, and in spite of a temperature of four degrees below zero, made all speed to a friend's house which was a considerable distance away, and next day dashed home again, barefoot as before. My father was not at home, but my mother, though she approved of my running away from a beating, scolded me, all the same, for running barefoot in the snow! Although I explained that I had not had time to put my boots on, she very nearly gave me a whipping.

Sometimes my father, when slightly drunk, would sing in a high almost womanish voice, which seemed as if it was some one else's and was oddly out of harmony with his appearance and character, a song consisting of a series of astonishingly meaningless words:

"Siksanikma,
Chetvertakma,
Tszanitma,
Souleimatma.
Ussum ta,
Bishtinikma!

EXTERIOR OF MY FIRST HOME IN KAZAN. DIRECTLY BEHIND ME IS THE ROOM
IN WHICH I WAS BORN

Dygin, dygin.
Dygin, dygin!"

I never summoned up pluck enough to ask him what these distorted half-Tartar words meant. And I could never grasp the meaning of a proverbial phrase he frequently repeated:

"Bokh Epimakh, vosmet na promakh!"

But he never spoke about God (*Bokh*) to me at all. He seldom went to church, but when he did he prayed very devoutly. Gazing steadfastly before him, he crossed himself and occasionally bowed down, but one felt that he was saying to himself all the prayers he knew. He probably did not know many, and I never heard him say them at home, at bedtime or in the morning.

In church, too, he said nothing to me, but would occasionally give me a cuff on the back of my head when, standing next to him, I began to look about me, observing for amusement what sort of beards, noses or eyes, people had.

"Stand still, Skvajina!" he would say in a whisper, rapping me on the head, and I at once stood still before the shrine with the dismal face of a devout worshipper.

Afterwards, when I went to work with my father at the Administration offices, I noticed that there was always a grave drawn on his blotter: a mound with a cross above it, and underneath it the words: "Here there are neither sufferings, nor grief, nor sighing, but life eternal."

*   *   *   *   *

Sometimes in winter bearded men in *lapti*[1] and peasant's garb would call on us; they smelt strongly of black bread and also of some other odour peculiar to people from Viatka, which may be due to Viatka people's eating a great deal of oatmeal. They were relatives of my father, his brother

[1] Lapti: Shoes made of braided strips of linden bark.

Dorimedont and his sons. They used to send me for vodka, and would spend a long time in drinking tea, talking about the harvests and the taxes, about how hard it was to live in the country, how some one's cattle had been taken away for nonpayment of taxes, or how a samovar (tea urn) had been taken from some one for the same reason.

"*Troudno!*" (Hard!)

That word was repeated so often, in such different tones. I reflected:

"It is a good thing that father lives in the town and we have neither cows nor horses, and no one can take away the samovar!"

I observed once that my father and mother were very much upset and kept on talking in whispers, frequently mentioning the word "Prokouror," [1] a word which seemed to me as strange as "Ieraksa."

"What does 'prokouror' mean?" I asked my mother. She explained the word, adding:

"The prokouror is greater than the governor!"

I already knew something about the governor. I had heard my father say to neighbours at the gates of our courtyard:

"Skariatin was governor then. He came and made the entire village come out into the street, and began to beat them all himself with his *Nagaika* (whip)!"

Hearing now that the prokouror was greater than the governor, I quite naturally began to think and anticipate that the prokouror would come some day to our town, make all the people come out into the street, and beat them with his own hands. I should catch it among the rest.

But the attorney was to be shown to me in just as powerful but in a kinder light. My mother's younger sister had been kidnapped by somebody and sold to a house of ill fame,

---

[1] District attorney.

and my father, hearing of it, appealed to the district attorney for her release from bondage. After a time Aunt Anna appeared in our room—a very pretty, merry, laughing girl, who was continually singing songs. I began to understand that not everything in life was so dreadful as it seems at first until one knows.

Carpenters and masons worked in our courtyard; I used to bring them paper for making cigarettes, and they rolled some tobacco up in a scrap of paper and offered it to me.

"Smoke. It clears one's chest!"

The bitter, greenish smoke of the cheap tobacco (called "Mahorka") did not please me, but one must get to know everything. I took the cigarette and smoked it!

I felt sick; experiencing frightful attacks of vomiting, I reflected, philosophically:

"So that is how one clears one's chest!"

On holidays the masons and carpenters drank themselves senseless and brawled; my father drank and created a disturbance with them. This disagreeably surprised me. My father was not on their level; he was dressed like a gentleman and wore a necktie of twisted cord, while they were quite simple folk. It did not seem proper for him to get drunk with them. . . .

One of the daughters of the landlord, who was a merchant named Lissitsin, played the piano, and the music seemed to me heavenly. At first I thought the young lady played on a charmanka [1]—that is to say, simply turned the handle, and the music made itself inside the case; but I soon discovered that the landlord's daughter beat out the music with her fingers.

"That is clever!" I thought. "If only I could learn to do that!"

Suddenly, as if by magic, it happened that some one living

[1] Street organ.

on our courtyard raffled an ancient piano; my father and mother took a ticket for me for one ruble and—I won it! I was wildly delighted and felt sure that I should now learn to play, but what was my disappointment when the instrument was locked up and in spite of my humble petitions I was not even allowed to touch it.

If I even went up to the instrument the grown-ups cried severely:

"Be careful; you will break it!"

On the other hand, when I fell ill I no longer slept on the floor, but on the piano. Because I lay for a long time on the instrument I used to imagine that if I opened the lid and made the attempt perhaps I should be able to play it.

I lay on the piano for a long time, and it seemed strange to me that I could sleep on it but must not play it! Soon afterwards the cumbrous instrument was sold for twenty-five or thirty rubles.

I was eight years old when, one Christmas, or perhaps Easter, I first saw the clown Yashka at a fair booth.

Yakov Ivanovitch Mamonov was celebrated at that time throughout the Volga country as a clown and "Butter-week showman." A stout old man with ridiculously angry eyes in his coarse face, with thick black moustaches which seemed as though they were cast-iron. "Yashka" possessed to perfection that heavy, bludgeonlike wit which is to this day the nourishment of the street and the town square. His frank jests and bold ridicule of the public, his thunderous, hoarse voice, his entire personality, produced a fascinating and overwhelming impression on me. The man appeared to me a fearless master and tamer of mankind—I was convinced that everybody, including even the police and the district attorney, was afraid of him.

I gazed on him open-mouthed, recollecting with delight his quaint sayings:

"Hey, sister, and you empty head, come up here and I'll give you a fairing!" he shouted to the crowd standing in front of his booth.

Pushing the players forward on to the terrace of the booth and holding a tattered doll in his hands, he yelled:

"Make way; bow to the ground. We are bringing the governor!"

Charmed by this street artist, I stood in front of the booth until my legs became benumbed and my eyes grew dim with the gay diversity of the strolling players' attire.

"How wonderful to be a man like Yashka!" I thought.

All the players of his troupe seemed to me to be people full of inexhaustible good spirits, who enjoyed clowning, joking, and laughing. I noticed more than once that when they came out on to the terrace of the booth vapour rose up from them as if from a samovar, and of course it never occurred to me that it was due to the evaporation of perspiration, called forth by excessively hard work and the painful effort of their muscles.

I cannot say with absolute certainty that it was Yakov Mamonov who gave the first impulse which awoke in me the desire for the life of art, but perhaps he, giving himself up to the task of diverting the mob, was the person to whom I was indebted for the early awakening of my interest in the theatre, in that scenic world which is so unlike the real one. I soon learned that Mamonov was a shoemaker by trade, and that he first began to appear on the stage with his wife and son and his apprentices, of whom he formed his first troupe. This information raised him still higher in my esti-mation—it is not everyone who can climb from his cellar to the stage! I used to spend entire days in the vicinity of the booth, and immensely regretted the approach of Lent and the end of Holy Week. Immediately after Easter, the square grew very empty and all the canvas was taken down from the booths; the slender wooden ribs were laid bare, and there was no one to be seen on the trampled snow, which was littered with the husks of sunflower seeds, with nut shells and the paper wrappings of cheap sweetmeats. The holiday time had gone by like a dream. But a little while ago the square had been filled with a gay and noisy life; I had wandered in the long corridors of the booths and from their round windows had seen fabulously beautiful cities, mountains, wonderful churches such as are not to be found in Kazan, and many extraordinary things only to be seen in dreams. And now the square was like a cemetery, though without graves or crosses.

*   *   *   *   *

We moved to the Tartar quarter, to a little room over a smithy; through the floor one could hear the hammers merrily and rhythmically striking on the iron and on the anvil. On the same courtyard there lived wheelwrights, carriage makers, and a working furrier—the delight of my heart. In the summer I used to sleep in the carriages which were brought to be mended, or else in some newly made carriage which smelt pleasantly of morocco leather, varnish, and turpentine.

The furrier was a black-haired black-eyed man with an Oriental face. He gave me work to do—laying out various skins on the roof to dry and afterwards beating them with slender supple sticks, for which he paid me five kopeks. This was great riches and good luck for me. For two kopeks I could go to the bathing enclosure on the Kaban Lake, where I swam in the "gentlemen's" enclosure until I was blue with cold. I could not take my brother and sister with me to the lake, because they were still too young. My brother Vasili, who had not long ago arrived in this world, was a lively boy, bright and promising. My little sister was quiet and thoughtful. I called her "Niunya." With my earnings I bought them *halva* (a Turkish sweetmeat), and we feasted, burying our young teeth in the rock-hard white mass. It was amusing when the queer stuff held one's jaws tightly stuck, and afterwards gradually took on a consistency like cobbler's wax and then melted, filling one's mouth with cloying sweetness.

I remember the jolly smith, a young fellow who set me to blow his bellows, and in return hammered out small flat pieces of iron for me to play *babki* (knucklebones) with. He did not drink vodka and was a very good singer; I have forgotten his name; he was very fond of me and I of him.

When the smith sang a song, my mother, sitting at her work at the window, would join in; and I liked very much the way the two voices harmonised. I tried to join in with them cautiously, fearing to spoil the harmony, but the smith encouraged me:

"Go on, Fedya, go on! Sing; you will be all the merrier for it. A song is like a bird—let it out and it flies away!"

Although my heart was light enough without singing, when fishing or lying on the grass in the fields I used to sing, and it seemed to me that when I stopped, the song still flew on like a living thing.

I rarely went to church, but once, when playing on a Saturday evening in the snow-covered square, not far from the church of St. Varlaam, I heard the bells calling worshippers to church and, feeling frozen, went inside to get warm. An all-night service was going on. I listened from the threshold to the harmonious singing. I pushed my way nearer to the singers, and found that men and boys were singing in the choir stalls. I observed that the boys held in their hands sheets of paper with something written on them; I had already heard that there existed written notes for singing, and had even seen somewhere or other the lined paper with black pothooks on it, which in my opinion nobody could possibly understand. But here I noticed something which was altogether incomprehensible: the boys held in their hands paper which certainly bore lines on it, but was otherwise quite devoid of characters and pothooks. It cost me a great deal of thought before I guessed that the notes were written on the other side of the paper, which was turned towards the singers. I had often heard choir singing, but had never before been able to get close to the singers. It was thrilling to see boys of my own age taking part in the service and for the first time I actually saw how they sang.

Soon after this we went to live in the Sukonnaya suburb, in two small rooms in a cellar basement. I think it was that very day that I heard the singing of psalms overhead and at once found out that over us there lived a choirmaster and that a rehearsal was going on. When the singing ceased and the choir singers had gone, I bravely went upstairs and there enquired of a man whom I could hardly see, owing to my diffidence and confusion, whether he would not take me, too, into the choir. He silently took down a violin from the wall and said to me:

"Sing to the fiddle!"

I earnestly sang a few notes in accord with the violin, and then the choirmaster said:

"You have a voice and an ear. I will write you some notes. Learn them!"

He wrote a bar of music on lined paper, explained to me the meaning of sharps, flats, and the keys. All this at once interested me. I speedily grasped the science, and after two all-night services I was already handing out the music sheets to the choir singers in accordance with the keys. Mother was immensely delighted with my success; father remained apparently indifferent, but none the less expressed the hope that if I sang well I should perhaps earn a ruble a month, anyway, to supplement his meagre earnings. And so it came out; some three months I sang gratis, and then the choirmaster gave me a salary of a ruble and a half a month.

The choirmaster was called Stcherbinin. He was a peculiar man. He wore his long hair combed back and used blue spectacles, which gave him a very severe and dignified aspect, although his face was horribly disfigured by smallpox. He wore a wide black garment without sleeves, a cape, a sort of bandit's hat on his head, and was very taciturn. But in spite of all his dignity he was as desperate a drinker as were all the dwellers in the Sukonnaya suburb, and as he worked as a clerk in the district courthouse the 20th of the month was also a disastrous day for him. Once again, I must say that in the Sukonnaya suburb, more than in other quarters of the town, after the 20th of the month, people became pitiful, wretched, and idiotic, carrying on a desperate revel in which all the evil elements of their characters predominated and during which they made use of all the obscene words they knew. I was sorry for the choirmaster, and when I saw him wildly drunk my heart ached for him.

On one occasion the clerks of the merchant Chernoyarov got up an evening party, to celebrate something or other, in the house of their employer, and asked Stcherbinin to find them boys who could sing. He selected me and two others. We all three went to the clerks'; they treated us with biscuits and tea, in which we might put as much sugar as our hearts desired. This was a notable luxury, because at home and even in the tavern, to which we boys used to go between the early and late services, we could not put sugar into our tea, but could only soak a small lump in it. But the clerks put as much as five lumps in a glass of tea! They were jolly fellows and talked pleasantly to us, giving us of their best with a good heart. In the evening there came to the party some important-looking people, the merchants and craftsmen. It was bright and gay, and altogether new and delightful to me. We sang a trio beginning with the words:

"Dark nights
The eyes of mortals . . ."

I remember it was called a "Christmas Hymn." For some incomprehensible reason the Stcherbinin choir was broken up, and the choirmaster had to give up his work in connection with it. It evidently weighed heavily on him, and he drank worse than ever. When drunk, he would call me to him, take his fiddle, and the three of us—that is, he, the fiddle and I—would sing—sometimes so well that one even wanted to weep for joy. Afterwards he would go to the saloon, and on his return would invite me to his rooms to sing. I don't recollect that he ever said anything very note-worthy to me or taught me, but evidently he liked me, as I did him. He was a lonely man, and of a gloomy character; he must have been one of those rare Russians who suffer in silence and are too proud to complain of their fate. Once towards evening he called me to him and said:

"Come along!"

"Where to?"

"To sing an all-night service."

"Where? With whom?"

"The two of us."

And we went by the ravines, along the river bank, past the brick sheds, to the Arskoe Polye, to the church of Barbara the Martyr, where the two of us sang the all-night service, treble and bass, and in the morning sang the morning services in the same church. In the same way we used for a long time to go together to sing in various churches, until Stcher-binin entered the Spassky Monastery as precentor of the Bishop's choir. Here I became an *ispolatchik*, receiving six rubles a month instead of a ruble and a half. This was great

THE OUPRAVA AT KAZAN

THE MARKET PLACE, KAZAN

earnings, and besides that I earned money at weddings, funerals, and Te Deums. I had to give the money to my parents, but of course I kept back part of it. Receiving a ruble and twenty kopeks for a funeral, I would keep back one half for myself to buy sweets. I enjoyed myself. "What a fine business singing is!" I thought. "A great pleasure to oneself, and besides that they pay you." I could go to the circus, and enjoy the talents of Yakov Ivanovitch Mamonov.

At Christmas, I, like all the choir boys, went to sing carols. We sang in chorus "Glory to God in the highest," the concerted piece of Bortniansky and the trio "Dark Nights." The people who had invited us were pleased; they gave us fifty kopeks. We sang at another place and received sixty kopeks; and in this way we got some six rubles on this sacred holiday. It was sufficient for the Christmas holdiays.

At Easter the choir boys also earned money by going about singing, and as the time drew near I determined to write a trio myself. Now, in the meantime I had fooled my parents to the extent of hiding bits of my earnings, with which I managed to buy a violin when I had scraped together the sum of a ruble and twenty kopeks. I somehow achieved the feat of learning the first position. So I took my violin, some lined paper, and began to compose a trio on the words, "Christ is risen from the dead." I composed the tune quite speedily; I wrote the part for the second voice without much difficulty, because, according to my ideas, it had of necessity to be a third apart from the first voice; but when I began to write the part for the third voice, to complete the harmony, I observed with the greatest disappointment that it all sounded wrong and false. Of course I was not aware of the existence of counterpoint, did not understand tonality, and therefore put down all sorts of queer accidental marks, sharps and flats, in front of every note. However, having somehow harmonised the second voice, I began to write the third. I tried it over. My bass harmonised with the first voice, but there was absolutely no harmony with the second. I struggled on with it, and finally overcame the whole difficulty and completed the trio; it sounded fairly correct and pleased the hearers, and the three of us earned a little more money with it.

The trio was written in lilac ink, which reminds me of some one's jesting lines:

Full of new emotions,
Ambition fresh within,
In ink of lilac colour
I boldly dip my pen.

My dreams have proved illusions,
And my strength exceeding slack,
So now I write in black ink,
As, before, I used lilac.

I long preserved my attempt at composition, but it got lost all the same along with my father's letters and my favourite book of Beranger's verses translated by Kurotchkin. The latter was a very tattered little book, the commencement of which was missing. I carried it everywhere with me for many years. I particularly liked the poem:

Rosy as an apple,
Dressed very carelessly,
Not excessively drunk,
But endlessly gay!

The hero of this impudent merry poem I long considered to be the most ideal of men—he seemed to be so unlike the people amongst whom I lived, and greatly to his advantage. . . .

The police threaten
To put him in prison.
But he, the queer fellow, laughs,
He says, "Ah, how funny
It is with them!"

In the Sukonnaya suburb people were unable to take up
a humorous attitude towards the police.

CHAPTER TWO

School Days—Hardships as an Apprentice—
Scarlet Fever—My Pals—I Develop an In-
terest in Literature—My Introduction to
the Theatre—At the Pawnbroker's.

THOUGH I had taken up singing, I continued to
attend a private school kept by a lady—Madame
V. . . —where boys and girls studied side by side.

I was fairly quick and easily learned my lessons, and was
consequently a careless, idle scholar, much preferring to
spend my time in skating—on one skate only, as a pair would
have cost me too dear. I frequently lost my schoolbooks,
and sometimes sold them to get the wherewithal to buy
candies, and the result was that I hardly ever knew my
lessons.

I used to sit next to a girl about two years older than myself, called Tanya. She used to help me out when I was in
difficulties. The assistance she gave me caused me to feel a
most ardent sympathy for her, and on one occasion in the
corridor, when we were changing classrooms, the warmth of
my gratitude led me to kiss her. Rather frightened, and
looking round to make sure we were not observed, she said:

"How can you? The teacher will see us. When we go
to play in the yard we will hide together, and then you can
kiss me. . . ."

I did not know that one ought not to kiss girls at my age,
and merely understood that one might not kiss them in front
of the teacher—presumably because that was not included in
the lessons she gave us. It dawned on me obscurely that
kisses were forbidden things when, kissing Tanya in a quiet

28

corner, I found out that it was much nicer than kissing in public. I began to seek for opportunities to be alone with Tanya, and we kissed each other as much as we wanted to. I think our kisses were nothing more than pure-hearted childish embraces—the mutual kindness which the human heart so longs for, whether young or old.

Of course the teacher soon caught us, and my little sweetheart and I were expelled from the school. I don't know whether my father and mother knew the reason; probably not, as otherwise I should have got a memorable beating.

But the incident did not pass without leaving traces in my heart; I had experienced that kisses were sweeter in secret, and when the teacher punished me it became clear to me that kissing was a matter to be done "under the rose." The incident awoke my curiosity about women and changed my attitude towards them. Until then I had felt no shame when I bathed in the river with my mother and other women, but after that day I refused to bathe with women.

I soon afterwards entered the Fourth Public School of the quarter, but very soon left it as a result of a strange occurrence: Once when on my way to school a big lad jumped out from the gateway of the Jouravliev house and struck me on the head with a stick, drawing blood, and then bolted.

I howled, then put some snow on the wound, and continued my way, wondering why anyone should have struck me with a stick. I told no one about it at school, nor yet at home. If my father had found me with a broken head he would have whipped me. The wound began to fester, but was not visible beneath my hair.

By mischance, a few days later, I got into trouble at school or else answered the teacher badly, and as ill luck would have it he was fond of what we called "pinching a partridge."

"Pinching a partridge" means taking a tuft of your hair between the thumb and first finger and pulling it upwards violently. The sensation produced is like having your neck broken. The teacher "pinched the partridge" just where my head was hurt. I howled with pain. Blood and suppurating matter flowed down my pate from the broken place. I ran home as fast as I could. My parents whipped me when I got home, for being an idle scholar, but I said:

"You may cut me in half, but I won't go to that school again!"

They called me a worthless creature and not a few other hard names; then my father decided that nothing good would come of me at school, and apprenticed me to the boot-maker Tonkov, my godfather. I had been at his house before that as a guest with my father and mother, and liked going there very much. A glass cupboard stood in his workshop, on the shelves of which were displayed boot trees and pieces of leather. The smell of the leather attracted me, and I used to want to play with the boot trees. Everything was very interesting. I was particularly fond of Mrs. Tonkov. Whenever I went there she used to give me nuts and sweet biscuits. She had a soft caressing voice which somehow intermingled in my mind with the smell of the biscuits; when she spoke it seemed to me as if sweet-smelling biscuits came from her lips instead of words. In after years, when I was already on the musical stage, I met her in Kazan, and when I talked to her this, as it were, edible voice of hers gave me just the same sensation of perfumed and delicate biscuits.

When he handed me over to the bootmaker, my father impressed upon me:

"Learn to make boots and you will be somebody in the world—a master craftsman. You will have money to support yourself, and even, perhaps, help others."

I was delighted to become a bootmaker, as I felt sure it was better than learning the multiplication table not only by rule but by skips.   Another source for rejoicing was that my mother made two aprons for me.

I remember that it was autumn.   The weather was frosty, and I went barefoot through the streets with my mother to the workshop.   I was wearing one of my new aprons, and put my hands behind the portion of it which covered my chest, just as I had seen the bootmakers do.   As I went, I looked around me to see what the good people of Kazan thought of me.   With time-honoured indifference to historical events, my fellow townspeople took no notice of me, though I felt convinced that everyone was reflecting:

"Hullo!   We have got another new craftsman now!"

My mother sighed.   In the market place she bought me five cucumbers for a kopek.   I put four of them behind my apron, and one in my mouth, out of which it stuck like a big green tongue as I walked along.

Tonkov was a big, sturdy, curly-headed man in a white shirt with satin trousers.   He received me kindly, saying:

"Look on today, and tomorrow you can begin to work."

I slept badly that night, being overcome with a desire to commence work.   In the morning we all got up at six.   I was fearfully sleepy.   I was given a glass of tea and some bread, and then my master showed me how to twist the waxed thread.

I set to work very zealously, but to my surprise I did not get on very well with it.   At first the workmen did not take much notice of me, but soon they began to call me a block-head.

When I had learned to twist the thread, I had to put in the bristles from both sides.   This turned out still more diffi-cult.   I felt very sleepy.   Still, I did not get beaten the first day.

I found the sewing easier than twisting the thread, but of course I did not master it without some encouragement imparted by means of blows. I was glad that the boss was my godfather, because the workmen were less hard on me for this reason. But I was not fated to become a bootmaker. Every Sunday, when the shop was closed, I went home to the *postaiali dvor* (a big courtyard where we lived and where waggons and carriages were continually passing in and out). There I used to play around with the other children in an atmosphere of squalor and horse manure. One day I heard that my little brother, Nicolai, was very ill, and on Sunday when I went home I found that he had died. Certainly my father was a drunkard who beat us all; still, underneath, he had a soft, kind heart, and when he lost his little son I realized that the blow had struck hard. I will never forget the day of the funeral. I did not see my father cry, but I knew that he was heartbroken as with slow proud steps he walked silently to the cemetery, his head bent and his bushy brows knit, carrying on his shoulder the rude wooden coffin, wrapped in a cloth, which held the tiny body.

Shortly afterwards, I caught cold and was soon seriously ill. I remember that when I went back to the shop my godfather gave me an apple. I bit a piece out of it, but it tasted horrible. I could do nothing but lie miserably on top of the hot stove—one of our Russian stoves built of bricks with a flat top.

As soon as my godfather realised how ill I was, he took me to the hospital, where I found my little sister was also a sufferer. My legs burned horribly, as though they had been scorched. A man in black sprinkled something on them from a pulveriser. The sensation was blissful, but when he stopped sprinkling them my legs began to burn again unbearably.

My mother, sitting on my sister's bed, said to some one: "My dear friends, how can they cut a person's throat!" Everything wavered about me. My head seemed full of fog, but I gathered that they wished to cut my sister's throat. I was not surprised, as I reflected that as we were in a hospital and not in a robbers' den, probably her throat must be cut because it was necessary. But my mother would not give her consent, and my sister died. It was now my turn.

But, thank God! after seven or eight days' grave danger I began to recover. My skin peeled off like a snake's, in big pieces. With my recovery my appetite began to torment me. I could not get enough to eat.

On one occasion a medical student from the university, who was on duty at the hospital, asked:

"Well, Feodor, what shall you eat today? There are cutlets, barley soup, and soup with chicken. Choose!"

I chose the soup with chicken, as I thought I should first of all get the soup, and then the chicken. I was bitterly disappointed when I was brought a plate of broth with a little bit of something of uncertain origin floating in it. I ate the broth and then asked timidly: "Isn't there any chicken?"

"What chicken?"

"They told me. . . ."

"Oh, so you thought you would get a whole chicken to eat! Well, you won't!"

"That's a pity," I said meekly.

When I got well my parents again apprenticed me to a bootmaker, but not to the same one. My father thought that my godfather was too easy-going with me and would never succeed in teaching me anything.

I was in for it properly in the hands of the bootmaker Andreiev. Though I knew how to twist the thread and to sew, he obliged me to wash the floor, put on and clean the samovar, go with his wife to the market and carry her heavy provision basket. Altogether, it was penal servitude. I was beaten mercilessly; indeed, I am astonished that they did not make a cripple of me with so much beating. I think it was not due to lack of zeal on their part, but to the strength of my bones.

To Americans, the art of bootmaking probably does not mean much, for in the United States machinery plays the leading part, but in Kazan on the Malaia Prolomnaia street everything from beginning to end was done by hand.

But I learned to do the work fairly well, and even began to do small repairs myself at holiday times; I mended downtrodden heels and put on patches. My only pleasure was when I used to go to the customers to deliver new boots or repairs. I used intentionally to take the very longest route, so as to be out of doors and at liberty for as long as possible. Sometimes a customer would give me five or ten kopeks by way of a tip. As I was always hungry, I bought myself white bread to eat with my tea.

"You will overeat yourself," said the workmen.

My master did not feed me badly, but very often I had not sufficient time to eat all I wanted to.

The way matters were arranged was very disadvantageous to me. They used to serve the cabbage soup in one big basin, and everyone had first of all to drink the soup, and then, when the foreman rapped his wooden spoon on the edge of the basin, one might take out a piece of meat. Naturally, one had to make haste to get out as large pieces as possible as quickly as one could. Well, when the grown-up workmen noticed that I ate quickly or swallowed the meat half chewed, the foreman would hit me on the head with his spoon.

"Don't hurry, you rascal!"

A skilful man can raise a good-sized lump on one's forehead with a wooden spoon!

During the autumn the life was still bearable. The evenings were long, and our thrifty master was unwilling to light the lamps, so that for an hour or so before it grew quite dark we worked in semiobscurity. One could rest a little. However, as Christmas drew near the work increased and we used to continue till twelve o'clock at night and got up at five in the morning. These late hours were called zasidki. This twenty-hour working day was too much for me. As things were I was nothing but skin and bones, and I now began to fear that even my bones would get thinner.

While working at the shop, I still continued my choir singing in my leisure hours, although only at the regular church services. I could not sing at weddings and funerals, owing to lack of time, and of course I could not sing at the night services, as I could hardly drag one foot after the other when evening came.

When the springtime came and it grew warmer, so that one could go barefoot in the streets, I told my father that I was too ill to work. I was not suffering from any well-defined illness, but I felt very exhausted, and hard swellings and yellowish spots made their appearance on my feet. They were not corns, but a sort of hardening underneath the skin. I felt no pain, but took advantage of their appearance to tell my father that I was suffering with my feet.

What was my consternation when my father took me to the hospital. As we went I reflected:

"Heavens! Whatever will happen now? The doctor will know that there is nothing wrong with my feet! Father will thrash me and send me back to the workshop, and there they will beat me, too. . . ."

But science saved me from any such martyrdom. The doctor felt my feet, summoned the students, and said something to them, then prescribed me an embrocation and forbade me to walk much. Going to the drug store with my father to get the embrocation, I limped still more, out of respect and gratitude to science. But as soon as my father had left me I ran home as fast as I could, and joyfully told my mother that I was sick, but that it was not serious, and that it was only necessary for me to use the embrocation. My mother sympathised with me. I rubbed my feet with the embrocation and started to go out of doors.

"Sit at home a little," said my mother; "you will rub off the embrocation."

I explained to her that it had already sunk in. Thus I took up once more my life of liberty with my merry companions.

Again, I could devote more time to my singing.

Unfortunately, I had learned to write fairly well at Mme. V's school, and this circumstance spoiled life for me.

"Nothing good will come of you, boy," said my father. "You have fooled about long enough. You write a good hand. Sit down at the table and write me out two or three sheets every day! It will soon be time for you to go with me to the Ouprava."

I sat down as I was bid. It was a tormentingly dull task, writing incomprehensible words in a careful hand, when my whole soul was in the streets, where the other boys were at play.

I forgot to mention that after my attack of scarlet fever, and before I went to work for the bootmaker Andreiev, my father apprenticed me to a wood carver. I was very unlucky there, too. My master fed me badly, and the work was too much for my strength. My master frequently took me with him to the market place, where he bought long planks of birchwood several inches thick. I had to drag these planks home. As I have said I was very thin, and my bones stuck out everywhere. Also, I was only ten years old. On one occasion I was taking some wood home and was so fatigued that I threw it down, turned my face to the fence, and wept.

A serious-looking gentleman approached me and asked

why I was crying, and when I told him what was the matter he took up the wood and carried it to the workshop, where, to my astonishment, he reproached my master severely.

"I will bring you up in court!" he cried.

My master listened to him in silence, but when the good man had gone he beat me savagely, saying:

"Complain, will you?"

I had not complained at all. I had only told the gentleman that I could not carry the wood and was afraid of being late at the workshop. After beating me, my master threatened that he would discharge me if such an unpleasant occurrence were to happen again. I cowered before him. But shortly afterwards my master, when he had done scolding me, turned his back, and I promptly put out my tongue at him, which he saw in a looking-glass. At the moment he said nothing to me, but next day, just before breakfast, when I was frightfully hungry, he told me:

"Take your things and be off with you! I don't want anyone like you."

I knew at once why he was discharging me, but what was I to tell my father?

I took my box and my bedding and went off home.

"Why have you come home?" asked my father.

"My master sent me away."

"Why?"

"I don't know."

My father whipped me as much as he thought I needed, and then went to see my master; but when he came back said not a word to me and did not beat me again.

After that my parents sent me to the Sixth Town School. The teacher, Bashmakov, was a lover of choir singing, and had a violin. As you know, I had long since taken a great fancy to the violin, and I still had mine, for which I had paid one ruble and twenty kopeks, although its strings were

broken. I now began to urge my father to buy me one, and
he finally got me a fiddle at the street market for two rubles.
And so I began to play by ear. This, however, resulted in
many beatings, for when I should have been preparing my
lessons at home, or studying at school, my mind was always
on my violin. What a pity! If I had not been beaten and
prevented from learning this beautiful instrument, I might
have been a violinist.

At that time I was eleven years old and I had a number
of young friends. Strange to say, they all died in early
manhood. The leader of our gang, Jenia Virilov, died after
he had become an officer in the army. Ivan Michailov, the
son of the caretaker at the Ouprava, because a hopeless
drunkard. Stepan Orininsky was killed. In the year of his
death he was a student at the Veterinary Institute. Ivan
D. became a village deacon. He got drunk while col-
lecting the church dues one day, fell out of a sleigh, and
froze to death. Strange that they all ended in such ways!

Jenia Virilov was the son of a retired army captain.
Though not rich, he was comfortably well off. I remember
going to dine at his house once. A sweet cake was served
for dessert. Of course I cleared my plate thoroughly, and
was very much surprised to observe that my friend left a
portion of cake on his plate; even though it was only a small
piece, still he left something. It stuck in my memory, as
it seemed to me that such behaviour must be a sign of Jenia's
gentle birth. He was the well-educated member of our
circle, and he strove to improve us. For instance, before we
became acquainted with Jenia, during the illuminations on
public holidays we used to go about the streets in a rowdy
band, putting out lamps, filling our mouths with kerosene
and then spitting out at a burning splinter, so that a cloud
of flame blazed up in the air. The great amusement of the
holidays was to enter into honourable combat with a band of

hooligans like ourselves. After such excursions some of us would go about with marks on our faces till the next holiday.

But Jenia persuaded us not to go about the streets barefoot, and to wear boots, if we had them, or at least something on our feet, and to give up fighting and behave respectably.

Ivan D. lived in my courtyard. He was a pupil in the ecclesiastical school. From him I learned the strange fact that the letters of the Latin alphabet were arranged in quite a different order to ours. I was greatly surprised at this, and still more at the noble sound of the language when I heard D. declaim Circero's oration against Catiline. I could not understand how the language could be beautiful although the letters were in such disorder! And why did they say "Catiline" and not simply "Caterina"? There are many surprising things in life when one is only eleven years old.

We also had a friend named Petrov, who was older than any of us. He worked in a notary's office. Petrov was of a literary turn, and was friendly with the librarian of the Noblemen's Club, from whom he procured various books. My companions read them eagerly, and I often heard them talk of Poushkin, Gogol, and Lermontov. I understood but little of what they said, and did not like to ask questions. But I was not inclined to be outstripped by my friends, and so subscribed to the library list and began to read for myself. I read the *Revisor* and *Marriage* of Gogol, and the first part of his *Dead Souls*. I was far from understanding all I read, but it seemed entertaining and clever.

D., who lived next door to me, and who used to sleep on the same stove with me in winter, was devoted to Mayne Reid. Together we read *Quarteronka*, *The Headless Horseman*, *The Dead Shot*, and many similar works. I confess that this sort of literature pleased me more than Gogol, and I sought after it eagerly. I used to take the library catalogue and select the books with the most attractive titles, such as *Felix Holt, the Radical* or *Fiacre No. 14, Michaud à la Patte Noire, La Chambre Rose, The Jack of Hearts Club.* If the book did not interest me at once I abandoned it and took another. In this way I read a great many novels describing rascals and robbers in cloaks and wide-brimmed hats, who awaited their victims in dark streets; duellists who killed their seven men in an evening; omnibuses, fiacres; twelve strokes on the bell in the tower of the Church of St.-Germain l'Auxerrois; and other horrors.

I read so much about Paris, where all these things happened, that when I really went there it seemed to me that I had already lived in the town and knew it well. (Oh, Paris! My dear Paris!)

* * * * *

I was twelve years old when I first went to a theatre. It so happened that in the church choir in which I sang there was an agreeable youth named Pankratiev. He was seventeen, but still sang soprano. He is now an archdeacon in the Kazan monastery.

Once, after the liturgy, Pankratiev asked me if I would not like to go to the theatre, as he had a spare twenty-kopek ticket. I knew the theatre as a large stone building with semicircular windows, through the dusty panes of which one could discern some sort of lumber piled up. I hardly thought that anything likely to interest me could take place there.

"What is going to happen there?" I asked

"'A Russian Wedding,' a matinée performance."

A wedding? I so often sang at weddings that the ceremony no longer excited my curiosity. If it had been a French wedding, I should have been more interested. Nevertheless, I purchased the ticket from Pankratiev, though not very willingly.

Thus I found myself in the gallery of the theatre. It was a holiday and there was a large audience. I had to stand, maintaining my position by holding on to the ceiling with my hands.

I looked down with astonishment into an immense well surrounded by semicircular benches, and saw that its dark floor was covered with rows of chairs, amongst which people were moving about. The theatre was lighted with gas, the smell of which, from association, has throughout life continued to be pleasant to me. The design on the curtain represented a quotation from Poushkin's *Russlan and Lludmilla:* "By the sea is a green oak with a golden chain upon it, and a trained cat tied by the golden chain prowls ceaselessly around it." The orchestra was playing. Suddenly the curtain shook, then went up, and I stood stupefied, enchanted. It was as if a fairy tale which I dimly recollected had suddenly come to life. In a wonderfully decorated room, magnificently dressed people wearing travelling costumes of the seventeenth or eighteenth century promenaded, conversing, as it seemed to me, in the most beautiful language. I did not understand all that they said. What I saw shook me to the depths of my being, and I looked on at these wonders unwinkingly, without a thought for anything else.

When the final curtain fell I still stood there, enchanted by a waking dream—a dream I had never dreamt before, but which I had always anticipated. People shouted, pushed me about, went out and came in again, but I still stood there. When they began to put out the lights I felt very sad. It seemed incredible that all that life could have come to an end. I had "pins and needles" in my arms and legs. I remember wavering on my feet when I got out into the street.

I realised that the theatre was incomparably more interesting than Yashka Mamonov's booth at the fair. It was strange to see that it was still daylight out of doors, and to notice the rays of the setting sun gleaming on the bronze statue of Derjavin, our great Russian poet. I went back to the theatre and bought a ticket for the evening performance.

In the evening they played "Medea," with Palchikova in the title rôle, and Strielsky as Jason. I had a comfortable seat and could place my elbows on the railing. Again I gazed without once removing my eyes from the stage, where the moon shone as if taken from the skies and where Medea suffered as she fled with her children; where the handsome Jason stormed and raved. I looked on literally open-mouthed. In the midst of an *entr'acte* I noticed suddenly that I was slobbering, which very much upset me. I looked round cautiously to see if those near me had observed it, but it seemed they had not.

"I must keep my mouth closed," said I to myself.

But when the curtain rose again my lips parted once more, quite against my will. I had to put my hand over my mouth.

The theatre made me quite beside myself. Going home through the empty streets, in which the infrequent lamps seemed to wink at one another sleepily, I stopped here and there, calling to mind the eloquent speeches of the actors and reciting them aloud, imitating the manner and gesture of each of them.

"I am a queen, but a woman and a mother!" I mouthed in the quiet of the night, to the surprise of the sleepy watch-men. A morose-looking passer-by stopped in front of me and enquired:

"What's the matter?"

I ran away from him in confusion, and he stood gazing after me, probably thinking, "The boy's drunk!"

When I got home I related to my mother what I had seen. I was tormented by a desire to impart to her even a little of the joy which overfilled my heart. I spoke of Medea, Jason, Caterina in "The Thunderstorm," told her how beautiful the people were in the theatre, recited their words; but I felt that none of it interested my mother and that it was all incomprehensible to her.

"So, so," she answered tranquilly, thinking about her own affairs.

I especially wanted to talk to her about love—the main pivot about which revolved all that elevated life of the theatre. But somehow it embarrassed me to talk of it and I could not tell her about it in a simple and comprehensible fashion. I myself did not understand why people talked so beautifully, loftily, and purely about love in the theatre, while in the Sukonnaya suburb love was a dirty, obscene business which called forth malicious jests. On the stage love is the occasion of great deeds, but in our street it led to brawling. Could there be two kinds of love? Could one be the greatest happiness in life, and the other only debauchery and sin?

At that age, of course, I did not reflect very much over this contradiction, but naturally I could not fail to notice it. It was too much before my eyes.

With all my desire to disclose to my mother that new world which so enchanted me, I was unable to do so. And when all was said, I myself did not know the reason for the very simplest things; for instance, why they spoke of Jason and not of Jacob, or of Medea and not of Maria? Where did it all take place? Who were these people? What was the "Golden Fleece," and where was "Colchis"?

"So, so," said my mother. "All the same, you don't need to go to the theatre. You will get out of the way of going to work again. As it is, your father is always saying that you do nothing. Of course I defend you, but it is true none the less that you are an idler."

I really did do nothing, and was an idle boy at school. When I asked my father if I might go to the theatre he would not let me, saying:

"You'll have to become a yard porter, boy, instead of going to the theatre. Be a porter, and you will at least have a crust of bread, lad. What good is there in the theatre? You did not choose to be a craftsman, and you'll end up in prison. See how the craftsmen live—well-fed, dressed, and shod."

Still, most of the workmen I had seen were ragged and barefoot, half starved and drunken, and I did not believe what my father told me.

"But I work; I copy out papers," said I. "Look what a lot I've written already. . . ."

He threatened me: "I'll set you to work as soon as you've finished the school! So you know what to expect, dolt!"

The theatre continued to attract me more and more, and I more and more often kept back the money I got by singing. I knew it was not right to do so, but I felt unable to go alone to the theatre. I felt that I must share my impressions with somebody.

I began to take with me to the play one or other of my friends, for whom I bought tickets. Most often I took with me Michailov, who was also very much in love with the theatre; and during the *entr'actes* we used to dispute hotly, judging the acting of the players and searching for the meaning of the play.

A touring opera company arrived and the price of the tickets went up to thirty kopeks. The opera astonished me; as a choir singer I was, of course, not surprised that people sang and that the words were not very easy to understand. At weddings I myself used to sing in the old Slavonic tongue; but I was surprised to find that a world existed in which people sang about everything instead of speaking, as they did in the streets and houses of Kazan. This songful existence could not fail to overwhelm me with astonishment. Uncommon people, adorned in an unusual manner, exchanged question and answer in song; reflected, grew wrathful, died, sat, stood in tuneful numbers; in solos, duets, choruses, and every possible way!

I was astonished at this manner of life, which delighted me uncommonly.

"Suppose everybody always sang everywhere," I mused, "in the street, in the baths, at their workshops."

For instance, the craftsmen would chant:

"Fedka, thread!" lengthening out the words. And I would answer:

"Here you are, Nicolai Evtropich!"

Or the policeman might seize a citizen by the collar and declaim in a bass voice:

"I'll take you to the police station!"

And the citizen would reply in a tenor:

"Go easy, go easy, good man!"

Musing on this charming idea, I naturally began to convert everyday life into opera. My father would say to me:

"Fedka, kvass!"

And I would answer in a high soprano:

"I'll bring some at once!"

"What are you shouting for?" he would ask. Or I would sing:

"Papa, get up to drink tea!"

He used to open his eyes wide and say to my mother:

"Did you ever see the like? That's what the theatre is bringing him to!"

The theatre became a necessity of life to me, and the rôle of spectator in the gallery no longer satisfied me. I wanted to get behind the scenes and find out where they got the moon from, where the people disappeared to, how towns and costumes were so quickly got up, what became of all that brilliant life after the performance.

I tried more than once to penetrate into that land of wonders, but harsh people drove me forth with blows. Once, however, I succeeded in attaining my desire. I opened a little door and found myself on a narrow dark staircase encumbered with various rubbish, broken frames, and rags of canvas. There it was—the road to the marvels!

Squeezing past these relics, I suddenly found myself underneath the stage, in the midst of a diabolical entanglement of ropes, beams of wood, machinery, all of which was in movement, shaking and screeching. In this maze, men with hammers and hatchets in their hands darted to and fro, shouting at one another. Slipping past them like a mouse, I climbed up on to the stage behind the scenes, and found myself, as if in a waking dream, in the company of red Indians, Spaniards, carpenters, and dishevelled people with copybooks in their hands. Although the Indians and the Spaniards spoke Russian like the carpenters, I was none the less fascinated by them, and gazed on their painted faces and gaudy costumes with the greatest delight. Amongst them jostled to and fro real firemen in brass helmets, and over my head there were people exercising on hand rings, training to man the ships' ropes (for the opera being presented was "L'Africaine"), reminding me of Yashka Mamonov. The whole produced an enchanting impression on me, which I shall never forget!

Soon after that I took part in a play as a super. I put on a dark smooth costume and had my face blacked with burnt cork, for which insult I was promised a reward of five kopeks. I submitted to being painted not only without any access of timidity, but with much joy, zealously shouted "Hurrah" in honour of Vasco da Gama, and altogether enjoyed myself immensely. But I was much upset when I discovered that it was not very easy to wash off the burnt cork!

On my way home I rubbed snow on my forehead and face till I had used up an entire snowdrift, but none the less showed a smutty face like a negro when I got in. My parents requested me very seriously to explain what it all meant. I told them, but they were not satisfied, and my father beat me severely, saying:

"You'll have to be a yard porter, boy!"

"Why a yard porter, exactly?" I asked myself more than once.

Of the artists of that time I best remember the bass Iliashevitch in the rôle of Mephistopheles. I had heard nothing but ill of the devil. He was to me an almost real personality, a force dwelling amongst mankind but hostile to the human race; an ill will which jestingly created greater confusion in a life which was already difficult and confused. Iliashevitch seemed to me to impart to the devil and all his doings an especial awe-inspiring feeling of conviction. To me he was both terrifying and incomprehensible, yet significant, both on the stage, when he appeared red as fire, singing sneeringly and in tones of thunder that "Men die for gold," and behind the scenes, when he spoke everyday words in ordinary human tones. His eyes, which seemed to shoot forth fiery-red sparks, frightened me to trembling, and I thought their strange glitter was a natural peculiarity of the actor's eyes until I discovered that it was produced by something stuck to his eyelashes.

Once when I was passing Iliashevitch's dressing room he said to me:

"Boy, take these twenty kopeks and buy me some grapes."

I dashed out of the theatre to the town square, where the Tartars sold fruit from trays, and bought some grapes. Iliashevitch gave me a little bunch of grapes for my pains.

I was overjoyed, and determined to take them home to my mother. I carried them about with me till the play was over, in fear of crushing them, but on the way home my childish curiosity, for I had never tasted grapes, overcame my love for my mother, and I ate them myself.

The idol of the public, and especially of the student youth of both sexes, was the tenor Zakrjevsky. He was adored; literally speaking, his admirers carried him in their arms; the young men took the horses out of his carriage and dragged it through the streets themselves. I remember with what awe I stood before the door, on which was a brass plate with the name, "Julian Fedorovitch Zakrjevsky."

I remember how my heart beat, anticipating that the door might suddenly open and I should see this universally idolised person!

Some years later I encountered Zakrjevsky, a semi-invalid, forgotten by everyone and almost a beggar. I had the sad honour of helping him a little and saw in his eyes tears of shame and gratitude, tears of anger and hopeless weakness. That was a sad encounter.

But such is the fate of the singer: he is the toy of the public, and nothing more. When his voice is gone the man is lost, he is forgotten by all, and abandoned like a wooden soldier which was once a child's favourite but of which it has grown tired. If you do not wish to suffer the same fate as the idol of my youth, "strike the iron while it is hot"; work while you have strength, unsparingly!

* * * * *

I finished my school days when I was thirteen, and to my parents' surprise I received a satisfactory testimonial on leaving. To tell the truth, I somewhat deceived my teachers. At the examination before leaving, the pupils had to write a story taken from their own lives. I felt convinced that I

could not write such a story, and made up my mind that it
would be much better to extract one from some book. So I
rewrote from some author or other a tale about a little boy
going with his grandfather to the forest for wood, and seeing
a snake by the way; how he killed the snake and what his
feelings were as he did so; what his grandfather said, where
the sun was shining, and so on. For this story, which I
handed in to the teacher with great trepidation, feeling
almost certain I should be detected in the deception, I got the
highest number of marks—that is to say, five! Honour and
glory to Learning! She was uncommonly gracious to me. I
involuntarily recollected what happened when my legs were
bad and I went to the doctor.

Besides the successful story, I also won the hearts of my
teachers at the examination by reading aloud the "Steppe"
of Koltsov and the "Borodino" of Lermontov, after the
manner of a small-town actor—that is, with gestures, groans,
and other methods appropriate to art! When reciting the
poem "Borodino" I called out "Uncle" and answered in a
genuine avuncular voice. The performance pleased my
teachers exceedingly; but my fellow pupils ridiculed me
afterwards, though I noticed that they listened to my reading with interest at the time. The reading seemed to them
to be improper, affected, and even something to be ashamed
of.

"Well," said my father, "now you are a finished scholar.
It is time you began to work. You do nothing but go to the
theatre, read books, and sing songs! You will have to give
up all that. . . ."

When drunk, he would call me to him, rap my pate with
his knuckles, and reiterate:

"You'll have to be a yard porter!"

Finally, he announced to me:

"I have found a place for you at Petchionkin's the pawnbroker's. You'll get no wages at first, but later on you will take what they choose to give you."

So I soon found myself behind the counter of a pawn-broker's shop, where I sat from nine till four o'clock every day. A great variety of dismal people used to bring rings, fur coats, spoons, watches, jackets, ikons (holy pictures); the valuer appraised the lot at a lump sum and stated a lesser amount which he would pay out by way of advance; disputes and haggling went on; people used bad language, wept, begged for a larger sum, pleading a mother's illness, the death of a son, and so forth; and meanwhile I made out the receipts and dreamed about the theatre. The lovely flower song from "Faust":

> Tell her, my flowers,
> How much I love her,

used to run through my head as I worked.

After working without wages for two months, I began to receive the sum of eight rubles per month. I detested my occupation profoundly, but was proud to be earning something and helping my mother to live. I worked hard, in spite of my distaste for my employment, and was well thought of by my master.

In the summer, a light opera company played in the Panaevsky Gardens, with them came *diseuses* and *chanson-niers*. Of course I used to visit the Gardens. I took a very great interest in the artists, but was somehow afraid of them and always watched them from a quiet corner. As I looked on I mused:

"What wonderful people! There goes a man who just now was a king, and now he is dressed like anyone else, drinks beer, and eats *sukhari* (dried bread)."

All the kings, Achilles, Pericles, Menelaus, and Lamber-tuccio from Boccaccio, as well as gipsy barons and governors, seemed to me equally interesting both on and off the stage. They were all of them merry buffoons and jesters. I thought theirs must be an easy life! While I sat all day at the pawn-broker's, where people groaned and cursed, complained and wept, all day and every day. And it was just the same out-side of the pawnbroker's in our Sukonnaya suburb.

I soon left Petchionkin's, why I can no longer precisely recall; but I am positive it was owing to the theatre, which diminished my enthusiasm for my work. Of course my father scolded me very severely, and forthwith sent me to school again, this time to a school of handicrafts in the small country town of Arsk. I don't think my father sent me there out of any wish to make me a craftsman, but chiefly because he knew there was no theatre there. Arsk is the meanest and most insignificant town on the face of the earth.

I left my parents for the first time and travelled alone with a country postman, a certain Holtzmann, who was a very decent fellow. It was wonderful dry autumn weather. The sunlight gilded the trees by the roadside, and threads of spiders' webbing floated in the blue translucent air "like threads from the water nymphs' spinning wheel." I seemed to be travelling towards some beautiful strange country, and I quietly rejoiced at leaving the Sukonnaya suburb, where life had become more and more disagreeable to me.

I chose the trade of carpenter for myself. It pleased me to find that the pupils in the senior classes might make boxes for their own use. But the handicraft soon began to seem a horrible one to me, for the carpenter who taught us used to beat the pupils—and myself oftener than anyone else—with all sorts of tools and materials, set squares and boards, and thought nothing of poking one in the stomach or rapping one on the head with a heavy plane. I asked to be trans-ferred to the bookbindery, merely because there were fewer heavy tools there, and a blow on the head with a book did

not cause one so much pain as a blow with a board an inch
or more in thickness. I very quickly learned how to bind a
book and used to do it fairly well.

Besides learning a handicraft, we had to work in the vege-
table gardens of the school. We used to pull and chop up
cabbages and pickle cucumbers. But it was all very dull and
I did not make friends with my fellow pupils. My only
pleasure was in going to the baths on Saturdays. We used
to stop in the steam bath until we were boiling hot, then rush
out of the baths quite nude and roll ourselves in the snow,
which fell early and very abundantly that winter. People
call it a dangerous practice, but we found it very good fun.

Once—I think it was on the winter's day of St. Nicholas—
I was sitting on the bench at the gates and thinking about
Kazan and the theatre, regretting that I was in this miserable,
humdrum Arsk. I had a few kopeks in my pocket, and suddenly made up my mind to go to Kazan, come what might!
I got up and set off, but I had not gone ten *versts*,[1] when
two men on horseback caught me up. They were the school
caretaker and a student of the senior class. They took me
back to the school, where I got a drubbing for running away.
I resigned myself to the idea that I should not get away from
Arsk before the spring.

Unexpectedly, a letter came from my father. My mother
was dangerously ill and there was no one to look after her.
I must go home immediately. I set off with some people
who were going the same way with carts. It was fearfully
cold travelling. I got quite benumbed, and we went at a
snail's pace. But what a pleasure it was to stop on our way,
to drink tea and eat black bread in the taverns!

My mother turned out to be really very ill indeed. She
cried out so much with pain that my heart nearly burst, and

---

[1] *Verst* is a Russian measurement of distance equal to a little less than
a mile.

I felt sure that she must die. But she was removed to the hospital and Professor Vinogradov there cured her. My mother spoke of him almost with awe to her last day.

My father found me a place as clerk in the office of the District Land Administration, and I went to work with him. We used to copy long reports with masses of figures, and frequently worked till late at night, sleeping on the office desks. My father, who worked at the secretary's desk, used to tell me stories about a former secretary who had the singular name of Pifiev. This man, it seemed, kept a strap at home with which, in his spare time, he taught his wife how she should behave.

My father was considered a good worker. Evidently the secretary valued him, for when he had drunk too much and became quarrelsome and impertinent, the official said nothing, but contented himself with winking and compressing his lips.

CHAPTER THREE

A Boyhood Sweetheart and a Duel—Medita-
tions on Love—A Barbaric Custom—I
Espouse the Cause of Woman—Pastimes—
My First Rôle—I Become a Copyist—We
Move to Astrakhan.

AS a result of reading thrilling novels and seeing so much
of life as it is represented in the theatre, I began to
think about love somewhat prematurely. My companions
were no more strangers than I to such thoughts. We all considered ourselves to be in love with Olga B., a pretty, placid
schoolgirl who walked with a waddling gait rather like a
duck, and looked on the whole world with indifferent gaze.
Goodness! how eagerly we awaited the approach of Easter,
when, according to the old Russian custom, we might exchange kisses with Olga after the midnight service! Not
only kisses, but the traditional salutations, "Christ is risen!"
"He is, in truth." Thus this custom was pagan on one side
and Christian on the other. I remember that opposite the
Church of the Descent of the Holy Ghost the Tartars traded
in cloth, silks, all sorts of haberdashery, soap, and wonderful
scent, of which one could buy a small bottle for three kopeks.
We bought some of this scent, and before the end of the
morning service we ran out on to the porch of the church,
where we all put scent on our teeth, lips, and the tips of our
tongues. The perfume produced a burning sensation, but
we smelt awfully nice! When Olga came out we went up
to her one after the other, like people getting tickets at a
theatre box office, said, "Christ is risen!" and cautiously em-

braced the lady of our hearts. She remained quite calm
and indifferent.

Jenia Virilov for some reason or other called her "Dulcinea Toboskaia," which sounded rather ugly to me. I cor-
rected him once, saying, "Tobolskaia, not Toboskaia!" I
thought it much more appropriate that she should be called
after the town of Tobolsk in Siberia.

"Shut up, if you don't know what it means," said he.

Our Dulcinea was the cause of my fighting a duel with
rapiers, as is meet for true knights. The duel occurred not
owing to any unavoidable necessity, but because we were inclined to it after reading Dumas and Ponson du Terrail.
Our clique made the acquaintance of a schoolboy who used
to steal muskets from his father, which he sold and spent
the money on buying beer for us. He was really a good
fellow, and we did not like him only because he paid for
our beer.

Well, on one occasion this youth permitted himself to
show insufficient respect to our young lady. It was not that
he did anything very special, but when one loves one cannot
help being jealous. It was happiness to any one of us to say
two or three words to Olga and to spend a moment in her
company. Unfortunately, I got even fewer of these
moments than any of my friends. I was the youngest and
least interesting of them all, but I was the one who told the
aforesaid youth to go to the deuce! He wanted to knock me
down, but my comrades stood up for me, declaring that if he
desired "satisfaction," any one of us was prepared to fight
him. He warmly agreed that a duel was unavoidable.

I was selected as the champion, since I could imitate
Mephistopheles, Faust, and Valentine, by bending a stick in
the manner of a duellist with a rapier, and making all sorts
of theatrical martial pirouettes and gestures with it. It was

unanimously resolved that I was the one who ought to run our insulter through the body.

Jenia brought us a couple of rapiers, which were hung usually as an ornament on the wall in his home. We took them to a smith to have them sharpened. I remember the blades of the rapiers were black, while their points shone as bright as silver.

We selected the Osokinskaya wood as the place of battle. The seconds of both parties were my friends, but they behaved with irreproachable correctness towards both the duellists. Altogether everything was arranged as it is in the very best romances.

"Don't try to do too much," said one of the seconds to us.

The other corroborated him, "Remember, there is no need to fight to the death!"

The duel was begun and ended in one minute, or maybe less. Striking our rapiers together once or twice, we lunged at each other as we liked best; my opponent aimed at my forehead, and I at his shoulder. Evidently he felt a good deal of pain, for he let go of his rapier, which hung down from my head. I at once pulled it out, and blood poured abundantly from the wound and ran into my eyes. Blood also ran down my opponent's arm. As we had agreed not to fight to the death, but only to the first drawing of blood, the seconds declared the duel terminated and began to bandage up our wounds, for which purpose one of them magnanimously tore strips from his cotton underclothing.

We duellists shook hands, and we all set off at once to steal apples from some one's orchard—which, of course, we did not consider to be really stealing—and in the evening I returned home very proud of myself, and was severely beaten. That was horrible. A person came home with the noblest feelings in his breast, only to have his trousers re-

moved and be beaten with rough cords. It was an unbearable act of oppression!

I don't know whether Olga knew about the duel, but probably some one told her. Anyhow, her attitude of indifference to me and my destinies did not undergo any change.

Love, both of the kind which was enacted in the theatre
and of the kind which troubled the Sukonnaya suburb, could
not but disturb my imagination. The girls of our neighbourhood used to sing, musingly:

> "Upon a silvery snow field
> Knelt a maid beneath the moon,
> And swore to Heaven that she would keep
> Her bower inviolate till death."

No doubt the words are stupid stuff, but they rang with a
sincerity of feeling which I understood. Further on in the
same song there were words which were not so stupid:

> "My love is stronger than the grave.
> I have yielded to it all myself.
> Love my strength has taken away,
> In its fires I have faded."

Although the song was sung by the faded village girls, it
nevertheless used to touch me to the heart.

I saw that everyone sought for love, and knew that all
suffered for it, both married and single, officials and mo-
distes, market-garden workers and labourers. In that direction there was much that was intimidating and that I could
not understand. Why did the girls and young women sing
about love so sadly and touchingly? Why did the youths
and many grown men talk to each other coarsely and jestingly about love and go to the bad houses on the "Sands"?
I knew what those houses were, and could not connect that
institution with the love which was spoken of in the "Dame
aux Camélias."

I sang at weddings, seeing brides who were really like white doves, and I observed that they nearly always wept. Village girls when they get married also weep and sing songs condemning married life. Thereafter they all, both town girls and country girls, "bear children in pain and sorrow." But none the less they all try to get married, all seek for love. The latter is in reality the chief thing in life.

Altogether, everything I knew with regard to the relations of the sexes seemed to be irreconcilably contradictory. It was obvious to me that in everyday life woman was merely a domestic animal, and the more valuable in proportion to the patience with which she toiled. At the same time I saw that woman everywhere brought holiday with her and that in her presence life became purer and more beautiful. I used to be present at the evening festivities which the men got up in the shops; the foremen and other workers, drunkards and foul-mouthed fellows, made us apprentices clear up the workshop, bought cakes, and sweetmeats, nuts and liquid refreshments, and invited girls—sempstresses, boxmakers, and housemaids—to the dances and games they arranged.

They used to play at "forfeits": a wild-looking fellow would select some girl and take her arm, while the others sang:

> "Heavens above, Heavens above!
> Whatever has come over me!
> Cheeks all covered o'er with blushes,
> Ruddy little lips!
>
> "Then her eyebrows and her eyes,
> They simply are a wonder!
> Kiss I will, and then once more,
> And be off then to my home!"

One ought to have seen the happy confusion of the boot-maker, tailor, or carpenter, when he clumsily and shamefacedly kissed his chosen maid; one ought to have seen her girlish blushes and the look in her eyes at that moment! It was a good thing in our lives, though it may now appear ridiculous; it wonderfully transfigured the laborious life in the semisubterranean workshops!

Through it all I felt that woman was the joy and the ruler of life! But at the same time many other things which coarsely humiliated her could not but strike the eye.

There was a certain custom which greatly surprised me. The sister of one of my friends married for love a young post-office clerk. I went to the wedding and looked on at the festivities. It was very merry and interesting. Late in the evening the young couple retired to their attic room, and I and my friend to the hayloft.

In the morning I was awakened by wild squeals, cries; in a word, an uproar as though some great disaster had occurred. I looked out into the courtyard and saw a scene which I shall never forget. Down there a number of intoxicated, half-dressed, dishevelled women were madly leaping and prancing. Some of them were dancing a wild jig, in which they lifted their skirts to their knees and even higher; others sang in high ear-piercing tones; still others were hammering pots and pans on the ground and the walls of the house or beating on frying pans and the like cooking utensils. A few were waving in the air a piece of linen upon which were stains. The crazy scene frightened me. Half-intoxicated men were laughing, shouting, and embracing the women, who continued to prance and dance about the courtyard like gnats over a pool. The young couple stood holding hands on the ancient staircase in front of the house, and looked on smilingly at the mad goings-on, in which there was much to make one blush. The women dancing in the yard shouted obscene words and showed their legs, and the men's comments were no less coarse. But the young couple were happy. I have never seen such happy eyes as they had that morning.

I asked my friend, who was older and more experienced than I, what they were doing.

"They are rejoicing," he answered. "Don't you hear what they are singing? That means my sister was an honest girl. 'The flowers have faded.' "

I asked in surprise: "Then is she less honourable now?"

My friend explained to me at great length the nature of maiden virtue. I listened with great interest, but none the less felt a certain embarrassment and shame. In all he said and everything that went on in the courtyard before my eyes I felt the existence of something wrong, a sort of derision of woman and of love.

I might not have related this incident, but I want to say that since then, whatever I have done, I have done in the cause of woman, for her soul and as her knight and champion; to win her regard and her love.

* * * * *

I have sailed over the beautiful Mediterranean and the Atlantic ocean, but I still remember with affection the tranquil dark lake of Kaban.

On summer evenings I particularly loved the lake. I used to walk along the shore, or climb into one of the great willow trees and sit there till daybreak like some nocturnal bird, musing and looking over the lake. Its quietude and stillness brought order into my thoughts, leading them away from the squalor in which the life of the Sukonnaya suburb flowed sluggishly onwards. Sometimes through the silence of the night a mournful but seldom sober voice would sound from the "Sands," where the fast houses were, singing the song which was then fashionable, about a maiden kneeling "beneath the moon, in a silvery snow field." A watchman would sound his rattle, and I used to listen for the meaning of this signal. If it rattled fast and for a long time, I knew there was a fire somewhere. Then I would get down from my tree and run posthaste to the fire, guided by the reflection in the sky. But if the watchman rattled slowly it meant that all was well and the thieves might continue their labours in peace, sure of the whereabouts of the threatening guardian, who was usually an old man of sixty at least, sickly and afflicted with deafness.

On one side of the Kaban Lake was the quiet Tartar village and the huge Krestovnikov factory, while on the other lay the "Sands," where people drank and brawled all night long. Between these two was the "Devil's Corner," where noisy bands of students, dressmakers, and all sorts of young men and women used to visit in rowing boats.

Sometimes my friends and I would go fishing. The great prize was the *sorojka,* a fish considered noble game and the catching of which was regarded as a piece of rare good luck. People with lively imaginations used to relate:

"Yesterday some one from the Sukonnaya caught a *podleshchik* weighing a pound and a half."

But I think no one ever met a person who said: "I have caught a *podleshchik* weighing a pound and a half!"

When we caught a fish we used to cook it on the spot, and if there was no other wood available we used to break out boards from the "Bishop's Bridge." Of course, breaking up the bridge was not a proper thing for us to do.

It was delightful on Kaban Lake in summer, but still better in winter, when we could skate over the blue ice, and when on holidays bouts of fisticuffs used to take place there. They call that an improper amusement, too. On the one hand we, that is to say, Russian Kazan, used to assemble, and on the other the good-natured Tartars. The small boys would begin the combat. While one was skating an agile

little Tartar boy would suddenly dash up, give one a blow
in the face, and away again with a taunting shout. And the
recipient would apply snow to his bleeding nose and reflect
without ill humour:

"Wait a bit, ugly; I'll show you!"

And in one's turn one would deal a blow to some unwary
Tartar boy. These lively cavalry engagements on skates and
singly, man to man, used to develop gradually, drawing into
the struggle ever greater forces, both Russian and Tartar.
People would throw off their skates, handing them over to a
friend to look after, and go into the fight on foot in mass
formation. Gradually the half-grown youths and, after
them, the young men would enter into the struggle, and
finally, in the very heat of battle, staid men of forty and
upwards. We used to fight desperately, sparing neither
ourselves nor the enemy. But even in the heat of battle we
never forgot the rules laid down of old—not to hit a man
who was down nor one squatting on his heels; not to use
one's feet nor to conceal heavy objects in one's mittens. Anyone caught with a five-kopek piece (a large copper coin), a
bullet, or a piece of iron hidden in his mittens got a drubbing
both from his own side and from the other.

The chief interest of these battles for us boys was centred
in the "strong men." The "strong men" on the Russian side
were two bath attendants, Merkulov and Jukovsky, both
of them already respectable old men; after them Sirotkin
and Pikulin, in whose house I lived in the Sukonnaya. Pikulin was a huge, broad-shouldered man, with curly red hair,
a pointed beard, and the clear eyes of a child. He kept a
number of pigeons for shooting, of which sport he was in-
ordinately fond. I used to help him to chase the birds;
climbing up on the roof with him, I would take off my
breeches, place them on a pole, and frighten off the "roof
sitters," or fat and lazy pigeons that would not take to their

wings. Of course standing on a roof without one's trousers, waving them wildly and whistling in ear-piercing tones, is improper, and I would not do it now for anything. But I would find some way to frighten the birds off, all the same!

Pikulin had such enormous hands and broad, spadelike wrists, that when I gave a pigeon to him it seemed as if he would gather me up in his grasp together with the snowy bird. I entertained a profound respect for him, as I did for all the "strong men," even those of the Tartar party, Sagatulin and Bagitov. When I saw these men, who were all of them good-natured and kind, knocking down Russian and Tartar boxers with their mighty blows, it recalled to my mind the stories of Bova and Yeruslan Lazarevitch, and my life, which was so lacking in beauty and forcefulness, took on an epic quality.

Legends grew up around these "strong men" which contributed to our boyish awe of them. It was said of Merkulov that the governor himself had forbidden him to fight and had even ordered to be indelibly stamped on both his hands the words "Forbidden to take part in boxing contests."

But on one occasion the Tartars were beginning to overwhelm the Russians and drove them back to the bridge over the Bulak Canal, which connected the Kaban Lake with the Kasanka River. All the Russian champions were badly knocked about and weary, and resolved to summon Merkulov to their assistance. As the police were keeping their eye on him, he was brought to the lake concealed in a barrel, as though a water carrier were coming for water. The strong man easily got into the barrel. He was short, and had bowed legs like a tailor. He climbed out of the barrel, and everyone, both Tartars and Russians, recognised him, the former with consternation, and the latter hailing him with delight:

"Merkulov!"

What power in a name!

The Tartars promptly retreated across the bridge and into their own village. In the heat of conflict fighters of both parties fell from the bridge into the Bulak, in which there flowed, even in winter, an unfreezing stream of warm dirty water from the baths situated on its banks. Passing over to their own side of the canal, the Tartars reassembled their forces, and the battle continued to rage in the streets of the village until the fire brigade came on the scene and deluged the combatants with water.

I went next day to see the place of battle. The damage done was considerable; the railings of the bridge were broken, and all the market booths were smashed up.

I believe this occurred in 1886. From that time they began to prohibit fighting on the Kaban Lake. Policemen visited the lake at holiday times and drove away the boys, who were the primary instigators, with whips.

I used to take delight in fires, too. They always bring into being an especially brilliant dramatic life of their own. The mere circumstance that people gathered at a conflagration in a different manner to that in which citizens came together in our Sukonnaya suburb, to deliberate upon the questions as to what tavern they should favour with their custom, or whom they should beat, was alone sufficient to make a holiday of the occasion. I recollect how magnificently the huge wooden four- or five-storyed Shamov mill on the Kasanka burned. The flames played with it as a cat plays with a mouse. White-hot sheets of iron from the roof were flung into the air like red birds, and the distant windows of the governor's palace on the hill shone with a blood-red reflection. The captain of the fire brigade, a little man, ran to and fro, streaming with perspiration, which ran down his face in black rivulets, and shouted:

"Pump, pump, you devils!" And he beat over the head everyone who came near him. The people had no desire to assist him and ran away in all directions. Many of them said openly:

"That's what they deserve! Let it burn!"

"It's insured!"

"You may bet they set it alight themselves!"

Almost everybody was glad that a rich man was being burned out, and no one regretted the labour converted into ashes.

It is jolly to watch a fire, but sad to reflect over it.

I was fond of going to the woods for mushrooms. We assembled, once, early in the morning, and had put on our lapti and picked up our baskets, when some one told us that there would very shortly be an eclipse of the sun. People had talked about it before, but not seriously, jesting and doubting:

"Probably it is some hoax invented by the students!"

But when a thin black hoop appeared on the sun's rim, the good folk of the Sukonnaya unwillingly bestirred themselves, saying:

"Look, it really seems as though there was something. . . ."

The sky was cloudless, the morning clear, when all at once a dull greyish shade began to come over everything. Some one had given us boys the hint to smoke pieces of glass and look at the sun through them. I did so, for one, and saw the sun expire, gradually becoming a black disc. I could not believe my eyes and put aside the smoked glass, but even without it the sun grew darker and smaller.

The world grew more and more grey and dull. The chill greyness made one's heart heavy. Cows lowed somewhere, but not in the usual way. People stood silent with their faces turned towards the sky. Their faces, too, were grey, and it seemed as though their eyes grew duller with the expiring sun. A terrified cat ran past me. A cock rushed crazily between people's feet. Then a moment came when the sun was not visible at all, but in its place a black disc about as big as a small frying pan hung in the sky, and from its rim pallid rays stuck out like red needles. It was awesome enough to make one cry!

But next moment a golden crescent of glittering light burned forth. The sun blazed out once more and the dismal shade began to melt away. The first to rejoice and hail him was the cock. Next the folk shook off their feeling of oppression and began to chatter. In a few minutes all was as before and already someone was shouting:

"I'll give it you. . . ."

My friends and I set off to gather mushrooms, some ten miles from the town, going by way of the Arskoye field, past the madhouse, where I once saw a madman, as I well remember. I had gone there with a choir to sing the funeral service for a deceased inmate. We arrived too soon and went into the garden. A pale, tired-looking man in a dressing gown and slippers and the usual underwear was quietly walking up and down the paths. We made up our minds that he was a madman, but he came up to us and began to ask me in a reasonable way who I was, why I had come there, where I sang, in what church, and whose compositions. He spoke in a perfectly natural way, and I had come to the conclusion that he must be a doctor, when suddenly, pointing to a short thick log of wood, he said:

"Let's roll it!"

"Where to? Why?" we asked.

"To beat the Saviour!" he explained in serious tones.

When we asked him why, he answered quietly and confidently:

"Christ, who has hindered me from living in the world."

The attendants came up just then and led him away.

The mad fantasy of the man greatly astonished me, as did the circumstance that, though he had lost his reason, he had nevertheless not forgotten the habit of all reasonable people of beating and fighting.

We got to the woods only as night was coming on, collected a few mushrooms, arranged our bivouac on the bank of a stream, then dug up some potatoes in a field, and, building ourselves a fire, boiled a stew in our kettle. We ate, and laid ourselves down around the fire, overlooking the stream, amongst the dark stems of the forest, talking and listening to gruesome stories.

I remember a dreadful tale being told about some students who were sitting in a beer shop and boasting that none of them was afraid of anything. One of them bragged that he could open a grave at midnight in the cemetery.

Now, I will stop a moment to tell you something about Russian cemeteries. They are the most beautiful spots imaginable, perpetual gardens, set deep in the woods, with beautiful trees and flowers in the greatest abundance. Charming pools and shady paths invite the visitor to rest or stroll. Of course these cemeteries are most beautiful in the spring, when their trees and shrubbery are alive with every variety of singing birds. So enchanting are these gardens of the dead that in the spring of the year they are often the favourite trysting places of young lovers. There, in the shimmering moonlight, while the nightingale's chant casts its magic spell, young men and women come to express the strongest desire of the living in the very midst of the dead!

But—to return to our students—

"One must not open graves!" said his friends. "They send you to Siberia for that."

But he persisted:

"Well, if you like, I'll lie down in a newly dug grave?"

They debated, and decided that he should go at night to one of the vaults in the cemetery and bring something thence, as a proof of his heroism—perhaps a lump of cement. He consented, and set off. His comrades determined to have some fun and followed him. They hid in various places amongst the graves and waited. Presently they saw him approach a freshly dug grave and prepare to descend into it. Then they began to mutter in unearthly voices and to groan, but he cried:

"Don't disturb yourselves, you dead folks; you won't frighten me. I am not afraid of you!"

He lay down in the grave, got out again and went towards a vault. Pelted by unseen hands, hooted at by voices, although apparently alone, he began to feel afraid and started running. His friends commenced throwing earth at him. Suddenly he fell with a shriek, and when his friends came to him he was dead. It seemed that a hoop from a barrel had lain in his path. He stepped on it, and turning it struck him sharply in the back. The shock and terror caused by this trifling occurrence killed him.

I listened with awe mingled with pleasure to this tale, which recalled to me vividly the stories of Kirilovna and my mother's village friends. When it became necessary to go into the wood for fuel, I begged that one of my companions should go with me, but they laughed and compelled me to go quite alone. I was frightened, but went and managed to gather some wood.

We did not sleep a minute that night, and next morning got up early and scattered through the woods, gathering mushrooms, and set out for home in the afternoon with full baskets. On the way we stopped and lay down to rest. I fell asleep, and my friends went on without waking me. When I woke up it was dark, the woods were all around me, and it seemed as if some one was noiselessly moving amongst the trees and silently ambushing me. I set off home swiftly, without looking round, and feeling as if my legs would fail me. The forest stirred behind me and trees seemed to block my path. I thought some one caught at my heels, breathing cold on my back and the nape of my neck. I still had to pass by the cemetery. The dead folk looked at me through its fence. They walked amongst the graves, shook the crosses, stood in white winding sheets beneath the birch trees. I tried not to see them, singing songs and talking to myself, but horrors crept out on me from all sides.

Of course I knew one ought not to be afraid of the dead; they were much better than the living; they did not drink nor swear nor fight. Yes, I knew all that, but presumably did not believe in it very strongly. I don't know how I found strength to get home, nor why my heart did not burst.

After that, however much I was urged to go for mushrooms to distant woods, I never went, but chose other places where there were fewer mushrooms, but where there was nothing at all to be afraid of.

* * * * *

I had an acquaintance by the name of Kamensky, a very theatrical youth of seventeen. He acted small parts in plays on the open-air stage in the Panaevsky Gardens. He told me one day:

"There is a splendid opportunity for you of getting on the stage! Our manager is very strict, but he is well disposed towards young people. Ask him to give you a chance!"

"But I can't act!"

"Never mind! Try! Perhaps he will give you a part with two or three words. . . ."

I went to the stage manager, and he at once offered me the part of the gendarme in the play "Gendarme Roger," a comedy translated from the French. I do not remember the name of its author. The play deals with thieves and tramps who are continually playing all sorts of tricks, whilst Gendarme Roger endeavours in vain to catch them. I was commissioned to play the part of this clumsy gendarme, and at once fell into a state of blissful and incessant agitation, due to my joy and the consciousness of the responsibility resting upon me.

We had to be at the rehearsal at eleven o'clock in the morning, at which hour I must be at my duties in the Ouprava. The natural consequence was that I was overcome by a severe headache. I put on the air of one tortured by unbearable sufferings, and told the accountant:

"Fedor Michailovitch, let me go home. My head aches frightfully!"

The accountant had keen, dark-brown eyes, and the glasses he wore increased their apparent size and the severity of his gaze. He looked at me for a few moments in silent contempt and, having crushed me with his gaze, said in tones which pierced me like a needle:

"Be off."

I went, feeling that he did not believe in my sufferings, but still keeping up my pose by placing my hand to my forehead, and taking care not to give myself away by hurrying. So that no one should notice which way I went, I stooped down as low as I could while passing the office windows of the Administration, when I got into the street.

It was agreeably gay in the Panaevsky Gardens. Birds fluttered about in the trees. Actresses strolled along the pathways with queenly gait, laughing and joking. I was already acquainted with some of them and even transcribed their parts for them, of which I was very proud.

I was stupidly and morbidly bashful; nevertheless, at the rehearsals, amongst people I knew who were dressed in their ordinary clothes, and behind the lowered curtain, I managed to get to work, grasped my part, and acted after a fashion.

The longed-for evening arrived. I came to the Gardens earlier than anyone else, went into the dressing room and put on a uniform of green calico with red collar and facings, with cloth gaiters, and plastered my face with various colours; but was not very well pleased with the effect of the whole when completed. My heart thumped uneasily and my legs were somewhat out of control.

The play began. I can't say what I felt that evening. I only recollect a number of horribly disagreeable sensations. It seemed as if my heart were taken out of my body and pierced and cut. I recollect being pushed on to the stage. "Now it is your turn!" some one said. I knew full well that I had to walk about, talk, and seem to be alive. But I was quite unable to move. My feet seemed to be stuck to the boards of the floor; my hands hung at my sides immovably; my tongue swelled up, choked up my mouth, and turned to wood. I could not say a word nor move a finger. Behind the scenes I heard various voices whispering:

"Speak, you fool! Say something!"

"Speak, ass!"

"Hit him with something or other. . . ."

Everything seemed to go round before my eyes; a huge deep mouth guffawed with many voices; the stage rocked. I felt as if I should sink through the floor or die.

The curtain fell, but I stood there immovable, as though turned to stone, until the stage manager, white with rage, began to beat me, tearing the gendarme's costume from my body. The gaiters and boots came off my feet by themselves, and finally falling into a patch of nettles I was pushed forth into the Gardens in my underwear, and a moment later my jacket and other garments were hurled forth after me. I crept away into a quiet corner of the Gardens, dressed myself, climbed over the fence and walked away, without observing where I went. I wept.

Later on I found myself in the Archangelskaya suburb at Kamensky's home, and sat there in a shed for two days without eating anything and afraid to show myself in the street. I thought that everyone in the town, even the women who hung out washing in the courtyards, must know what a howling mess I had made of things and how I had been beaten.

At length I determined to go home, and on the way recollected that I had not been to work for three days. When I got home my parents enquired where I had been. I invented some story or other to account for my absence, but my mother told me sadly:

"They'll be sure to discharge you from your work. The caretaker came and asked where you were."

Next day I went to the Ouprava, nevertheless, and asked the caretaker, Stephen, how matters stood.

"They've already engaged some one else in your place," he told me.

I sat with him for a while in his place under the staircase, and then went home.

* * * * *

Things were very bad at home. My father got drunk almost every day now; my mother went out charring by the day, but was rapidly losing her strength. I continued to sing in the church choir, but my earnings were small. Besides that, my voice broke. I was already fifteen years old, and my boyish soprano was about to disappear.

It occurred to me to petition the Law Courts for a job, in the Palais de Justice, as a copyist. I was hired and sat day in and day out, transcribing the judgments of the court. The work was so arduous that I seldom finished in office hours, but was obliged to take some material home with me.

The officials in the Palais de Justice, all except little clerks or copyists like me, wore frock coats or coats with bright buttons. Everything was very severe and respectable, inspiring me with a feeling that I should not long be a servant in the Temple of Justice. Here in the Law Courts I experienced for the first time the pleasure of drinking coffee, which had till then been unknown to me. The caretakers used to bring round coffee with cream for five kopeks a glass. My salary was fifteen rubles a month, and of course I could not indulge in coffee every day. But I used to stay behind and do the turn of night duty for the others, for which I received fifty kopeks from my fellow employees, and I drank coffee much more frequently than some of them who received pretty good salaries.

The chief clerk, a very handsome man with gray hair and a goatee, always seemed to me a very important person. He brushed his hair backwards from his forehead, and wore eyeglasses in a gold frame on a broad black ribbon. His brown eyes were shadowed by thick eyebrows, and he spoke in the grandiloquent tones affected by Kisselevsky, a once well-known "gentleman actor." The chief clerk, too, appeared to me to be a "gentleman," and reminded me of a marquis from one of Dumas' novels. I mention him with so much detail because I never have been able to understand how anyone with such a magnificent exterior could drive me from the Law Courts in so coarse a fashion.

On one occasion, when unable to finish my task, after receiving my salary, I went to purchase tea, sugar, and various provisions to take home with me, also buying some books from a bookseller. I drove home in a cab, and suddenly discovered, to my dismay, that I had lost the bundle of papers from the Law Courts which I had been carrying with me. I was horrorstruck, and felt as though the earth had opened beneath my feet, leaving me hanging in the air

like a worthless feather. I rushed back to all the shops
where I had made purchases, promenaded the streets, enquired of passers-by whether they had not picked up a bundle of papers, and no doubt did a lot of stupid things, but
I did not find the documents. I spent the rest of the day
in a state of stupor, and did not sleep a wink that night.
Next day I went to the Law Courts and told the caretakers
of my misfortune. The account produced a profound impression on them. Shaking and scratching their heads, they
said in significant tones:

"Mm . . . yes! That's bad, brother!"

My friend Zaitsev arrived. He was the person who had
incited me to petition for employment in the Law Courts.
When I told him of my loss, he also said: "Yes. Yes . . ."
and put on such a countenance that I at once understood
that if I was not exiled forthwith to Siberia, to the mines,
I should certainly not escape imprisonment in any event.

I did not go upstairs into the offices, but hung about
downstairs with the caretakers. The staircase was so wide
and impressive that it semed to lure all mortals on and up
till they came beneath the sword of the blind goddess.

After sitting some five minutes or so with the caretakers,
I heard proceeding from the summit of the staircase the
fine velvety voice of the chief clerk:

"Where is that anathema? Where is that pig? . . .
that . . !"

He swore foully, without any restraint of language, and
sparing neither his tongue nor his throat. Cringing, I crept
forth from underneath the staircase and stood at its foot by
the first stair. The chief clerk stood at the top with Jove's
threatening aspect; his gold eyeglasses glittered; the broad
ribbon on which they hung shook; the skirts of his frock-
coat flew out like the wings of a black cock. He spun on
his heels, stamped his feet, and hurled his words at me like

thunderbolts. The scene had in it something Roman or Olympian; it was magnificently picturesque.

"Be off!" thundered the chief clerk, and turning to the caretakers, who were standing drawn up rigidly against the wall behind my back, said: "Why are you standing there, the deuce take you? Beat the swine! Chase him away! Don't oblige me to come downstairs or I shall kill him! Away with you, accursed ugly mug!"

I guessed in the end that it really probably would be better for him if I went away, and I darted into the street as quickly as I could. Of course I was not sure that that would be the end of it all, but my fright diminished and was easier to bear. I was greatly astonished at the marquis-like chief clerk, whose appearance was so magnificent, but who swore like any dweller in the Sukonnaya suburb.

My father and mother were waiting for me at home. I had to live somehow, and must find work. My mother baked a sort of cakes, and sold them in slices in the streets. One could not earn enough to live on in that way. I could no longer sing in the choir, having now altogether lost my childish voice. For entire days I wandered, half starved, through the streets, looking for work, which was not to be found. I used to go down to the banks of the Volga, to the quays, and look on for hours at the noisy, incessant toil of hundreds of men. Steamers came swimming up like great swans. The men working on the cranes sang continually the song "Dubinushka":

> "Oh, thou mother Volga,
> Oh, thou river broad and long,
> Thou hast rocked us, thou hast rolled us,
> Till our strength is gone!"

Sometimes they also sang that other Volga song, the now celebrated "Song of the Volga Boatmen."

On the deep hot sand of the bank, Tartars traded in their wooden shops in Russian-leather goods, Kazan soap, and Bokhara cloth. Russians sold rolls of bread, sausages, and all sorts of comestibles. Everything was vivid and appetising and had a holiday air, while I wandered like one accursed, yearning for something to do and eating my heart out with pity for my poor mother. I felt that I must get away somewhere, that the town was an unlucky place for me. I only wanted to get away, no matter whither. . . .

When my desire to go away had ripened into a firm determination, I succeeded in persuading my father and mother to remove to Astrakhan. We sold all we had, and steamed away down the Volga in the fourth class on the steamboat *Zeveke*, a boat built in the old-fashioned style with the propeller at the stern.

CHAPTER FOUR

Astrakhan and the "Arcadia"—Life on the Volga—I Join the Chorus of an Operetta Company, and Sign My First Contract—Promotion and a Debut—I Begin My Concert Career—Barnstorming—An Attack by Cossacks.

I WAS greatly charmed with the inexpressible tranquil beauty of the Volga, that queen of our rivers. I don't think I slept a single night of the voyage, as I feared to let slip some wonderful thing that I ought to have seen. A much-travelled man with whom I got into conversation told me of the Caucasus, of its snowy mountains reaching to the clouds, of the heat, of its people, who even in the height of summer went about in sheepskin headgear, which was just the very thing that saved them from sunstroke. Delightful prospects opened before my mind's eye. Some of the stories I heard had a strange, almost a legendary, quality, and gave me sensations of boyish delight. How big the world was! One could wander far.

Astrakhan accorded us but a poor reception. I had depicted the town to myself as something out of the ordinary. The very name seemed to promise marvels. To my surprise, I found it worse, in external appearance, than Kazan, and my very first view of it was enough to recall me from the ecstatic frame of mind induced by the voyage down the Volga.

Leaving my father on the quay, my mother and I went to look for a lodging. The sandy streets were like a furnace, and the stone built houses threw off the heat as though they breathed it out. Fish scales glittered everywhere, and the smell of fish, both fresh and dried, was all-pervasive. We soon found a little two-roomed hovel, which we rented for two rubles. It was hidden in the corner of a big courtyard which was very dirty and where the flies were so numerous that one thought they must be manufactured for exportation. Waggon drivers and porters lived in the courtyard among the flies. Old carriages, broken-down waggons, sacking, planks, and assorted rubbish could be seen piled up in corners. After the spaciousness of the Volga the squalid confinement of our new home particularly tried my soul.

The next day I went with my father to look for work. We called at offices and shops—in fact, wherever we could get the door open. Everywhere we were received very politely and kindly, and everywhere we were told to "make written application for employment."

I believe I sent in some scores of written applications to various official departments and personages, but to this day I have never had a single reply. We had no money, and we quietly, but none the less surely, starved. The taciturn steadfastness of my mother, the stubborn firmness with which she contended with poverty and need, astounded me. Amongst our Russian women we have such singular characters, who all their lives struggle tirelessly against their bitter necessities without hope of overcoming them, bearing fate's blows without complaint and with a martyr's courage. My mother was of their race. She began once more to bake and sell *pirajgi* (pastry filled with fish or berries). How I longed to eat half a dozen of those pastries! But my mother guarded them as a miser does his treasure, never even permitting so much as a fly to alight on them. One cannot live by selling pastry in the street. Later my mother got work at washing dishes on the steamers, and used to bring home remnants of food of various kinds—bones with a little meat still adhering to them, scraps of cutlets, fowls, or fish, bits of bread. That did not happen very often, however. We just starved.

I was walking in the fields one day with my father, when he suddenly sank to the ground.

"I can go no further," he said.

I knew that his weakness was the result of hunger. I sat down on the ground beside him for a long time, overwhelmed with a boundless despair.

Somehow or other I got my father back to our refuge in the town and then in the falling dusk, resumed my melancholy reflections. What was to be done?

Across the square from our courtyard was a red brick church with a little chapel which was open day and night. The light streaming through the windows from its many candles attracted my attention.

"God! God!" I thought. "I will ask Him to help us!"

Crossing the square, I entered the chapel. My weary eyes immediately fell upon the holy ikon of the Virgin with the Saviour at her breast. Then I remembered that I had humbly dedicated myself to the cause of woman, to be her knight, her defender and her champion.

"Now I am too utterly broken to be of help, but I will appeal to woman, to the Madonna," I resolved, and fell on my knees before the ikon.

"Woman, Holy Woman," I prayed, "Thou who art first among all women of Heaven and earth, if Thou canst hear and feel and understand, help us!"

I don't know how long I stayed on my knees. I only know that tears streamed from my eyes and that a faint sense of renewed courage stole over me.

*　　*　　*　　*　　*

My voice was of some assistance to me, for it was now gradually becoming a barytone. I began to sing at a church, where I was paid a ruble and a half for an all-night liturgy.

There was a pleasure garden at Astrakhan called the "Arcadia." I went there and enquired whether I could not be taken on in the chorus. A short clean-shaven man dressed in a pongee suit and a panama hat, was pointed out to me as the manager, Cherkasov.

"How old are you?" he asked me, to which I replied that I was seventeen, adding a year to my real age.

He looked at me, reflected, and then said:

"Well, if you want to sing, you can come and sing. You will be given a costume, but I shan't pay you anything. Business is bad and I haven't any money."

I was glad even of that; although my parents and I could not get a living on those terms, my engagement none the less imparted a rosier hue to our misfortunes. The choir-mistress, Madam J., gave me a score, in which were written the words:

When folk gather in the square,
Here and there,
What a bustle, hither, thither!

How splendid it all seemed to me! It was the chorus from "Carmen." That evening, dressed as a soldier or a peasant (I forget which) I dwelt in Spain. The weather was warm; the stars were shining; folk in bright costumes danced and sang. I sang and danced, too, though there was a disagreeable sinking sensation in my stomach. Still, I felt very well, very light and joyous.

When I went home, however, and showed my father the score, boasting that I was going to be employed in the thèatre, he was dreadfully vexed, stamped his foot, cuffed my head severely, and tore the music into tatters.

"Why did you drag us here to die of hunger?" he shouted. "You rascal, you want nothing but the theatre, I know! Curse the theatre. . . ."

What was I to do? How could I return to the theatre without my part? I did not go back to the theatre, and in my anger at my father resolved to go away to Nijny Novgorod, to the Fair. In the Panaevsky Gardens at Kazan, I had listened to many comedians who told stories, sang songs, and delivered themselves of timely patter. From them I had acquired a number of stories and anecdotes, which I used sometimes to recite to the evident pleasure of my listeners. I determined to go to the Fair, and appear on the stage there as a comedian in one of the open-air theatres. I had saved a few kopeks from the money I had earned by singing. I borrowed a little more money for the journey, enough to make the sum of two rubles.

My father and mother decided that it would perhaps be better if I were to go away; there would be one mouth less to be fed and there was no visible benefit from my presence. So I soon found myself once more on a steamer, this time a tugboat which hauled a number of barges. On holidays the sailors on the barges sang songs and played the accordion, and women in gaudy skirts danced. It was a careless, merry life. As I could sing folk songs, the sailors welcomed me amongst them and took a great fancy to me. I ate and drank with them.

Our steamer proceeded without haste, though at a businesslike pace. We took goods on board, unloaded again, leaving our barges at some quays and taking on others, with more sailors and women and accordions. My voyage as far as Saratov was a jolly artistic promenade; we all sang and danced. I had plenty to eat and was content. At Saratov the steamer stopped a whole day. I went into the town, and came across a pleasure garden on the river bank, over the entrance to which was the sign, "Otchkin's Pleasure Garden and Open-Air Theatre."

"What if I were to try appearing here?" I mused.

I went into the garden and asked for the proprietor, saying that I wished to appear on the open-air stage. I was told to wait.

At length a man in a white shirt and dinner jacket, and wearing a gorgeous necktie, made his appearance, surveyed me with indifferent gaze, and enquired:

"What do you want?"

"Don't you need a comedian?" said I.

He reflected. I experienced a qualm of uneasiness. What if he were to take me at my word and require me to appear on the stage that very evening, and if I were to fail again as shamefully as I had done at the Panaevsky Gardens?

At length this brilliantly attired person made up his mind.

"No, I don't want anyone," he said with conviction, and went away. Sincerely grateful to him for his refusal, I continued my stroll through the town.

"But suppose I get an engagement on the stage at Nijny," I reflected, "and lose my head again!"

Matters appeared to me by no means so easy as they had done when I made my plans at Astrakhan.

The tug changed its contingent of barges. Again there were fresh sailors, with other women and other songs. But somehow I found it more difficult to get along. I had already spent all my money, and the new crew was not so good-natured as the first one had been. At Samara I begged the stevedores to let me work with them.

"All right, get to work," said they.

They were loading flour. The very first day the great sacks, each of them weighing six poods, or nearly 220 pounds, nearly made me faint with the effort of raising them.

By evening my neck and back ached and my legs were giving away under me, as though I had been beaten with the shaft of a cart. I found that I lacked the strength to carry sixty or eighty sacks, so was told that I need only help load these on the men's shoulders, for which I would be paid twenty kopeks a day.

When I went to work, next day, I could hardly walk, and the stevedores laughed at me:

"You'll have to get used to breaking your back at this job, clown."

It was well that even in making sport of me they were good-natured and did not deeply wound my feelings.

Besides the flour, the barges took on board watermelons, and when we left Samara the work was lighter, and I was consequently more cheerful. A man with a long pointed beard, who was in charge of us, made us unload watermelons at almost every quay we came to. We stood in a line on the gangways from the barges to the shore and threw the melons from hand to hand with jokes and merry horseplay. If one did not keep one's eyes open and failed to catch a melon, it fell into the water or broke on the gangway, and the bearded man would give the culprit a blow on the head. Every way of life has its own laws! For this work I got twenty kopeks and a couple of watermelons. That was splendid. I bought five kopeks' worth of bread and ate it with the melons, and swelled up so much, in consequence, that I felt like a well-to-do tradesman.

During this voyage I lived for the first time in the midst of the riverside folk and gained a knowledge of their way of life. It seemed to me that there were all sorts of people amongst them, but they were a decent, jolly, good-natured tribe for all that.

We came at length to Kazan. I was delighted to see my native town again, though it had not been gracious to me.

I smelt once more the thick odour of naphtha, which somehow or other I had not noticed anywhere on the voyage, except at Astrakhan. The smell of naphtha was thicker, however, at Kazan, which, of course, was hardly a meritorious quality, but it was sweet to me as the "smoke of my fatherland." Leaving my belongings in charge of a clerk on the steamer, I went ashore early in the morning to call on a friend who had formerly supplied me with books from the library of the Noble Assembly, who loved to recite poetry, and even wrote verse of a very poor quality himself.

My friend greeted me with glee. In the evening we looked up two other old comrades and went to an inn, where we played billiards and where I got intoxicated for the first time in my life, in honour of the "joyful reunion with my friends." When we got out into the street again we became mixed up in a row with a night watchman, who of course got the worst of it, but his fellows came to his assistance and overwhelmed us. We were arrested and taken to the police station. I was younger than any of my friends, but proved myself a greater ruffian than they. I spoke impertinently to the police officer in charge of the station, swore, and altogether my behaviour was as perfect a picture of the chief clerk's at the Palais de Justice as could be imagined. My conduct brought about its natural consequences: instead of being content with drawing up a record of the incident in writing and locking us up till we were sober, the police officer summoned two soldiers, who belaboured us for all they were worth and then pushed us into the street. I cannot say that I remember these doings with pleasure, but conscience forbids me to be silent about them. I spent the night at my friend's house. He asked his mother, a good pious woman, who went at five o'clock every morning to hear the first liturgy, to wake me up. My steamer was due to leave at seven in the morning.

Naturally I overslept myself, although the good woman woke me up as she had promised. The steamer took its departure, and incidentally went off with all my belongings— my treasured copy of Béranger's poems, the trio "Christ Is Risen" which I had composed in violet ink, and everything else that I set store by.

I remained at my friend's home in Kazan. He had no objection, but his pious mother forthwith began to poison my existence, hinting transparently that there are far too many good-for-nothing fellows with hearty appetites in the world, and that it would be better if the earth were to open and swallow them up. I set earnestly about looking for work, and after long searching got a job copying documents at eight kopeks a sheet in the Ecclesiastical Court, called formally the Consistorial Court. These documents were chiefly to do with divorces, and in the course of my labours I made acquaintance with the incredible, amazing squalor and filth which the consistorial officials were not ashamed to make public. They were all of them the most thoroughgoing drunkards I have ever seen. They used to drink themselves into epileptic fits, into a state of trembling and wild imbecility, which horrified me.

Only one of them, the secretary, was anything like a decent human being, and he overdid the part. He wore an official uniform, a frock coat like that worn by the Jupiter of the Palais de Justice, and made use of powerful scents. His voice was soft and insinuating, his movements had in them something catlike, even a little womanish. It seemed to me that the man could draw my soul out of me so adroitly that I should never notice it. He used to question husbands and wives who sought for a divorce.

I transcribed about four sheets a day, but reckoned up twice as many in my account. One of the tipsy employees gave me the hint to do this. I calculated that I had earned in this way eighteen rubles, but was paid only eight rubles altogether for the month, and, to my surprise, not a word was said to me about the inaccuracy of my account. They were magnanimous people!

I was already seventeen years of age. A light-opera company was appearing at the Panaevsky Gardens. Naturally I hung about there every evening, and one day a chorus singer told me:

"Semenov-Samarsky is getting a chorus together to appear at Ufa. Ask him to take you on!"

I knew Semenov-Samarsky as an artist, and adored him. He was a good-looking man with large jet-black moustaches. He wore a top hat and carried a cane and light-coloured gloves. He had imposing dark eyes and the airs of a high-born gentleman. On the stage he was as much in his element as a fish is in water, and used to sing in a very expressive barytone voice the waltz from the "Beggar Student":

> "I kissed her ardently,
> But only on the shoulder!"

The ladies melted before him like wax before a fire.

Plucking up courage, I went up to him in the Gardens, and took off my cap.

"What do you want?" said he. "Oh! Come to me at the hotel tomorrow!"

I went next day to his hotel, but the doorkeeper would not let me go up to his room. I begged and entreated him, almost with tears, and in the end tormented him so much that, after expectorating in disgust, he sent a boy to ask Semenov-Samarsky whether he wished to see a long-legged, ill-fed, ragged fellow who was waiting downstairs.

"Send him up," said the boy when he came back.

I found Semenov in his dressing gown, his face covered with powder. He looked like a miller who was resting after the day's work, and who had not yet had time to wash. Facing him at the table sat a young man, evidently from the Caucasus, while a lady reclined indolently on a sofa.

I was very bashful, and particularly so in the presence of ladies. My heart quaked; I feared that I should not be able to utter a word, with a lady in the room.

Semenov-Samarsky enquired of me kindly as to the extent of my musical knowledge.

It did not surprise me that such a gentleman should address me so politely, for I thought so refined a man could not do otherwise; but his question alarmed me. I knew nothing, but made up my mind to put on a bold front, and said:

"I know 'Traviata' and 'Carmen.'"

"Yes, but mine is a light-opera company."

"I know 'Les Cloches de Corneville,'" I went on, enumerating all the operettas I could call to mind, but failed to produce any impression.

"How old are you?" he asked me.

"Nineteen," I lied shamelessly.

"And what is your singing voice?"

"First bass."

The kindness of his manner gave me increased courage. Finally he said:

"You know, I can't pay you the salary that chorus singers with a good _répertoire_ receive . . ."

"I don't want it. I'll come without pay!" I blurted out.

This astonished everybody. They all three stared at me in silence. I explained further:

"I haven't any money, of course, but perhaps you will give me something?"

"Fifteen rubles a month," said he.

"You see," I retorted, "I must have enough to live on.

If I can live on ten rubles a month at Ufa, then give me ten, but if I shall need sixteen or seventeen rubles . . ."

The Caucasian laughed and said to Semenov-Samarsky:

"Give him twenty rubles! What difference does it make?"

"Sign," said the manager, pushing a document towards me. And I signed my first theatrical contract with a hand "trembling for joy."

A little stout man named Neuberg, a member of the chorus, came into the room and greeted the manager with an independent air:

"Good morning, Semeon Yakovlevitch!"

He signed a contract for forty rubles a month.

"In two days' time," said Semenov-Samarsky, "I will give you a ticket to Ufa and an advance."

"Advance?" I did not know what the word meant, but it sounded all right. I sensed that it meant something good.

I went out with Neuberg. He had been a member of the chorus in the Serebriakov Opera Company, which I had been very eager to join when I was fifteen, but which did not engage me because my voice broke that year. This little fellow Neuberg afterwards proved a very good friend to me.

When I got home, or rather to Petrov's house, I summoned my friends and showed them with great pride the document which had made me a servant in the temple of Thalia and Melpomene. My friends had been very skeptical and vexatious in the attitude they adopted towards my theatrical ambitions, but now it was my turn to triumph and recall to them how they had ridiculed me. Sometimes when we were playing hopscotch I had used to sing snatches of opera, at which they would laugh, much to my disgust. "Just you wait awhile," I used to say. "In another three years I shall be singing in the 'Demon,' by Rubinstein!"

Three years later I really did sing, though it was Mephistopheles and not the "Demon."

The two days soon passed, and having received an advance of six rubles and a second-class ticket on one of Yakimov's steamers, I was on my way to Ufa.

It was the month of September and the weather was cold and misty. I had no overcoat. Petrov's mother gave me an old shawl, which I put around my shoulders. I was in great spirits; for the first time in my life I travelled second-class and on such a journey—to serve the cause of Art!

On the Bielaya River our steamer went aground twice, and the captain unceremoniously told the second and third class passengers to "take a walk along the bank." It was bitterly cold. To warm myself, I turned cartwheels on the haystacks on the bank and performed other acrobatic feats, while some peasants near at hand, who were loading the hay to take to their village, made fun of me:

"Look! Look! What's come over the gentleman!"

"Gentleman!" thought I to myself.

That night I could not sleep, and went on deck to look at the river and the stars. I thought of my father and mother, from whom I had heard nothing for a long time, and only knew that they had left Astrakhan and gone to Samara.

Feeling gloomy, I sang a popular Russian song:

"Ah, thou night, dark night,"

and wept.

Suddenly I heard a voice in the darkness:

"Who is that singing?"

I was startled. Could it be that it was forbidden to sing at night on passenger steamers?

"It is I," I answered.

"Who is I?"

"Chaliapine," I replied.

The Caucasian, Penaiev—the same man who had said, "Give him twenty rubles a month," a very good fellow— came up to me. Evidently he noticed that I had been crying, and said in a friendly way:

"You have a fine voice. Why are you sitting here all alone? Come along with us. We have a merchant with us who has invited us to supper. Come on."

"Won't he send us away?"

"No. It's all right. He's drunk."

In his large first-class cabin there sat at the table a fat, red-faced trader, obviously very drunk and lyrically inclined. In front of him were bottles of vodka, wine, caviar, fish, bread, and in fact everything one could think of to eat and drink. He was staring before him with dull eyes and puddling his fingers in a little pool of wine on the table. One could see that he was feeling bored. Penaiev introduced me to him and he at once poured me out a glass of vodka.

At the end of the supper the merchant asked me:

"Who are you? An actor?"

"Yes. I am just beginning my career."

"So—you are an actor. Well—smell my fingers," he muttered in a burly tone, sticking out a huge paw. "What do they smell of?"

I sniffed humbly and replied hesitatingly:

"I d-o-n-'t know. I think perhaps of fish."

The man looked at me with a frown and shouted:

"They smell of woolen stockings!"

I have never been able to understand exactly why he asked me that strange question.

However, in Russia, simple people who were born peasants have great regard for swollen pocketbooks. As for me, perhaps I am wrong, but I think that when the pocketbook is thin its owner is apt to be unassuming in his relations with others, but when the pocketbook becomes swollen there is a noticeable inclination on the part of the owner to become intolerably arrogant. It seems to me that this evening with the ignorant Russian merchant had a special significance.

At length our steamer arrived at the quayside where we were to disembark for Ufa, early one morning. The town was some five or six miles away. It was abominably muddy and wet underfoot, and rain was spattering down. I took my belongings under my arm—the chief treasure amongst them was a pearl-gray necktie which I had carefully pinned to the wall of my cabin throughout the journey—and set out on foot for the town, accompanied by Neuberg. We were an odd pair, one long and thin, the other short and fat.

When we got to the town we went to the hotel where Semenov-Samarsky was staying, but the porter told us loftily:

"We don't take in such dirty fellows."

We took off our boots and went barefooted upstairs to our manager's room. As at Kazan, he was in his dressing gown, smothered in powder. He laughed at the sight of us, and then asked us to take tea with him.

The same day Neuberg and I found rooms in the house of one of the musicians connected with the theatre, at fourteen rubles a month each. For this sum we were also to receive tea, dinner, and supper. I went at once to Semenov-Samarsky and told him:

"I have fixed myself up for fourteen rubles a month; the other six rubles I don't need. I joined you not for the sake of the money, but for the pleasure of working in the theatre."

"You are a queer fellow," he told me.

The rehearsals began. We were seventeen men and twenty women in the chorus. We practised to a violin played by the choirmaster, a nice good-natured fellow, but a terrible drunkard. All at once, much to my alarm, a rumour circulated that the manager had been going through the list of members of the chorus and that some who were not wanted would be discharged. I felt sure that I should be one of them, but when it was proposed to dismiss me the choirmaster said:

"No, we must keep that boy. He has quite a good voice and I think he is capable."

I felt as though the weight of the Urals had fallen from my shoulders.

The season began with an operetta, "The Singer from Palermo." Naturally, I was more excited than anyone. My goodness! what a pleasure it was to me to see my name on the posters: "Second basses of the chorus: Afanassiev and Chaliapine."

The costumes for the chorus in "The Singer from Palermo" were Spanish, divided into two groups, nobles and peasants. The peasant dress consisted of stockings and shoes, braided breeches, a short jacket, broad sash, and white collar. The nobles' costume was of cheap plush with short puffed breeches, a coat with a collar and short cape. In addition we wore hats of cardboard covered with plush or satin. The shoes worn by nobles and peasants were alike, which somewhat offended my sense of reality as a former shoemaker. But I consoled myself with the reflection that things on the stage could not be exactly as in real life. I put on a Spanish costume, made myself little moustaches, and a chin beard, darkened my eyebrows, reddened my lips, and in fact painted myself all I knew to make myself look like a handsome Spaniard.

I was unbelievably thin. For the first time in my life I donned tights, and I felt as though I had nothing on at all. I was much embarrassed. When the chorus had to go on the stage I stood in the front row and assumed a proper Spanish pose, with one foot advanced, arms akimbo, and head proudly thrown back; but it proved to much for my strength to maintain the attitude. The leg which I had thrown forward trembled excessively. I changed over, supporting my weight on it and advancing the other leg instead. It began to tremble in its turn, in spite of all my endeavours to overcome it. Then I hid shamefully behind the other members of the chorus.

The curtain rose, and we all sang:

> "One, two, three,
> Come, make haste,
> In the cards your fortune see . . ."

I trembled inwardly, too, with fear and joy. I felt as though I were in a dream. The audience shouted and applauded and I was almost weeping with emotion. The footlights danced before my eyes. The black yawning mouth of the auditorium, filled with uproar and clapping white hands, seemed at once delightful and threatening.

In a month's time I could maintain any pose I wished on the stage. My legs did not tremble and my mind was at ease. They began to give me small parts with two or three words to say. I walked on to the centre of the stage and thunderously announced to the hero of an operetta:

> "Some one from beneath the earth
> Wishes to see you!"

or something of that sort. The members of the company and even the workmen were kind and good to me. I was so fond of the theatre that I worked for everybody with equal pleasure. I poured oil into the lamps, cleaned the glasses, swept the stage, helped to arrange the decorations. I even manufactured Bengal lights with our prompter. Semenov-Samarsky was also very pleased with me.

It was determined to put on the opera "Galka," by the Polish composer Moniushko, for Christmas. The part of the Stolnik, a very rich nobleman, Galka's father, was to be sung by the stage manager, a tall man with a coarse face and lantern jaws—a very disagreeable person. He was continually making things unpleasant for everybody, gossiping and telling lies. When rehearsing his part he sang out of tune and time, and finally, two days before the general rehearsal, declared that he was not going to sing, that his contract only bound him to take part in light opera and not in grand opera. This put the company in an awkward position. There was no one to take his place.

Unexpectedly Semenov-Samarsky called me to his dressing room and enquired:

"Chaliapine, can you sing the Stolnik's part?"

I was alarmed, for I knew it was a responsible rôle. I felt that I ought to say: "No, I cannot," but involuntarily the words slipped out:

"Very well. I can sing it."

"Good! Take the music and learn it by tomorrow."

I felt as if I had had my head chopped off. I almost ran home in my haste to study the part, and spent the night over the music, incidentally preventing my roommate from sleeping.

Next day at rehearsal I sang the whole of the part, though with fear and trembling, and not without making some mistakes. My comrades encouragingly clapped me on the back and praised me. I did not see any envy amongst them at all. That was the only season in my career when I neither saw nor felt the envy of a fellow actor, nor even suspected its existence on the stage.

Right up to the moment when the opera commenced I felt as though I were walking on air, at least three inches

above the ground, and that day I began to make up at five
o'clock in the afternoon. I had a difficult task to make myself look like a respectable Stolnik. I put on a false nose,
moustaches, and eyebrows, and painted my face to make it
look old, attaining a fairly satisfactory result. The great
problem, however, was how to do away with my meagreness.
I put on a contrivance to make myself look stouter, but the
effect was terrible—my body looked as though I were suffering from dropsy, and my arms and legs looked like match
sticks. It was enough to make anyone cry!

I felt inclined to slip away from the theatre without saying a word to anyone, and make off to Kazan once more.

I recollected how I had been chased off the stage in the
Panaevsky Gardens, and felt sure that my début here would
end similarly. But it was too late to run away. At that
moment some one came up behind me, clapped me on the
back, and said in friendly tones:

"There's nothing to be afraid of! Put a bright face on it
all! Everything will go off splendidly!"

I looked round. The speaker was Semenov-Samarsky,
dressed for his part of Yanush. Taking heart, I went on to
the stage, on each side of which were arranged a table and
two armchairs. My fellow actors were promenading to and
fro, jesting and laughing carelessly. I envied them their
self-possession. Sitting down in an armchair, I did my best
to make myself look as fat as possible.

The curtain wavered, the lamp seemed to dance, and a
yellow fog obscured my vision. I sat as though stuck to
my chair, hearing nothing, and only when Dzemba had
finished singing did I begin to sing automatically, but in an
unsteady voice:

> "I raise to you my goblet, brothers,
>   For your sympathy and friendship,"

and the chorus replied:

"Good luck to you!"

I rose from my chair and walked, with legs that felt like cotton wool, towards the prompter, with the manner of one going to capital punishment. At rehearsal the conductor of the orchestra had impressed upon me:

"When you sing, whatever you do, keep your eyes on me!"

I now gazed on him with the unwinking stare of a startled cow, and, keeping in time with the beat of his bâton, began my aria in mazurka time:

"Friends, this is happiness indeed.
I am lost when I would most
Like to thank you for your toast.
Yes, to thank you for your kindness too much eloquence I need!"

Obviously the Stolnik addressed these remarks to his guests, but I stood with my back to my guests and not only paid no attention to them, but even forgot that anyone else was on the stage except myself—a very unhappy man at that moment! With my eyes fixed on the conductor, I sang on, and endeavoured to produce a few gestures. I had observed that the soloists waved their arms about and in general did not stand stockstill. My arms, however, appeared to have become unbelievably heavy and capable of movement only from wrist to elbow. I stretched them out at my sides, and alternately placed first one and then the other on my stomach. Luckily my voice did not fail me. When I had concluded my song, applause broke out. I was astonished, and thought it must be intended for some one else, but the conductor whispered:

"Bow, you idiot! Bow!"

I then began to bow zealously in all directions, and as I did so walked backwards towards my chair. One of the

members of the chorus, Sakharov, who had a small business
as a manufacturer of rubber stamps and who was very free
in his manners when on the stage, for some reason, while
I was singing, moved my chair to one side, I, of course, sat
down on the floor and my feet went up in the air most
idiotically. Thunderous laughter rang through the theatre,
and the applause again burst forth. I was overwhelmed
with confusion, but got up, put the chair back in its place, and
sat down in it, firmly this time. I sat there and my tears
ran down my cheeks, washing off my make-up. I was vexed
at my own clumsiness, and also at the audience, which applauded both my singing and my tumble with equal zest.
During the *entr'acte* everyone did his best to comfort me,
but without effect, and I sang through the rest of the opera
mechanically, without enthusiasm, convinced that I had no
gift for the stage.

When the opera was over, however, Semenov-Samarsky
said a few flattering words to me, but forbore any mention
of my clumsy mishap, and this somewhat tranquillised me.
"Galka" was staged three times in all. I sang the Stolnik's
rôle with success, and the next time I retired backwards I
took care to feel for my chair with my hands.

After that I was entrusted with the part of Fernando in
"Trovatore," and Semenov-Samarsky offered me an extra
five rubles a month. I refused the addition to my salary,
saying:

"The fact of acting is sufficient reward to me for my
work."

However, Semenov-Samarsky pressed me to take the
money, assuring me that I should find some use for it.

I sang with more self-confidence in "Trovatore," and
even began to believe that perhaps I was no worse than other
members of the chorus. I walked the boards with as much
assurance as they did.

The Caucasian, Penaev, was a very good friend to me. He lived with a very jealous, quarrelsome lady, and although generally good-natured, he was quick-tempered. There were scenes between them almost every day, and about once a week they used to separate and remove to different lodgings, only to become reconciled within a few days. On each occasion I had to help them to remove and return, dragging trunks, hatboxes, etc., from one apartment to another. I did this willingly because I was fond of Penaev.

It was winter, but I went about without an overcoat and was obliged to wear my shawl. I was unable to buy an overcoat. I had not even the money to purchase necessary underclothing, as practically all my spare cash went in treating my friends. My boots were coming to pieces; the sole of one of them was loose, and the upper leathers of the other were broken.

After one of his reconciliations with his mistress, Penaev celebrated the occasion by giving me an overcoat. It was rather short for me, but buttoned well around me, as the owner was considerably stouter than I.

Shortly afterwards, however, a street row occurred, in which I took part to the best of my powers. In the struggle all the lining and wadding was torn out of one of the sleeves, so to have them both alike I tore the lining from the other sleeve and wore the overcoat slung over my shoulders like a cape, buttoning only the top button. I looked like a scarecrow.

*   *   *   *   *

Things were going splendidly at the theatre. The company, including the chorus, got on well together. All worked excellently. It often happened that after the performance we stayed behind to rehearse the next play to be staged, until four or five o'clock in the morning. The management provided us with a bottle of beer each, with bread and sausages, and we sang our parts through after an informal supper. We enjoyed the life very much.

Towards the end of the season Semenov-Samarsky said to me:

"You have been a very useful member of the company, Chaliapine, and I wish to thank you and to suggest that you should have a benefit night. Choose what piece you would like to have played, and we will stage it on Sunday afternoon. You will get part of the receipts."

I was greatly surprised; but in the course of the season my self-confidence had grown till, I think, it bordered on impudence. I had for long harbored in my soul a longing to sing the part of the Unknown Stranger in the "Grave of the Askolds," a rôle which Semenov-Samarsky always sang himself. I told him of my wish, and he very kindly consented.

On the Sunday I put on a black beard, girdled myself with a red sash, and went on to the stage with an oar in my hand.

The part of the Unknown Stranger begins in prose. As soon as I began to speak I realised that I was talking with a strong middle Volga accent—that is to say, making my "o's" very round and full. This upset me and I very nearly broke down, but the audience applauded me all the same after my aria, "Our fathers in the olden time" ("*V starini jivali diaydi*").

My own accents horrified me when I had to speak a passage in Act II which contains a lot of "o" sounds, and the audience laughed.

I made up my mind after that to learn to speak "like a gentleman"—*i.e.*, flattening the "o's" to sound like "a's."

After the benefit Semenov-Samarsky brought me an envelope containing fifty rubles, presented by members of the audience, besides which some one gave me a silver watch with a steel chain. I also got thirty rubles out of the receipts. In a word, I was rich, never having had so much money before in my life, not to mention the watch.

The season came to an end and our company broke up. The conductor asked me to help him with the luggage, and gave me a nearly new cap with a broad peak. The cap not only pleased me, but it was a pleasure to receive a present from some one before whom all trembled. I bought myself a shaggy dark-brown camel's-hair coat, a leather jacket with red flannel lining, such as is worn in Russia by engine drivers, boots, gloves, and a cane. I dressed myself up in all this grandeur, and promenaded the main street of Ufa, called, if I remember correctly, Kazanskaia, and whenever anyone coming the other way appeared to me to be worthy of attention, I carelessly drew out my watch and looked to see what time it was! I was very anxious to let everyone know I had a watch!

I felt myself to be an absolutely happy man. Besides all my other good luck, Semenov-Samarsky summoned me to him and told me:

"I am going to Zlato-ust with some of the other actors. We propose to play portions of some light operas there, and also to give a concert. Can you sing any concert songs at all?"

Naturally, I was wildly delighted. I knew the arias of Russlan, from "Russlan and Lludmilla": "Oh, field, field," "They feel the truth," "Our fathers in the olden time," and Koslov's song: "If I had known."

"Excellent!" said Semenov-Samarsky, and added, with a slight smile, that Tania R. was going, too.

I felt that my happiness was now complete. Tania R., a moderately-good actress in our company, was a woman of thirty or so, a chestnut blonde with wonderful blue eyes and a very pretty oval face. I was not indifferent to her, but I did not dare to tell her so nor even let her see. I feared that she might notice the tenderness with which I regarded her. Her attitude to me was kind and unaffected, like that of an elder sister.

I at once went and offered to help her pack, and begged permission to see her safely in the train, which she graciously gave.

I saw her comfortably settled in her sleeping compartment, made the sign of the cross, saying, "Sleep well. God keep you!" then went into the corridor and thence on to the open platform of the car. It was my first railway journey. The ground seemed to slip by like a grey torrent; trees darted past; sparks flew through the air like threads of gold. It was snowing, but the weather was not very cold. The roofs of the villages humped up through the snow; distant churches moved slowly along the horizon; haystacks seemed to swim over the fields. I stayed out there till morning, thinking of Tania and of the happiness of loving a woman.

We arrived at Zlato-ust in the morning. I settled Tania in her hotel, and took a room for myself next to that occupied by the object of my adoration. I very shortly heard a masculine voice, joyful exclamations, and merry laughter in her room. Jealousy awoke in my heart, but when Tania called me to her room and made me acquainted with this rival, my jealousy at once expired. He turned out to be a very pleasant, jolly fellow, and moreover he was Tania's husband, which was, of course, an additional merit. To complete the matter, he was a comedian, and at that epoch I wanted to know all the actors in the world and it was an honour and a joy to me to make the acquaintance of any one of them.

We were to give our performance in the town arsenal. It was resolved to put on an act from "Bluebeard," but at the last moment it turned out that Semenov-Samarsky had forgotten to bring any crêpe with him and had nothing to make a blue beard out of.

I therefore cut off a good big bunch of my long locks, dyed them blue, and offered them to Samarsky. He was much touched by my act, not knowing that he had but to ask me for my finger or ear and I would have given him either of them.

"But, Chaliapine," said he, with a smile, "you can't appear at the concert like an engine driver, in a leathern jacket, and with an unnatural bald spot on your head. Take my frock coat, and curl your hair, too."

I did as he wished, and for the first time in my life appeared in public in a dress coat. The audience gazed at me very joyously, and I heard jeering remarks passed amongst those near at hand. I know the coat did not fit me, and I probably looked like a stork in a waistcoat. Still, I was not in the least embarrassed.

I sang "They feel the truth," and was rewarded with friendly applause. The audience also liked the aria of Russlan and Koslov's romance. I was in a highly emotional state, but sang well.

During the *entr'acte* a stout, breathless, perspiring, bald man in military attire, and with enormous moustaches, came up to me and said, not without manifestations of surprise:

"I thought you were going to sing treble."

"What an idea!" said I. "How old do you think I am?"

"Fifteen or thereabouts."

"I shall be twenty very shortly," said I with some vexation.

"Well, I never did! You have a fine voice for your age! We could do with a fellow like you!"

"Where is that, then?"

"In the police! I am a police officer."

Semenov-Samarsky gave me fifteen rubles for my share in the concert. It seemed to me an enormous sum for a single evening, and I felt as if I was being petted like a spoiled child.

On my return to Ufa I became conscious of my loneliness, and felt as sad as though I were in a cemetery. The theatre stood untenanted. None of the actors had remained, and the entire town gave one the impression of age-long workadayness.

You remember, dear readers, how the Fair grounds in Kazan resembled a cemetery after Yashka Mamonov and his gay comrades had departed. How sad it was to see the bare ribs of the booths which had once been magic palaces. In Kazan all was over for everyone. But here I felt with all my heart and soul that all was over for me.

It was Holy Week and the sad church bells seemed to say:

"Enough, you masqueraders. Come and present yourself before God, with all your sins."

Perhaps all the characters I had assumed in the theatre were sins from a religious point of view, but to me these masks were ikons, and to feel, even for one moment, that this enchanted life was over made me the prey of indescribable tortures.

*   *   *   *   *

I lodged with a washerwoman in a large house on the steep bank of the Bielaya River. The building, which was plastered with lean-to structures and other additions, was jam-full, like a tin of caviar, with theatrical carpenters, workmen, restaurant waiters, and other poor folk of the sort that find happiness in getting drunk. To one who had tasted the evanescent but brilliant delights of theatre life it was not a very cheerful existence amongst them. My lot was somewhat alleviated by the circumstance that the washerwoman's daughter, a very pretty, though smallpox-marked, soldier's wife, took a great deal of trouble in looking after me. I remember that she used to feed me on some special cutlets of her own, which fairly swam in butter. They were not very tasty, and indeed my stomach almost turned at them, but I ate them merely for the sake of not upsetting her.

Week after week went by, and my money flowed away rapidly. I had to look for work. Unexpectedly a fine carriage drove into our dirty courtyard. A very well-dressed man sat in it, driving the well-fed beautiful horse. I was dumb with astonishment when I learned that he was asking for me. I went out to speak to him and found that it was the lawyer R., whom I had frequently seen in the theatre. He shook hands with me, saying that he wished to speak to me "on business." Feeling unable to invite him to my poor bare room, I stood before him like a post in the yard, and he explained to me that the local circle of art lovers was thinking of getting up a play and concert and counted on my kind participation. I was flattered, and consented with the greatest pleasure, at once commencing to prepare for the performance, but to my horror I caught cold two days before the appointed evening and my voice became hoarse.

What was to be done? No matter what I did to my throat, gargling with Glaubers' salts and swallowing raw eggs, nothing did any good. I recollected, very unfortunately, as it turned out, that a mixture containing raw eggs, cognac, and burnt sugar relieves hoarseness. I went at once to a public house, bought half a bottle of rum for thirty-five kopeks, poured it into a basin, added several eggs, and then ground up some lump sugar in a cloth and roasted it in a metal spoon over a candle. I swallowed some of the strong-smelling liquid, which tasted disgusting, and then made a trial of my voice. It seemed to me that my hoarseness was going off, and by rehearsal time that evening I was confident that my voice sounded perfectly good. R. sent me a dress coat. I put it on, placing the bottle containing the remainder of my mixture in one of the pockets, and set off for the scene of action.

But when I got out of doors I suddenly became conscious that I was slightly intoxicated, but did not draw from the fact the conclusions I should have done, and boldly made my appearance at the Noble Assembly Rooms, and was, I think, very free in my conversation with R., whom I met on the staircase leading up to the hall.

"Good evening, Mr. R.! How are you? Well, so here I am!"

The lawyer looked me up and down, and enquired, with alarm, as it seemed to me:

"What is the matter?"

"Nothing! Why?"

"Aren't you well?"

"Yes, I am quite well!"

But I felt that there was something in his enquiries which threatened me with disagreeable consequences. And so it turned out. The lawyer said to me severely:

"You are really ill! You ought to go home at once and lie down!"

In confusion, I then drew from my pocket the bottle containing my accursed witches' brew—they called it "gogle-moggle"—and said:

"I assure you I am quite well! But perhaps this mixture . . ."

He took the bottle from me and continued to urge me to go home. With painful feelings I returned into the street, conscious of having made a sad mess of things. When I got home I threw myself down to sleep off my sorrow, and two days passed before I could make up my mind to show myself to R., during which time I gazed sadly on his dress coat, hanging on the wall of my room. Finally I plucked up courage, wrapped the coat up in paper and took it to its owner. To my surprise, R. met me with a hearty welcome, laughing and saying:

"Well, young man, a nice mixture you invented! I don't advise you to make use of household remedies another time, or else you will poison yourself!"

"But, Sir, everyone said gogle-moggle did one's voice good!"

"Never mind. Come to rehearsal tomorrow!"

I went home on the wings of joy, and two days later sang Mephistopheles in the church scene from Gounod's "Faust" with success.

The amateurs of the club, the general public who formed the bulk of the audience, and even the president of the District Land Administration himself praised my voice exceedingly, saying that I had gifts for the stage and that I ought to study. Somebody proposed that a collection should be made of subscriptions and that I should be sent to St. Petersburg or Moscow to study, but later on it was resolved that it would be better if I did not leave Ufa, but remained there to take part in amateur dramatic performances and work as an employee at the Rural Administration, where the president would give me a job at twenty-five or thirty rubles a month. I was to sing and to work at the Administration, and meanwhile my well-wishers would collect a sufficient sum of money for my journey to the capital to study.

I was very undesirous of employment at the Administration offices, but, lured by the prospect of studying, I set to work again to transcribe dull documents which were meaningless to me. I noticed from the very first day that all the other employees adopted a very suspicious, almost hostile attitude towards me. This was very hard for a person as jolly and fond of company as myself, not to mention that such a state of affairs was something entirely new to me; I had never experienced such unfriendliness. Noticing that the employees were cautious of talking in front of me and that they interrupted a conversation as soon as I made my appearance amongst them, I suffered great vexation of spirit and wondered whatever was the matter. Did they take me for a spy sent by their superiors?

When I could bear it no longer, I said candidly to one of them, a young fellow:

"You know, it seems to me that you all take me for a person appointed to look after you and spy upon you. Let me tell you that I am here only because they have promised to send me to the Conservatoire. Personally I hate the Administration, pens and ink, and all your statistics."

The youth believed me, invited me to his home, and, no doubt as a mark of especial confidence, played tunes for me on his guitar.

Thereafter the attitude of my fellow clerks towards me took a sudden turn in my favour. One of the employees even told me with charming simplicity:

"We really did think you were a spy. How could we do otherwise? The president of the Administration himself shakes hands with you every morning. He never gives his hand to one of us!"

That just shows how superiors can compromise an employee!

My life was quiet and dull. My fellow lodger at the washerwoman's was a crippled official. He had had one leg cut off. He was a quiet, kind man, evidently having suffered much misfortune in life. When going to bed he always used to say: "Chaliapine, purr something for me!" I used to sing songs for him in a low voice. He would fall into a doze, or at other times would join in, wonderfully out of tune.

One remembers hundreds and thousands of such mild, inoffensive people, who seem as though intimidated by life, lonely dwellers in the wilderness, and one grows sad at heart. People have a bad time of it in life!

The washerwoman's daughter was also a very unfortunate woman and appeared to be hysterical. She talked very little, took dark views of everything, and worked like a horse. Sometimes she used to get drunk, sang songs, danced like a Cossack, and swore at the labourers and workfolk who inhabited the house in words which the censor would not pass at all.

I moved from the washerwoman's dwelling and took a room in the house of a head clerk. He also played the guitar. I think that at that epoch all the inhabitants of Ufa played the guitar. The head clerk made music quietly and meditatively, raising his eyes to the sky and gazing unwinkingly, like a wooden doll. He lived with his wife, but they had no children. Life flowed on in dull quietude. It seemed as though they both, and I with them, were slowly going to sleep. Having found out that I could sing, the clerk forthwith taught me a very strange song, "Spring does not come for me," which contained the words:

> "Not for me does the rose, in the garden growing,
> Put forth its perfumed flower.
> My toil unknown for aye must perish.
> Spring will not come for me!"

When I sang this melancholy ditty the clerk used to make sudden gestures, dash tears from his eyes with his fingers, go out into the vestibule through the door, come back, and altogether behave in a very high-strung way. The song moved him especially when he was intoxicated, which did not occur only on the 20th of the month with him. He once said to me, sadly envying:

"You are lucky to be able to sing! I used to have a voice when I was young, but I have drunk it away."

This quiet existence began to choke me. I felt that nothing would come of the promises of the amateur club. There began to be disagreements in the club, and performances and concerts ceased to be gotten up. And May had come.

A Little Russian company appeared in the summer garden theatre. I went to the gardens at once and made the acquaintance of some of the chorus. They were all very jolly people, in open jackets, with embroidered shirts and bright-coloured ribbons instead of neckties. I did not quite understand their language. I had heard the Little Russian tongue before, but somehow did not believe that it was a genuine language. I thought people spoke like that "intentionally," in order to seem different to others. I was surprised to find that there were entire plays performed in this language.

I was pleased to see these fresh people, who were so unlike the folk of quiet, grey Ufa, and I delighted to hear their new and interesting songs.

I told the chorus singers that I was an actor, too, in a way, that I had played at that very theatre, and had even had a benefit performance and received a present—my watch.

They did not seem to put much faith in what I said. They only clicked their teeth with their tongues and said:

"Yes? Hmm. . . ."

I told them that it was proposed to send me to the Conservatoire—which I did not believe in myself. The Conservatoire did not make the chorus take a greater interest in me. Then I sang something for them once in a public house.

"Listen," said they: "Why don't you join us?"

"But what about the Conservatoire?"

"To the deuce with the Conservatoire! It is better to be with us. We travel from town to town. It is jolly and an easy life!"

Reflecting that the prospect seemed attractive, I went to the manager of the company. He heard me out and said:

"All right, join us! We will give you forty rubles a month."

It was a good salary! I had quite made up my mind to join the Little Russians, when I suddenly felt a twinge of compassion for the head clerk with his guitar and his wife, who looked after me so well, as though she were my mother, and for the young and pretty lady teacher who used to come out into the courtyard with a book in her hand when I began to sing. I was not acquainted with her and had never even heard her voice, but I regretted leaving her behind at Ufa. Also the president of the Administration repeated to me that it had been decided to send me to study.

The company played a few pieces and went away to Zlato-ust, whence they were to go to Samara. The day after their departure I woke early in the morning with a feeling of oppressive yearning for the theatre. I felt that I could no longer stay in Ufa. But I had nothing to go away with. However, the same day I got an advance of fifteen rubles at the Administration, purchased some tobacco, and in the evening went to sleep in the hayloft earlier than usual. I could not make up my mind to tell the head clerk that I was leaving the town, but before going to bed

I felt such a sudden burst of tenderness for him and his wife that I kissed them with feelings of the warmest gratitude. I was incredibly sorry for these people, not only because they had been kind to me, but somehow or other quite apart from that. I lay down in the hayloft for an hour and a half, and then got down quietly, taking with me my tobacco and cigarette papers, but leaving behind me my coverlet and pillow and all my belongings, and went down to the steamer quay in the quiet of the night. At seven o'clock next morning I was already on board a steamer, worrying over the thought that I had taken an advance at the Administration which I should hardly be able to repay.

When we got to Kazan I found that Lubimov's light opera company was playing in the Panaevsky Gardens. I went to ask for an engagement, and found Lubimov in his dressing gown, sitting at table and eating a salad. It was the first time I had seen a human being eating green grass plenteously covered with vinegar and oil. Lubimov showed himself a humorist with a sardonic turn.

"You want to sing in the chorus?" said he. "Sing, then! Sing as much as you like and when you like! Night or day. But I shan't pay you anything for it. Excuse me. I haven't anything to pay those who are singing for me now!"

He was very excited, I don't know why, and he began once more to fill his mouth with grass.

Without loss of time I again took the steamer for Samara, hoping to come up with the Little Russian company there. My father and mother were living there. I had written them more than once that I was getting on very well and that I was already quite rich. They had replied that things were going badly with them, but that "never mind," they would be able to live somehow or other.

I travelled in a dark blue cheviot jacket, buttoned over my bare body. I covered my chest and throat with a rubber "dicky" and collar. My tie was also of rubber, but very pretty, with bright spots.

When I got to Samara, I was ashamed to appear before my parents dressed up and without a job.

"Feodor, are you working?" they would ask.

So I waited from eight in the morning until ten, when it was time to go to the theatre.

There I said to the manager of the Little Russians, in the humblest tones I could master:

"I am ready to go to work now."

"We don't want you now," he answered jeeringly.

I must have gone rather white, for he added: "We don't know what to do with our own people," but, looking at me, made me an offer on the spot:

"I'll take you for twenty rubles a month!"

"The devil you will!" I thought, but forthwith signed the contract, took an advance of five rubles, and hurried off to see my parents.

They were not at home. My little brother was playing in the tiny dirty courtyard. He took me into a little, desolate room, like a beggar's. It was clear that my parents were living in extreme poverty. How could I help them? My father came in; he looked older and thinner. He did not display any very great joy at seeing me, and listened indifferently to my account of how I was living and what I intended to do.

"We are getting on badly, very badly," said he, without looking at me. "I have no regular employment . . ."

Looking through the window, I saw my mother enter the yard with a bundle over her shoulder covered with canvas; then she entered the room, greeted me joyfully, and with looks of embarrassment set down her bundle and pushed it into a corner.

"Yes," said my father, "our poverty has driven your

mother to begging. All day long she wanders about, asking alms in the name of Christ!"

The incident weighed on my heart. It was sad to feel myself powerless, unable to help.

I spent two days at Samara, and then went with the company to Buzuluk, a little town where huge swine wander through the streets. Pigs, fowl, and sheep also promenaded in the little gardens of the Public Assembly Rooms.

From Buzuluk we went to Uralsk, to play there in the presence of the heir to the throne, the Tsarevitch, but, as we had some time to spare, we determined to go to Orenburg, and set out over the steppes in country carts.

It was broiling summer weather, and we were tormented with thirst. On both sides of the road lay heaps of watermelons. Of course we chorus singers took advantage of this luscious gift of Heaven. To avoid the heat we travelled by night, and suddenly one night we were stopped by the howling of some horsemen who had caught up with us and were firing off muskets. What was it? We thought they must be robbers.

The manager of the company hastily commanded:

"Take your weapons! Arm!"

We hurriedly got out of the carts our stage-property arms—blunt iron sabres, broken muskets, etc., and hastened to take cover behind the carts. The women cried and screamed, and the horsemen, who had surrounded us on all hands, began to fire at our caravan. It was lucky it was dark, and moreover they must have fired at us with blank cartridges. We saw nothing but the flashes of their muskets as they fired, and the black silhouettes of their horses. I confess I was frightened, although in general I am not a coward. I involuntarily reflected:

"My life's lost for nothing!"

The manager courageously commanded:

"Don't yield, you devils! Don't yield! Stand your ground to the last! We must keep our end up till daylight!"

But there was no one to fight with. The horsemen did not attack us, but remained at a distance and continued to fire. We stood thus under arms till daybreak with all our train. When dawn broke we selected spokesmen and sent them to the enemy with white handkerchiefs in their hands. Seeing this, the horsemen gathered in a crowd. Some of them dismounted and entered into a lively argument with our ambassadors.

Finally our spokesmen returned and informed us that we all had to pay the Cossacks twenty kopeks a head for stealing their melons. Was that all? We at once complied with the demands of the brave army, and were once more in a position to resume our journey.

While we had been engaged in this "cruel" battle and during the time that our ambassadors were treating with the enemy, one of the women in our company, whose nerves had been upset by the noise and the shooting, gave premature birth to a child. So, in the midst of our troubles, the invincible forces of nature once more asserted themselves. We stood awestricken around the cart where lay the mother and child and where those among us, with a little experience in such matters, had given every possible assistance. And the good, red sun smiled down a radiant welcome to the little newcomer who in spite of everything had managed to make his entrance into the world.

*   *   *   *   *

It was strange, but all the way to Orenburg we had trouble with the Cossacks. It was as thought we were travelling through a hostile country which was about to declare war upon Russia.

CHAPTER FIVE

*More Barnstorming—My Mother's Death—
I Leave the Little Russians—In the Under-
world at Baku—Starving in Tiflis—Diphtheria—Usatov's Lessons in Singing and
Manners—I Move Towards Success—Moscow.*

F R O M the city of Orenburg we went to Uralsk, a town
which surprised me by its abundance of dirt and its
lack of vegetation. In the middle of the town square stood
a red-brick building, which proved to be the theatre. Its in-
terior was inconvenient and smelt disgustingly of dead rats
and was as close as a steam bath. We gave one performance
in this mausoleum for deceased rodents, and the next day the
Tsarevitch arrived. This was the future Emperor, Nicholas
II of all the Russias. We were summoned by the Ataman
of the Cossacks, with whom he lunched, to sing on an open-
air stage. Our chorus was not a large one, but was wonderfully good. Every member sang with a real love for his
work and understanding of it. I was first bass and sang the
beautiful southern songs with the greatest ardour.

The celebrations in honour of the Tsarevitch took place
in the Ataman's vast courtyard, which was planted with
withered trees. Beneath their sparse and dusty verdure a
white canvas tent had been set up, in which rows of magnificently dressed ladies and gentlemen sat at table. It was
strange to see so much splendour in this humdrum town,
which had the air of having been built in a hurry. Two
little girls with their hair flowing loose down their backs

presented the Tsarevitch with flowers, while a very stout man in a Cossack *caftan* sobbed with emotion.

We sang for some three hours, and were rewarded with a royal gift of two rubles each. The manager received a ring set with red and green stones. The town was liberally adorned with flags, and the old-fashioned bearded townsmen and Cossacks were in holiday mood, but struck me as excessively staid and dull. We members of the chorus who found ourselves by mere chance in this town, found ourselves a little out of this holiday. We looked around for lodgings and found a refuge in a large room over the ground floor of an inn. The windows of this barracks-like room looked out on the market square. Some one of our company suggested that we should get up a merrymaking of our own, pool what money we had, buy vodka, bread, sausages, and cakes and invite some of the young market women to join us. We followed this pleasant suggestion. The young women were not at all surprised at our invitation and gladly came to share our revelry. We danced, drank, and sang. Towards morning our festivities quite resembled an orgy in ancient Rome. The next day I woke up feeling very ill, and, as usual after indulging in such carouses, I wondered with shame and sorrow what Tania R. would have thought could she have known of the scene in which I had just taken part.

From Uralsk we returned once more to Samara, whence we went to Astrakhan, also giving performances at Petrovsk, Temir-Khan-Shura, and Uzan-Ada, on the Caspian.

I don't know why, but the memory of our fleeting visit to Temir-Khan-Shura, a city of the Caucasians, surrounded by imposing mountains remains with me to this day. We sang and danced at a little club run by officers of the Imperial army. I remember the atmosphere in that room, the flushed faces of the officers and women. Everyone was in love.

Ah, love! love—in the steppes, in the mountains, in the streets, in Imperial palaces! . . . . .

Meanwhile, I lived the pleasantly varied life of a tramp, which gave me many new impressions. By this time I could speak and sing in the Little Russian or Ukraine tongue with perfect freedom, and was entrusted with small independent rôles. I was contented with this rapidly flowing existence, and only rarely felt a longing for anything different. Only, sometimes I felt a great yearning for something unknown and indescribable.

The great ironworks at Kizil-Arvat made a deep impression upon me. There I saw the molten metal flow like thick red oil, and was astonished to see a workman roll up his sleeve and plunge his arm into the molten stream right up to the elbow, drawing it out again not even burned. He actually laughed. The thing was quite incomprehensible to me until one of our actors, Ivanenko, gave me some explanation of how it was possible to do it.

This Ivanenko was a splendid fellow and a fine artist, but like most good Russians, he drank unsparingly. He played so finely, with such truth and sincerity, that I used to feel tears of delight well into my eyes. There was a song of his in "The Prisoners" which moved me particularly:

"*Oi, zishlà zaryà ta vècherovaya*" ("The evening sun is setting").

I always endeavoured to be agreeable and useful to him, but I hated to see him drunk.

"The stage is not the Sukonnaya Sloboda," I reflected. "There is no need to drink!"

But many of the artists drank a great deal too much.

I had a friend, Kolya Kusnetsov, who was a fellow towns-man of mine, since he hailed from Kazan. He was a meticulously clean, methodical man, and always carried clean sheets with him in his baggage, though not one of the other members of the chorus had them. I used to notice how long he kept his clothes clean and unspotted.

It may seem that I am relating a lot of trifles about people of no importance; but these trifles meant much to me, for by observing them I educated myself. We all learn from little things. What Shakespeare, Tolstoy and other geniuses of world-wide renown teach us does not take a very firm hold on our minds, but life's trifles penetrate into the mind as dust does into velvet, sometimes poisoning the spirit and sometimes ennobling it. Besides that, I want to talk about good people of no importance in the world. The great people will speak for themselves. Nobody remembers these little people who live unknown and perish in silence, though they too can love, and comprehend the beautiful, and feel a thirst for the higher life.

Kolya Kusnetsov was in love with one of the actresses of our company. I was playing billiards one day at a café in Askhabad, when he came in and suggested to me that we should go to watch a ball which some officers were getting up. The ball took place in the courtyard of the Officers' Club, but we of course were not admitted. We climbed on the fence, however, and looked on at the dancers, amongst whom was the actress of whom Kolya was enamoured. Perching on the fence like a magpie, I noticed Kolya drinking something out of a bottle, and a few moments later he fell off the fence.

Thinking he must have taken poison, I jumped down and was very near calling out for assistance.

Happily it turned out that he had only attempted to drown his jealous emotions by swallowing a Gargantuan dose of vodka. I took him home, and he cried all night.

"Love is certainly no laughing matter!" I reflected, but I rather envied one who could love so ardently.

On the journey from Askhabad to Chardjoui I had an

adventure which was both unpleasant and ludicrous. I was eating bread and sausages with garlic in a third-class railway carriage, when D., the *entrepreneur* of our company, a monstrously fat man, entered:

"Throw that beastly sausage out of the window. It stinks!" he ordered.

"Why should I throw it away? I prefer to eat it."

D. lost his temper and shouted:

"How dare you eat that stinking stuff in my presence?"

I retorted that it did not matter to him, travelling in a first-class compartment, what people ate in the third class; or something of that sort. He waxed still more furious. Just then the train stopped at a station, and D. pushed me out of the car on to the platform. The engine whistle blew and the train moved off, leaving me on the platform of a little wayside station, amongst a lot of black-bearded Asiatics in long gowns and turbans who stared at me in a manner by no means friendly.

Not knowing what else to do, I determined to pursue the train on foot. I had not a kopek in my possession. The afternoon wore on, but a thick heat haze continued to lie over the sands on both sides of the railway track. Perspiration streamed from me as I walked, and I kept my eyes very wide open, as I had been told that tigers and other unpleasant beasts haunted those regions. Lizards scurried across the track. The great red disc of the sun descended far away over the steppe behind the sand dunes, and the sky flushed crimson like molten iron. I felt like some unhappy Robinson Crusoe prior to his encounter with his man Friday. I struggled on, and finally reached a station where a train was standing, crept in when no one was looking, and rode without a ticket to Chardjoui, where I found the Little Russians and rejoined them. D. pretended not to notice me, and I acted as though nothing had happened. I was very much afraid that he would abandon me in that country, where there were tigers, great hairy poisonous spiders, scorpions, tarantulas, fevers, and last but not least, speechless swarthy people in long robes and turbans, with white teeth like cannibals, and a strange look in their eyes, which made one's flesh creep.

Like a sweet and vivid dream I remember Samarkand with its wonderful mosques and the boys in white robes in the courtyards of the mosques. It was hot and still. The boys swayed to and fro as they chanted the Koran. Somewhere in the distance a donkey brayed, a camel groaned. Orientals went noiselessly as shadows through the little narrow streets between the low white walls of the houses. The muezzins chanted their calls sleepily.

While walking along the street some Sart would approach one and in broken Russian offer a little girl, indicating her age on his fingers:

"Ten years old. Would you like her? Awfully nice. A lively one, too. . . . Eleven years old, say?"

I fled from these traders, who inspired me with fear.

After a long tour in the Asiatic provinces of the Russian Empire we returned to Baku. There I read on the posters that Madame Lassalle's French Light Opera Company was playing in the Tagievsky Theatre. Amongst the artists enumerated were Semenov-Samarsky and his wife—Madame Stanislavskaya-Durand. I went at once to see Semenov-Samarsky, who received me joyfully and promised to get me an engagement in the French company.

Life was not too easy with the Little Russians, and I was glad of the chance to leave them; but when I told the manager's wife, Madame D., of my intentions, that lady, who both on the boards and in real life was a comic old woman, was very vexed, saying:

"We wanted to make a man of you, and what's the result? Nothing but a pig!"

Such scenes were no novelty for me, but as the Little Russians had appeared to look on me with indifference, and I had never felt that they were trying to make anything in particular of me, the lady's unexpected wrath astonished me. I was still more surprised when D. refused to surrender my passport to me. When I insisted, he threateningly suggested:

"Let's go to the police station. I'll give you your passport there!"

I suddenly realized with pride how much they needed me in his company!

I agreed, and we went; but on the way he began threatening me, repeating:

"We shall see what will be the outcome at the police station! You'll see!"

I began to be alarmed, as I knew how the police dealt with people; and as though to let me know what I had to expect, when we got to the police station they were beating somebody, who cried out wildly for help and begged for mercy. Oh, my dear police! I don't know whether they are like this in every country. In consternation I told the manager that I did not want my passport, as I would stay with the troupe. We went back to the theatre almost friends. D. was very much pleased. However, I soon afterwards ceased to take part in the performances of the Little Russian company, owing to the following sad occurance:

One evening, while playing the rôle of Peter in "Natalka of Poltava," I was handed a telegram which read:

Mother dead. Send money. Father.

I had no money, of course, and, in fact, was in debt to the manager. I sat for a while in a corner and sorrowed, but at last made up my mind to ask D. for an advance on my salary. For only twenty-five rubles a month I was playing responsible parts, though some of the chorus got forty rubles a month. The manager gave me two rubles after hearing my request. I asked for more, but he refused.

Rebelling at his callousness, I ceased to attend the performances of the company, which shortly afterwards left Baku. I remained in the town without a passport, and joined the chorus of the French Light Opera Company, which, as a matter of fact, included only three or four Frenchmen, the remainder being Jews and Russians. The company was doing thoroughly badly. Nevertheless, we merrily sang all sorts of foreign-sounding words at random, such as:

"Colorado, Niagara, Mississippi, Charpentier, and Eau-de-vie. . . ."

The good people of Baku were not well up in foreign languages, and the nonsense we sang was cheerfully accepted for the purest Parisian French. I was not paid any salary, but the manager considered it unbecoming for a member of the chorus of a French light opera company to go about in a mountaineer's shaggy sheepskin cloak, and gave me a note to take to a shop, where I was given a cloth coat lined with wadding.

The company in the end broke down altogether, and I was left literally in the street. I was obliged to sell my coat, and to be very cautious in eating and drinking. In fact, I could afford only bread and tea. Winter had began and in Baku it was very disagreeable. The wind was cold; sleet alternated with the endless rains. It was impossible to sleep on the benches in the gardens. Two comrades and I used to take refuge in the wooden circus building, which was untenanted at that time. All three of us slept in the gallery, wrapped in my sheepskin. The cloak was very large, yet not big enough for three of us, and probably for that reason my companions suddenly disappeared, without saying a word to me. I was now quite alone and could sleep in more comfort. Still, it was more difficult for me to live than it had been before, and I came very near being entangled in an affair which might have taken me far beyond the Urals at government expense, though by no means in the rôle of a singer.

I don't recall what were the circumstances under which I made the acquaintance of a young man who said that he had been an actor. He was bolder and more resourceful than I, and was therefore able to live in apartments and hotels without a kopek in his pocket. He highly recommended this mode of life to me, and I agreed to try it. We took a room together, and occupied it for a day. The landlord demanded money from us, which we promised to pay, and stayed another day, after which we took our departure, when no one was looking, and found another hotel.

On one occasion, however, my friend went out alone and did not come back, and the landlord told me that he would not let me out of the house nor give me anything to eat until I paid him. What was I to do? I remained a hungry prisoner for two days, then resolved to escape. The room had a small balcony which opened on to a courtyard, but there were people in the yard both night and day. At length I observed that a cornice below my window was continued until it joined a wall. The wall, it is true, was as high as the third floor up, and was very nearly on a level with the roof. However, what will not a man do when he is hungry? I got out of the window on to the cornice that night and crawled along to the wall, which I bestraddled. Seeing from my perch a dark heap down below, which I took to be a pile of manure, I jumped down. It turned out to be a heap of broken fragments of tin plate and pieces of iron. I found myself in a dark empty courtyard, whence I made my way into the street. I went to one of those dark dens in Baku which I had visited previously when in difficulties. The place to which I now repaired was always full of ragged fellows. I sang for them, and they gave me food and drink. I think there were escaped convicts amongst them. Most of these people had no proper names, and merely went by nicknames. One called "Klik" ("Tusk"), a black-bearded, curly-headed man, with several teeth knocked out, a low forehead, and grey eyes with a strangely arresting expression in them, particularly attractd me. His uncombed hair fell in a sheaf over his eyes. He habitually spoke with authority and evidently commanded the respect of all his fellows. I was convinced that he had escaped from some convict prison.

He was always very well disposed towards me, called me "the singer," and used frequently to urge me to sing. I sang for him, and he would burst into tears, sobbing sometimes, even, like a woman weeping for some one beloved who has died suddenly. I liked this characteristic in him, and almost became sincerely attached to him.

A day came, however, when he proposed to several of the "boys," myself among them, to go at nightfall to the square where the circus stood, with the object of cutting the throat of a certain market trader who went about in much-darned and patched clothing, but who, we were assured by "Klik," carried a lot of money sewn up in his patches. The "boys" gave this proposal their unqualified approval, and "Klik" allotted to each one his special duty. It was all done as simply as though robbery and murder were perfectly customary and lawful, even though by no means easy undertakings. My task was to be to stand at a corner and keep an eye on the police. I could not refuse, for although these people were very good to me, if I were to refuse to take part in the business they would of course have knocked me about frightfully.

When the day came on which the trader was to be murdered, I did not turn up at the lurking place of the gang, and never showed myself there again, fearing that I should be called a "traitor," or, still worse, a spy.

In bidding farewell to these people, however, I lost all chance I had of eating and drinking. I offered my services as a singer in the cathedral choir, but without success. I was so ragged and dirty that I was probably taken for a drunkard and a thief. I got work with the porters on the quay of the Caucasus and Mercury Steamship Company, at thirty kopeks a day. This helped me to live, but cholera broke out and speedily took on the character of a frightful epidemic; people doubled up in agonies and fell down in the streets. Persian corpses lay about till the soldiers, smeared over with tar as a protection against infection, could remove them for burial. Death walked about the town as though he were the governor. The porters took fright and left their work. I was left once more without work or bread, and, like every one else, could get nothing but the badly distilled sea water which everybody in the town had to drink. Temporarily, chaos reigned in Baku. The authorities ran away. The townsfolk died by hundreds every day, like flies in autumn. The life of the town came to a full stop; only at the railway station was there any activity, and there it simply boiled over in a continual uproar of departure; but even there I could get no work.

All at once Fortune smiled on me. I found in the street a calico handkerchief with a knot at one corner, in which were four twenty-kopek pieces. I hurried straightway to eat *liali kebab* in a Persian restaurant; ate my fill, went to the station, and offered the conductor of an outgoing train all the money that was left to me if he would take me to Tiflis. The conductor showed himself a good-hearted man, and took from me only thirty kopeks for the journey to Tiflis. I rode on the brake platform of a freight train.

On my arrival in Tiflis I learned that Semenov-Samarsky was in the town, and that an officer by the name of Klucharev was assembling an opera company for Batoum. The company included Vanderik and Flasha-Vanderik. Amongst the chorus I found Neuberg and the two friends who had abandoned me at Baku.

It was Lent, and, by the law of the Orthodox Church, singing in Russian was forbidden. The opera company was therefore called "Italian," though the only two Italians in it were a flautist in the orchestra and a member of the chorus named Ponte, an old acquaintance of mine at Baku and a very good fellow. Very shortly I was called on to sing the part of Oroveso in "Norma," for which purpose I was obliged to copy the whole of my part, which was of course written in Italian, into Russian letters. You can imagine how sweet the tongue of Italy sounded on my lips, for of course I did not know a word of the language!

From Batoum we went to Kutais, where I sang, not without honour, the parts of the Cardinal in "Jedovka" ("The Jewess") and Valentine in "Faust." Soon after this one of our company—the deuce take him!—ran away with the wife of Klucharev, and the company consequently went to pieces.

I returned to Tiflis with Neuberg, Krivoshein and Sessin, all members of the chorus, and we all lived together. Sessin was the most remarkable of any type I have met in my long experience with human nature. He was modest, sensitive, talked and sang in mezza, and in general possessed a moderato temperament. He distinguished himself by his marvellous ability for acquiring a *fiancée* wherever he went. He never hurt the young women, only exploited them for food and money. Thus while courting them he was of course able to eat and drink, and occasionally, as bridegroom-to-be, he could borrow a little money from his future wife's parents. On our arrival in Tiflis he at once looked up a sweetheart, very fortunately for us, as almost every day he brought home from her house cutlets, fruits, and bread, besides furnishing us with five-kopek and ten-kopek pieces. Perhaps some will find an excuse for his conduct in the fact that he was a poor actor, pinned down by the managers to an infinitesimal salary, and only by such methods could he manage to procure a little more food for his friends. It was regrettable—at least for us—that his love affair in Tiflis soon ceased to be successful, and he disappeared from the town. We found it difficult to get on without our "bridegroom."

My comrades very soon arranged their affairs, while I, being more indolent and not so clever, remained alone and hungry. The landlady was a good-hearted woman and did not press very much for her money, and, benumbed by my misfortunes, I slept away my time. When one is asleep one does not feel hungry. Occasionally I slept for more than forty-eight hours at a time.

I had got used to going hungry for two days at a time, but now I had to live without food for three days and sometimes four. That was too much for me.

I sought for work, but in vain. My clothes were tattered, I had no underlinen, but still possessed a presentable hat, and when I went once to a sawmill to ask for something to do, the workmen laughed at me for a "gentleman." To be sure, I had a hat, but I think it was more my manners and general appearance than the hat which impressed them.

It was particularly disagreeable and trying to have to starve in Tiflis, because there people do all their roasting and boiling out of doors. Various odours of cooking teased one's sense of smell, and no one who has not experienced the sensation can conceive of what the odour of food means to a starving man. Starvation makes a wolf ten times stronger and fifty times more intelligent, while the effect of acute hunger upon a human being is one of profound humiliation.

I used to have fits of despair and wild rage. Many times I was even on the point of turning beggar, but this I could not quite bring myself to do. One idea haunted me. It was to go into a shop that dealt in firearms, ask to be shown a revolver, and then, when I had it in my hands, shoot myself. In fact, all I could think of was to end my life in some fashion or other. Actually, I really wanted very much to go on living, but how was this to be done?

As I stood at the door of a firearms shop, a familiar voice sounded in my ears. I turned and recognised the Italian, Ponte.

"What's the matter with you?" he asked in tones of alarm. "Why are you looking like that?"

I was so glad to meet a friend that for a few moments emotions made me speechless. Then I told him the story of my miseries. When he heard that I had been four days without food, Ponte took me home. At his house, his wife immediately set a dish of macaroni before me. I ate a fabulous quantity, though I felt a certain shame in doing so before the eyes of Madame Ponte.

The meeting with the Italian, his hospitality, and the macaroni all gave me new strength. The very next day I read an announcement that an amateur performance would be given in some gardens. I went to the gardens, and encountered at the entrance an eccentrically dressed man whom I took for a circus artist. For some reason or other he took notice of me and asked who I was and what was my business. I told him, and this person, who turned out to be the actor Okhotin, led me to a distant pathway in the gardens and asked me to sing something. Then, after reflecting, he said that he would give me a Russian costume, in which I should appear on the open-air stage in the gardens.

The gardens were small and uninteresting, and people seldom cared to go there. However, I sang zealously and received two rubles a performance, appearing twice a week. While there I made the acquaintance of some employees in the offices of the Trans-Caucasian Railway, when relating anecdotes to amuse them in return for their hospitality, I once told them something of my own misfortunes. The story called forth general sympathy. Learning that I knew something of office work, my hearers suggested that I should apply for employment to the chief accountant of the railway. I did so, and was given a clerkship at thirty rubles a month.

I longed to get back to the theatre, and when a former comrade in the chorus came to me with a proposal that we should get up a concert at Kodjhori, a village of summer villas about twenty-five miles from Tiflis, I gladly agreed, procured two days' leave of absence from work, and set out on foot to Kodjhori with other singers. There were eight or so of us under the leadership of choirmaster Karl Vend, a nice fellow, but a terrible drunkard. The concert, however, never came off, owing to the profound indifference of the public and also because, unfortunately for us, the heavens broke up in a sort of prehistoric deluge and hurricane.

I have seen some fine downpours in my time, but never experienced anything so horrible as I did on that occasion. Trees crashed to the ground; foaming torrents rushed from the mountains, hurtling great stones along in their course; the howling wind almost knocked us over. The rain came down in streams as thick as a man's arm. Through this deluge Vend and I were obliged to make our way back to Tiflis, as we feared to overstay our leave of absence from work. I feared that more than anyone else. We appeared to make hardly any progress at all, and sometimes had to creep on all fours, lest the wind and water should force us from the path and throw us over the precipice which it bordered. However, we got home safely. I dried my clothes and went to my work, but by midday felt that I had caught a chill and that my throat was sore. I was despatched at once to the railway hospital, and given a room to myself. I was told I had diphtheria.

The long days in the hospital were very tedious, and it seemed as though I had been forgotten. The doctor never came, and I lounged all day long on my bed, clad in a kind of dressing gown which had the appearance of convict garb. I was hungry, and felt perfectly well, but was given only the thinnest of soup. I begged to be sent home, but the caretaker told me that the doctor would come in a week or so, and then perhaps I might be allowed to go. A week, and even then only "perhaps"!

"To the devil with them," I thought and decided to slip away from the place. I quietly got my clothes out of the cupboard where they had been hung, put them on, climbed through the window, and went home.

Next day, however, when I went to the office, I was not allowed to work, as the hospital had given notice of my escape. Almost with tears in my eyes, I argued with my superiors that I was quite well, and in the end got them to send me to a doctor, who certified that there was nothing the matter with me.

Not long afterwards I received a letter from Semenov-Samarsky, who wrote that he could find me an engagement at one hundred rubles a month in Perovsky's opera company at Kazan. I could have an advance to pay the expenses of my journey. I joyfully wired back, "Waiting advance," and shortly received a remittance of twenty-five rubles from Kazan. The same day I gave up my employment.

However, the unexpected happened. My fellow employees had frequently remarked on my fine voice, saying that I ought to study singing seriously under their local Professor Usatov, formerly an artist of the Imperial Theatres. On the day I was to leave Tiflis I suddenly made up my mind to go and see this singing teacher, thinking that in any event I should lose nothing by doing so.

When I entered his house a pack of pug dogs scurried around me, and then a short round man with the turned-up twisted moustaches of a stage brigand appeared, his cheeks blue from much shaving.

He enquired, not very courteously, what I wanted, and on my explaining, said:

"Very well. Let's go and howl a bit!"

He ushered me into his drawing-room, sat down at the piano, and made me run through a few arpeggios. My voice sounded well. He asked me to sing something from an opera.

As I imagined that my voice was a barytone, I proposed that I should sing the aria of Valentine from "Faust," but when, on a high note, I began to hold it *fermato,* the professor ceased playing and prodded me in the side with one finger so hard that it hurt. I broke off the note, there was a moment of complete silence. Usatov gazed at the keys of the piano, and I looked at him, thinking that matters seemed ominous. The pause was painfully prolonged. Finally I lost patience, and enquired:

"Well, do you think I might study singing?"

Usatov looked at me and answered decisively:

"You must."

I at once cheered up and told him that I was on the point of going to Kazan to sing in opera there, that I should get a hundred rubles a month, which for five months would mean five hundred rubles, out of which my living expenses would be one hundred rubles; that thus there would remain four hundred rubles, and with the money I would return to Tiflis to study singing. He said, however:

"Give up the idea! You won't save anything, and, anyway, it is hardly likely you will ever get your salary! I know that sort of business. Stay here and study with me. I won't take any money from you for lessons!"

I was astounded, for it was the first time that anyone had made me such an offer. Usatov went on:

"Your chief is a friend of mine. I will write to him to take you back again."

Inspired by my unexpected good fortune, I rushed with Usatov's letter to my chief, but found that I had already been replaced. This took the wind out of my sails, and I returned to Usatov, who thereupon gave me a note to the owner of a wholesale business in pharmaceutical goods. This man, who looked like an Oriental, read the letter and asked me whether I knew any other language than Russian.

I told him that I understood Little Russian, but he said that was of no use to him, and asked me further whether I did not know any Latin. Of course I had to answer, "No."

"That's a pity," said he. "Well, I will pay you ten rubles a month, and here is two months' pay in advance.

"What must I do?" I enquired.

"Nothing. You must study singing, and I shall pay you ten rubles a month for doing so."

It was all quite like a fairy tale. One man was going to teach me for nothing, and the other would pay me for learning!

Together with the advance received from Kazan, I now had forty-five rubles in my pocket. Usatov told me to rent a good room and hire a piano. If I returned the advance received from Semenov-Samarsky, I should be unable to do so. I therefore wrote to Kazan to say that I had suddenly fallen ill and could not come.

I did wrong in acting thus, certainly; but I have since consoled myself with the thought that many people often do much worse things for less elevated reasons.

* * * * *

My studies with Usatov led to my meeting his other pupils, some fifteen in all. They were people of the most diverse fortunes and social standing. Amongst them were officers, civil employees, and aristocrats. One of them was Joseph Komarovsky, who later became assistant to the stage manager of the Great Theatre (Bolshoi Teater) in Moscow; another was the bass, Starichenko, a very self-confident and ridiculously conceited individual; a third, Paul Agnivtsev, afterwards went out of his mind. The latter had a wonderful voice, which I loved to hear, and I always used to observe with delight his elegant and restrained manners when in society.

Everything in Usatov's house was strange and unfamiliar to me; the furniture and pictures and the hardwood floor, even the tea and sandwiches which his wife, Maria Petrovna, knew so well how to prepare. I was very much surprised, too, to notice how my fellow pupils laughed and chattered without embarrassment in the presence of the professor and his wife, relating anecdotes, and altogether behaving with perfect freedom, like equals. I had never before seen such relations amongst people with whom I was acquainted, and although I enjoyed the gracious atmosphere of equality which they created, I could not muster up sufficient courage to adopt them myself. My clothes were very frayed and dirty, and, though I frequently went to the baths, I could not keep myself clean. I had only one shirt, which I washed myself in the river Kura and dried over the lamp in my room.

Once at my lesson Usatov said to me:

"Listen, Chaliapine, my wife will give you underclothing and socks; you must turn yourself out better!"

I took the bundle of clothing with deepest gratitude and came to my next lesson well dressed and shaved. Usatov proposed that I should stay to dinner. I thanked him, but did not accept. The truth is, the prospect was altogether too much for me. I had seen how they dined, with a maid waiting at table and giving the diners different plates in succession; while the table was furnished with table napkins and a variety of knives, forks, and spoons. How was I to know which spoon to use for what dish, or what any particular knife was intended to cut?

Later on, however, the Usatovs made me dine with them, and I suffered not a few torments when I did so. Dishes were served that I had never seen in my life. I did not know how they should be eaten. A green fluid [1] was served with a hard-boiled egg floating in it, which, when I touched it with my spoon, jumped from the plate on to the table-cloth, whence I picked it up with my fingers and put it back in the soup. My hosts looked on at my proceedings in silence, but with evident disapproval. However, after suffering similar martyrdoms on several occasions, I learned how to eat without embarrassing my neighbours by, for instance, putting my fingers in the salt cellar, or using my nails to remove remnants of meat from my teeth. But it cost me dear! Moreover, Usatov had a noble habit of pointing out my faults with a charming directness, which used to make me feel dizzy.

"Chaliapine, you must not snuffle during dinner!" he would advise me.

I had no handkerchief, and when a steaming aromatic dish was served, how could I help snuffling?

[1] Green Stchi, a common Russian soup made of spinach or sorrel.

WITH A FELLOW STUDENT AT USATOV'S

"If you eat with your knife you will cut your mouth to your ears," he used to say.

He also spent much time in teaching me to sit upright at table, not to eat fish with my knife, etc., etc., and altogether zealously undertook my social education.

He made me learn an aria from "Fenella," and Bakhmetiev's song, "Beard, my beard," and when I had quite mastered them sent me to make acquaintance with a club of music lovers in the Artzruka house on Griboyedovsky Street. This club used to get up plays acted by students and amateurs, and was quite independent of the well-known "Tiflis Artistic Club." I became acquainted with the leading amateurs of the club, and began to be present at their frequent evening meetings.

At one of the concerts a black-eyed young lady in *pincenez*, with a piquant little turned-up nose and attired in some filmy confection, sang a song about moonlight and boats on the water. The young lady seemed to me to be a heavenly beauty, and her soft, delicately modulated voice delighted my ear. I applauded her, oblivious to everything else, and went home from the concert in an ecstatic frame of mind.

"What lucky fellows there are in the world!" I thought when I saw her give her hand to some one to kiss as she left the stage.

Usatov told me that the club was going to help me and that they would give me a monthly stipend of fifteen rubles, in return for which I should occasionally appear in the club's concerts and amateur theatricals. He gave me a dress coat, though, unfortunately, he was short and stout and I was tall and thin. However, I knew a tailor, who altered it to fit me fairly well.

At my début on the stage of the club I sang "Beard, my beard" (*"Boroda-l', moya borodoushka"*). The audience laughed, although good-naturedly. I thought they were laughing at my dress coat, but it turned out that their merriment was occasioned by the circumstance that, while I sang very touchingly about my beard, there was not a trace of hair on my face. I looked quite like a boy on the stage. However, I was warmly applauded at the end of my song, and as I bowed my acknowledgments I saw in the audience the young lady who had captivated my fancy.

"There is the person for whom I must sing!" I resolved. The question was, what to sing? I determined on "All ages are obedient to love" from "Eugen Onegin," and gave it when called on for an encore.

It seemed to me that the young lady applauded more enthusiastically than anyone else in the audience.

After the concert there was a dance, and the lady who had played the accompaniments offered to introduce me to the young lady I had noticed. I silently consented, and crossed the polished floor to the other side, where she was standing, feeling as if my legs had gone bandy and were giving way under me. The young lady warmly shook my hand and complimented me. I said something pointless in reply, feeling like a clumsy fool.

If she had asked me to escort her on foot from Tiflis to Archangel I should have agreed without a second thought, or if I had known where she lived I should have prowled about beneath her windows. I was in love with all the energy of my youth.

The Italian, Farina, a member of the club, came up to me and told me that I was to receive fifteen rubles a month from them, and asked me to help them in every way to the best of my ability. Of course I was delighted to consent, and began to take an active part forthwith in all the doings of the club. I sang at concerts, acted in dramas, taking the rôles of Rasgulaiev in "Poverty is not a Crime," of Neschastlivtsev in "The Forest," of Peter in "Natalka of Poltava," besides assisting with the decorations, cleaning the lamps, looking after the scenery and stage properties, and altogether throwing myself heart and soul into the work.

Meanwhile, I continued my studies under Professor Usatov, who was extremely severe and did not stand much on ceremony, especially with such pupils as myself. If I did anything badly, he would scrape some snuff out of a tin box with his conductor's bâton, and loudly blow his nose after snuffing it up; at other times he used to puff away at a cigarette as thick as my finger. These were signs that he was dissatisfied and vexed.

If he detected that a pupil's voice was weakening, Usatov used to hammer the singer on the chest and shout:

"Sustain it, the deuce take you! Hold it!"

It was a long time before I comprehended what he meant by "sustaining." At length I grasped that it was necessary to support the sound on one's breathing and concentrate it.

Distracted by my work in the club and carried off my feet by my newborn passion, I began to study less zealously and frequently failed to master my lessons thoroughly. When this occurred I adopted the stratagem of placing the music open on the piano, and reading it from a distance by gazing at the sheet obliquely from my post at one side of the piano. Usatov noticed this, however, and on one occasion adroitly placed himself between me and the music, so as to obscure my view of it. I ceased singing, and without ceremony he began to beat me with his bâton, saying:

"You don't do anything, you idler!"

I got hammered so frequently that I was obliged to adopt measures of defence. The piano stood a few inches away from the wall, so I moved it a little farther, and the next time Usatov offered to set upon me with his bâton, I got behind the piano. He was stout and could not get at me, being reduced to shouting and stamping his foot. He got so angry on one occasion, however, that he threw the music at me and cried in a rage:

"Come out of that, you young devil! Come out! I know your game!"

I came out, and he beat me with his bâton to his entire satisfaction, after which we resumed the lesson.

In after years, when we ran across each other again, we recalled these lessons reinforced with the stick, and we both had a hearty laugh over the past. A first-rate fellow was my old teacher!

Usatov coached me in the third act of "Russalka" ("The Water Nymph") for a performance at the Musical Club, and also Mephistopheles' serenade from "Faust," and a trio. I was so tall and thin that I looked quite ridiculous in the costume of Mephistopheles, but the audience liked my singing. The impression I produced was particularly strong when I sang the Miller's song from "Russalka": "I have grown old and foolish." I remember now the silence in the hall when I sang that phrase. I received tremendous applause when I had concluded, and the audience even rose from its seats. Next day I read in the newspaper *Caucasus* a paragraph in which the writer compared me to the celebrated Petrov. The notice was signed "Karganov," whom I knew to be a well-known connoisseur and lover of music. He afterwards wrote a book about Beethoven.

When I read this criticism I recognised with an inward thrill that the improbable and unexpected had happened to me—something that I had never even dreamed of. I knew that I had sung the Miller well, better even than I had ever sung before, but it still seemed to me that the critic exaggerated my gifts. I was confused and intimidated by this first praise in the press, foreseeing how much would be demanded of me in the future. Usatov praised me, too, saying:

"Well, idler!" clapping me on the back. "So that is how matters stand now!"

I could not bring myself to tell him that I had read Karganov's notice. That was altogether too much for my modesty.

I continued to meet the lady of my heart. Her father, a lawyer, took very little notice of her doings. She lived with her mother in a small but prettily furnished flat. Her mother was a woman, evidently of simple extraction, whose views on life were of an extremely practical cast. I very soon noticed that her favourites were wealthy Armenians who paid court to her daughter. Altogether there was something queer and rather disagreeable about the mother.

My sweetheart, Mademoiselle X., was a student at the Conservatory of Music in Petrograd, and played the piano. She amused me with lively descriptions of Petrograd, telling me what a fine city it was, and of the joys of sleighing in winter. She was a very pleasant, interesting girl, but she had a proud look in her eyes, which seemed ready to dart forth glances of scorn at all times.

* * * * *

Towards the end of the summer a rumour started that Lubimov and Forcatti's opera company would appear in the state theatre that winter. At that time I still did not know a single opera thoroughly, but nevertheless I asked Usatov whether I might not try to make an appearance on the stage.

"Why not?" said he. "Make the attempt. You can sing on the stage and continue to study with me. Only, you must learn a few operas. 'Russalka' and 'Faust'—those are your great stand-bys, so believe me! You must also learn thoroughly the 'Life for the Tsar.'"

I learned by heart the three operas he named. One fine morning Lubimov came to Usatov's to hear Agnivtsev and

myself sing. He liked Agnivtsev's voice and made a contract
with him for two hundred and fifty rubles a month. I did
not please him, although I sang the third act from "Russalka," for which I usually got more praise than for anything else.

"I am far from being an actor yet," I sadly reflected.

However, some one or other advised Lubimov to hear me
again at the amateur club. He did so, and was better pleased
with my singing than he had been previously.

"I am willing to pay you one hundred and fifty rubles a
month," he proposed to me.

"Well," I reflected, "I'd have agreed to the half of that!"
Without further discussion, we signed a contract. I began
to attend rehearsals, where on one occasion I heard the
orchestra conductor, Truffi, say to somebody in his broken
Russian:

"What a fine voice that boy has!"

I was greatly pleased.

*   *   *   *   *

The season began with "Aïda." All went well till all of a
sudden Amneris got her dress caught in the scenery and
could not get it loose. I was taking the part of the Chief
Priest. I raised her train to help her to free herself. The
next day I read in the paper a severe reproof from a critic:
it was altogther out of the question that the Chief Priest
should bear Amneris's train.

It soon came about that the entire bass *répertoire* reposed
on my shoulders. Then, unexpectedly for me I occupied the
chief place in the operas. This state of affairs was especially
contributed to by the production of Leoncavallo's "Pagliacci," which was then staged for the first time in Tiflis. The
rôle of Tonio was well suited to the range of my voice, and
I acted the part, on the whole, quite successfully. The opera

was put on a number of times, and always met with great approval.

I was continually preparing new parts. I would receive a part one day and be expected to sing it the next evening. If I had not already acquired a certain habit of the stage and ability to meet its demands, this urgent hurried work would probably have been both trying and ruinous to my talent. But I had already long since become an *habitué* of the boards. I had gained the power of not losing my head before an audience, and was too much in love with my work ever to be frivolous about it. Although I had not really sufficient time to study new rôles thoroughly, I learned them, so to say, "on the run," studying them in the night hours. I threw my whole soul into each one of them.

Meanwhile I continued to go to Usatov's for my lessons. He sometimes praised me, and sometimes administered severe reproof. I always listened with attention and affection to the teachings of this man, who had drawn me out of the mire and now devoted his labour, energy, and knowledge to my improvement, absolutely without any thought of his own advantage. As a teacher of singing he was, so to say, a teacher of the mechanics of the art, instilling into his pupils its technique. He knew music well and loved it deeply. He often used to call all of us pupils together and tell us about some musical work, explaining to us its merits, pointing out its defects, and thus educating our taste.

On one occasion the tavern scene from "Boris Godounov" was staged at the Musical Club. I took the part of the chief of police. When Varlaam began to sing his long-drawn, apparently meaningless song, while on the background of its long-drawn accords the Pretender converses with the innkeeper, I suddenly felt that I was experiencing something unusual. I sensed in the strange music something wonderfully familiar, something to which I was no stranger. It seemed to me that all my tangled difficult career had gone on to just such an accompaniment. It had always followed me about—nay, it lived in my own soul, and more—it was everywhere in the world I knew. I say this now, but at that moment I simply felt a strange mystic union of sadness and delight. I wanted to weep and to laugh. I felt for the first time that music is the voice of the world's soul, its wordless song.

On one of the last days of the season I was given a benefit performance for having "given more of my services than had been expected of me," as the manager of the company said. I staged two operas in one evening—"Pagliacci" and the whole of "Faust." I could bear fatigue like a camel, and could sing for entire days. I even used to get ordered out of lodgings through my passion for singing.

On the day before the benefit performance General Ernst, the commander of the Tiflis garrison, died. He was an unbelievably thin, bony man, like a living skeleton, with an earth-coloured face and dead-looking eyes. A great many laughable stories used to be told about him; for instance, he was driving along a street one day in bad weather, when he espied a military clerk in galoshes and white gloves:

"Halt!" cried Ernst. "Take off those galoshes!"

The soldier clerk halted and stood to attention in the mud.

"Rub the mud off your galoshes with your hands!"

The clerk obediently rubbed the mud from his galoshes with his gloved hands.

"Put on your galoshes and consider yourself under arrest for two days."

During the time that he was a director of the Imperial Theatres, it was said that when he used to storm at his wife she would sit down at the piano and play the National Anthem, which obliged the general to come to attention at once.

At the theatre he always occupied a box over the orchestra, just above the drums and brass. Noticing on one occasion that the wind instruments were silent after playing for a short time, he came to the conclusion that such conduct was disorderly, called for the manager of the theatre, and enquired:

"Why are the wind instruments not playing?"

"There is a pause in their score."

"What? Do they draw their salaries with pauses too?"

"They get their salaries in the same way as everyone else."

"Be good enough to tell them to play without pauses next time! I won't put up with idlers!"

When I sang the part of General Gremin, in "Eugen Onegin" Ernst asked some one or other:

"Who is that young man?"

When he was told, he remarked:

"Hm! that's strange! I thought he must be the son of a general. He certainly plays the part very well."

Afterwards he came behind the scenes and praised me, but remarked that my costume was incomplete; certain indispensable military decorations were lacking.

"And your gloves are rotten, too! Next time you sing the rôle of General Gremin I will give you decorations and gloves!"

True to his word, on the next occasion he came to the theatre long before the performance was due to commence, requested me to put on my costume, and began to order me about, prodding me with one finger in the ribs, chest, and shoulders to emphasise his words:

"Eyes front! Half turn to the right! Turn! March!"

I turned, marched, came to attention, and received the general's approval. He then drew forth from a handkerchief a star and a cross, placed the decorations on my breast, and said in an embarrassed fashion:

"Listen, Chaliapine. Don't forget to give me back the decorations afterwards!"

"Of course not, Your Excellency!"

With increasing embarrassment the general explained:

"There was a fellow, also a bass singer, here, to whom I gave some decorations, and you know, he sold them—to buy drink, probably, the deuce take him! Anyway, he didn't bring them back, you know. . . ."

Well, this oddity died just on the eve of my benefit; and I was much alarmed lest the performance should be cancelled for that day. However, there was no postponement, and the performance was very successful. There was a large audience; and I was presented with a gold watch and a silver goblet, besides receiving three hundred rubles out of the receipts.

Usatov removed the inscription "To Usatov" from a riband which had been presented to him at some time or other, replaced it by the words "To Chaliapine," and brought it to me with a laurel wreath.

I was very proud of that!

The season came to an end. What was to come next? Naturally, I wanted to go to Moscow, the centre of artistic life in Russia. Usatov approved my determination, and furnished me with letters to Pchelnikov, the manager of the administrative offices of the Imperial Theatres, to the orchestral conductor Altani, to the stage manager Bartsal, and also to some one else whose name I cannot recollect at the moment.

Early one morning in the middle of May, Agnivtsev and I went to the post-horse station. Agnivtsev had not got on in opera, and had given up singing in the height of the season. Mlle. X. and her mother came to the station. I endeavoured to persuade her to go with me, but she refused. Her attitude towards me had long since come to resemble the curiosity with which people watch an acrobat at the circus, wondering whether he will break his neck today or tomorrow. I was conscious of this, and it hurt me, but I loved the girl all the same. When the galloping horses hurried us along Olginskaia Street and out on to the Georgian Military Road, my heart was heavy.

It was my first journey over this famous thoroughfare, and I had heard a great deal about its extraordinary beauties, but I was sad and preoccupied at leaving Mademoiselle X. and it was only after we had passed Ananour that the magnificent Caucasian scenery made me forget myself and my unfortunate romance.

*　*　*　*　*

After this lengthy journey Agnivtsev and I determined to hold a concert at Vladikavkaz, give the local public an opportunity to admire our art and, incidentally, replenish our pocketbooks by earning a few rubles. We engaged a hall and went to the necessary expense of having tickets and posters printed. But, alas! when on the morning upon which the concert was to take place we went eagerly to the box office to ask for news of the seat sale, the young woman in charge of the tickets, who looked very much like a witch, said acidly:

"Not a single ticket has been sold!"

However, we were not discouraged. Agnivtsev suggested that we should go to Stavropol, where an officer to whom he was related lived, who could help us. Travelling over a dull dusty road, we arrived at the even duller city, and at once went to see Agnivtsev's relative. He received us warmly and hospitably, and willingly exerted himself to arrange a concert, while Agnivtsev and I went in search of an accompanist.

We were told that a pianist who had been a pupil of

Rubinstein resided in the town, and were given her address. We found it to be a little house with a glazed veranda. We entered into conversation with a woman holding a dirty duster in her hand and with her skirt tucked up to her knees. She told us that her mistress was sick in bed at the moment, but she would let her know that visitors had arrived. Ushering us into a room, she disappeared. We sat down to wait. Deep sighs and groans penetrated through the wall to our ears. At length the door opened, and a woman with a bluish face and eyes enlarged by sickness entered the room.

"It is true I am a pupil of Anton Grigorievitch Rubinstein, but I cannot accompany nor play any music at all at present!" she announced, and at once left the room.

We went out, somewhat surprised at our reception. At the gate we again met the woman with her skirts tucked up. When I asked what was the matter with her mistress, the woman informed me calmly:

"She is going to have a baby."

I confess that this excellent intention seemed to us very ill-timed and much upset us.

However, Agnivtsev's relative sent us to another accompanist. It would seem that at that time all the musicians of Stavropol were ladies! This time we encountered a young blonde with abundant hair, who was evidently blessed with a very joyous disposition. She laughed at everything we said to her.

"So you want me to play accompaniments for you?" she said, giggling. "Do you know I have played with Josef Lhevinne? Yes, with Lhevinne himself!"

We were rather stumped by this, as we did not know who Lhevinne was at that time. However, we very earnestly begged her to assist us, but she answered very definitely:

"I can't accompany unknown artists! But I will give you a note to a girl . . ." laying emphasis on the last two words.

We gratefully accepted the note and set out to find the "girl." On the outskirts of the town we found ourselves in a deserted street and confronted by a long fence behind which a low irregularly built house stood in the midst of long grass. A dog lay on the porch steps. Washing was hanging out in the yard. We knocked for a long time, in turns, at the closed gates. At length a very suspicious woman admitted us into the courtyard after making very detailed enquiries as to who we were and what we wanted; and then summoned to the porch a decrepit old woman, with head shaking on her shoulders, as though palsied.

Agnivtsev, having been an officer in the army, bowed elegantly and clicked his heels together before her, and enquired whether Mademoiselle So-and-so lived there?

"What do you want of her?"

"We have a letter to her."

Thinking the old woman must be the accompanist's grandmother, Agnivtsev gave her the blonde young lady's missive. We were surprised to see her open it.

"I beg your pardon," said Agnivtsev, "the letter is addressed to Miss——"

"I am she," said the old woman, not without hauteur.

Then it dawned on us why the blonde had laughed so gaily when she recommended us to appeal to this "girl." The old woman told us, when she had read the note, that it was thirty years since she had touched the piano.

It seemed we were in an impasse. However, some kind person informed us that there was still another accompanist in the town. We found her living in an out-of-the-way place, and she turned out to be a very pleasant, agreeable woman, the wife of a district inspector of police. She was blonde, dreamy and shy. When she heard our request she blushed furiously and explained:

"You see, I have not had very much teaching. I play

only for my own pleasure, and I hardly think I should be suitable for you."

We entreated her to show us what she could do. She played very badly, without any idea of rhythm or of the movement of a piece. She read badly, too; however, we succeeded in teaching her a little of what we required. I was sufficiently musical to delay my *tempo* when she went wrong; but when Agnivtsev had once begun to sing he would go on to the end, taking no notice of the accompaniment and not attempting to keep time with it. I determined that during the concert I would sit beside the lady at the piano and point with my finger to the note which Agnivtsev might happen to reach while she was struggling to read the music.

In spite of everything, the concert took place and was not unsuccessful. Our accompanist's husband was particularly pleased!

Next day we took third-class tickets on the Moscow train. On the way certain kind gentlemen induced me to play cards. The game seemed so simple and interesting that I expected to win all kinds of money, but I soon realized that it was much simpler for the gentlemen who had suggested this pastime than for me! I lost two hundred and fifty rubles!

The loss of my money made me very sad. To console me my noble partners in the game said:

"Never mind! We will have dinner at the next station, meet afterwards for another game, and you will have better luck!"

Not only did this meeting never take place, but within a few minutes those noble gentlemen disappeared from the train entirely and I never saw them again.

Naturally I arrived in Moscow feeling very depressed.

*   *   *   *   *

Moscow, of course, overwhelmed us provincials with its variety, bustle, and uproar. As soon as we had engaged a room for ourselves, I hurried off to look at the Great Theatre. Its columns and the four horses of the façade produced a grandiose impression on me. I felt myself to be small and insignificant before such a temple of art.

Next morning I paid a visit to the office of the Imperial Theatres. Porters with eagles embroidered on their uniforms were sitting in the vestibule, obviously bored to death. People ran about with papers in their hands and pens behind their ears. It was all very unlike a theatre. A doorkeeper took my letter of introduction, turned it over in his hands uncertainly, and enquired indolently:

"Who is the Usatov you say this is from? Wait here a little!"

I sat down on a chest that also served as a bench, a typical article of furniture in a purely governmental institution, which is generally the receptacle for candles, boot brushes, and dusters. An hour, two hours, went by. At length I begged the porter to remind M. Pchelnikov about me. After objecting for some time he at length consented to do so, went away, and returned after an absence of about an hour, when he informed me that M. Pchelnikov could not receive me and had instructed him to say that at present, in the summer, all the government theatres were closed.

This statement had the ring of finality even though it was not very polite!

I next went to see Altani, a conductor, and Avramenko, a director of the chorus, and was received more politely. They also told me that the season was over, and that in the Imperial theatres the auditions were held in Lent. The Lenten season had already begun for me, by the way! I had hardly any money left! Agnivtsev and I registered our names at Madame Razsokhine's Theatrical Agency. I gave the agency my photographs, posters, and press-cuttings. Madame Razsokhine expressed a wish to hear my voice, and was evidently pleased with it.

"Excellent!" said she. "We will find you a theatre!"

Very soon all my money was gone. Agnivtsev and I used to dine at a tavern for fifty kopeks. I had never confessed to my friend that I had lost so much money at cards and was still unwilling to do so. Soon necessity forced me to refuse to dine with him. But it was dull sitting alone and dinnerless in a little poky room; and when I had spent two days in this manner I told him of my predicament. He scolded me a good deal, but urged me to dine at his expense, saying that I could repay him later on when I had the money to do so.

Pavlusha Agnivtsev was a very agreeable good fellow, but he was quite vexatiously punctilious in his accounts. If he spent seven kopeks he promptly debited me with three and a half kopeks in his little notebook. It was the right thing to do, of course, but wearisome in the extreme!

"Write me down for four kopeks!" I begged him, but he replied very reasonably:

"But why? Half of seven is three and a half; half of five is two and a half . . ." and so on.

To escape from my friend's notions of arithmetic I used to go to the Sparrow Hills, where I could look on the splendour of Moscow, which like everything else in the world appeared more beautiful from a distance than close to. Sitting there alone, I thought sadly and uneasily about my past life. I remembered Tiflis where I had spent so many happy hours and—Mademoiselle X.! For a time, I wrote her long letters, but the intervals between her replies grew long as weeks went by, and I was forced to realize that the first love of my life had been but a sorry story!

A month passed. At the beginning of July a note came from Madame Razsokhine asking me to call at her office. I snatched up my music and fairly ran all the way! A huge, curly-headed man with a handsome flowing beard sat in the hall. He looked like the Russian legendary bandit Tchurkin; his great broad chest was covered with about three pounds of assorted trinkets. From under his bushy eyebrows he looked sternly, almost angrily, at everybody. In fact, he had every air of being a most important personage, which indeed he was, for this man, they told me, was Lentovsky, the famous Moscow impresario!

I had already heard this name, which was celebrated in Russia, and I was rather afraid of him. Lentovsky looked me up and down and said to Madame Razsokhine:

"He might do."

"Sing," said Madame Razsokhine.

I sang an aria from "Don Carlos," with eyes fixed on the back of my accompanist's neck. After listening for a few minutes, Lentovsky said:

"Enough. Well, what do you know and what can you do?"

I told him the extent of my knowledge, but that I did not know what it might be possible for me to do!

"Have you sung 'The Tales of Hoffmann?' "

"No," said I.

"You will take the part of Doctor Miracle. Take the music and learn it. Here are one hundred rubles. Afterwards you will go to Petersburg to sing at 'Arcadia.' "

Everything—Lentovsky's laconic style, the hundred rubles, his bushy eyebrows, and the trinkets with which his person was adorned, produced a crushing impression on me. So that was how Moscow impresarios behaved! I signed the contract without even having read it, and hurried off home in a happy frame of mind. Shortly afterwards I signed a further contract for a winter season at Kazan, with Unkovsky, but was told at the office that he demanded a guarantee that I would really come, and I must therefore put my signature to a bill of exchange for six hundred rubles.

I signed, and set out for Petrograd, after bidding a friendly farewell to Agnivtsev.

My poor friend had continuous bad luck. In later years his voice even changed from barytone to tenor. After a trying life, full of misfortunes and disappointments, he went raving mad and died while acting as rural overseer in Siberia.

CHAPTER SIX

Petrograd—I Become an Artist of the Imperial Theatres—Dalsky—First Appearances at the Mariensky—New Acquaintances—Hotel Palais Royal—Nijny Novgorod and Mamontov—An Italian Ballet Troupe—I Join Mamontov's Company at Moscow—Pskovitianka—Paris—Marriage—Boris Godounov—Friendship with Stassov.

ON THE journey to Petrograd I imagined to myself the town set on a hill, and thought to see it white and clean, half-buried in foliage. I thought it could not be otherwise, since the Tsars lived there.

It was rather disappointing to see the numerous factory chimneys and the pall of smoke over the roofs, but the peculiar sullen beauty of the town created a vivid impression.

"Arcadia" I also expected to be a garden of unheard-of elegance and beauty, but it turned out to be something after the style of the Panaevsky Gardens in Kazan, just as closely built up with various structures, which displayed the same sort of wooden elegance. There were performances going on in the garden. The splendid *diseuse*, Paola Cortes, was singing in the open-air theatre. I went to hear her every day, for it was the first time I had seen such a talented woman. I did not understand what she sang, but admired her voice, intonations, and gestures. Her chansonettes penetrated farther than the mere sense of hearing.

A fortnight went by. Lentovsky turned up, and a series of disorderly rehearsals and confused performances took place. It appeared that the owner of the enterprise was not

Lentovsky, but the proprietor of a restaurant, and not only disputes but actual brawls at once began to occur between him and Lentovsky. The "celebrated Moscow impresario" thrashed the caterer more than once, and being occupied with so doing did not pay much attention to opera. He was also distracted by a vaudeville entertainment, "The Magic Pills," for which he had called in some very clever acrobats. They climbed up trees, were swallowed up in the earth to the accompaniment of thunder and lightning, got drowned, crushed, or hung. It was all very amusing, but in superabundance rather boring.

I took the part of Miracle, but the "Tales of Hoffmann" did not meet with any success. The public stayed away from the gardens. I was to have received three hundred rubles a month, but got nothing beyond the one hundred rubles which had been given me in Moscow. I frequently asked the "celebrated *entrepreneur*" to give me two or three rubles, and he never gave me more than fifty kopeks. I got tired of going hungry, besides being ashamed to do so in the capital.

Towards the end of the season I had an amusing but rather unpleasant experience. I made the acquaintance in the gardens of two ladies, and was driving with them one day in an open carriage or *izvozchick*. The cab was much too small to hold three people, so I was obliged to sit on the floor and let my feet dangle outside. In turning a corner the driver accidentally brought my feet into contact with a lamp-post. I cried out with the pain, but felt still worse when I noticed that my boot had been knocked to pieces. The ladies took me to their flat and rubbed my injured foot, but they could not mend my boot! I begged and prayed Lentovsky to give me sufficient money to buy a new pair of boots, but he would not do so. Luckily, I had a new pair of rubber galoshes, which were as bright externally as patent leather.

I walked about the streets of the capital in them for many months.

The season at "Arcadia" ended disastrously. I needed to pay my fare to Kazan, but could not get the money. Some one suggested I should join a society of operatic artists, which was going to arrange a series of performances in the Panaevsky theatre in Petrograd.

I said that I had signed a contract for Kazan; but my friend told me that I did not need to trouble my head about that.

That seemed strange to me, for I felt sure that if I had signed an agreement I must needs fulfil it, besides which I had signed a bill of exchange for six hundred rubles. I reflected.

I was not anxious to leave Petrograd. I liked its wide streets, the electric lamps, the river, the theatres, and the general tone of life in the capital.

In the end I went to the Panaevsky theatre, where all the members of the partnership had already assembled, with conductor Truffi, an old acquaintance of mine, at their head. I told them I was willing to join the company, and they received me with open arms.

We were busy with our preliminary preparations, signing papers, getting funds from somewhere or other, and rehearsing, when the death of Tsar Alexander III occurred and it was announced that all the theatres were to be closed for six weeks. This was an unexpected blow. However, we approached various influential people and were graciously accorded permission to sing.

Our performances were very successful. I had the good luck to attract speedily the attention of the public, and various well-known personalities in the musical world began to call on me behind the scenes. Everyone liked the way in which I sang Bertrand in "Robert le Diable." V. V.

Andreiev, the famous Balalaika artist told me that the authorities of the Mariensky theatre were taking an interest in me, and soon afterwards I was invited to call there and sing something in the presence of Napravnik, the celebrated Czecho-Slovakian conductor.

I ought to say that on one occasion, when I sang the "Conjuration of the Fowers" from "Faust," the audience unanimously, and greatly to my surprise, demanded an encore. My comrades on the boards were also much surprised, as hitherto no one appeared ever to have taken much notice of this aria. Well, when I resolved to call on Napravnik, V. V. Andreiev recommended me to select the "Conjuration of the Flowers" for performance. Napravnik was a man with a very dry manner, very uncommunicative and restrained in his speech. One never knew whether anything pleased him or not. He listened to my singing without a word of comment. Shortly afterwards, however, I learned that it was proposed to arrange an audition for me on the stage of the Mariensky theatre, in the presence of the manager. I knew that the Mariensky theatre required a bass singer, as the celebrated Melnikov had then already ended his career.

Naturally, I did not expect to take his place, and was in a great to-do when I was asked to prepare for my audition the aria of Russlan, which was one for which Melnikov had usually received the greatest praise. The audition took place, but apparently my critics and judges were not satisfied with my singing of the aria of Russlan. They asked me to sing something else as well, and I sang the fourth act from "A Life for the Tsar," both the aria and the recitative. I sang the aria in the same manner as all other artists did, but executed the recitative after my own fashion, in the same style as that in which I sing now. Apparently the impression produced on my judges was favourable. I recollect the tenor Figner coming to shake my hand, with tears in his eyes. He was a singer of long experience. Next day I was asked to sign a contract, and thus became a member of the artistic staff of the Imperial Theatres.

Was I glad of it? I don't remember, but I don't think I was very greatly rejoiced at the event, for at that time I had many reasons for satisfaction.

I continued to sing at the Panaevsky theatre, and zealously enlarged the circle of my acquaintances. I became very friendly with V. V. Andreiev, at whose flat painters, singers, and musicians used to assemble on Fridays. These receptions opened a new world to me. I drank in the knowledge of the beauties of art. I saw painters design their works, heard musical and theatrical celebrities sing and recite, listened to discussions on music. I looked on and listened eagerly, learning busily from observation. Very often at the conclusion of these Friday receptions we all used to go in a body to Leiner's restaurant, celebrated as the favoured meeting place of the artistic world in Petrograd, where we continued to chat and sing till the early hours of the morning, and sometimes till daybreak. There I made the acquaintance of Mamont Dalsky, a tragedian attached to the Alexandrinsky theatre, one of the other Imperial Theatres devoted to the drama. Dalsky, then a young man and in the heyday of his popularity with the public, was a Russian nobleman. His real name was Neiolov.

I frequently sang at students' concerts and at charitable entertainments. V. I. Kachalov—the same Kachalov who has since appeared in America with Stanislavsky's Moscow Art theatre studio—was then a student and wearing the uniform of his university. He frequently organised these concerts. On one occasion he came to fetch me in a closed carriage. This pleased me very much, for hitherto I had seen only great ladies and prelates drive in closed carriages, the usual conveyances in Russia being open cabs. Now it was my turn to drive in state.

Well, well, I was young then and, I must say, naïve to a degree! Kachalov tried to talk to me, but I answered at random, looking out of the windows, deep in recollections of my childhood, of Kazan, and the nights I had slept in carriages of the same type when I used to work for the skin dresser. This carriage, like the carriages of my childhood, also, had an agreeable odour of leather, varnish, and some special fragrance besides.

When I stepped on to the concert platform of the Noble Assembly Building of Petrograd (DVORANSKOE SO-BRANIE), where I was to sing, I was astonished by the magnificent look of the hall, with its columns, and by the sight of the great audience. My heart quivered with fright which soon turned to pleasure. I sang with great enthusiasm, being particularly successful with "The Two Grenadiers." There was a tremendous uproar of applause in the hall. I was not allowed to leave the platform, and was obliged to sing every number two or three times. I was ready and willing to go on singing till morning, so touching was the enthusiasm of the audience.

Friends congratulated me sincerely on my success. Everyone said that it would be of great service to my career in the Imperial Theatres. Naturally, I was more than delighted, and I more and more frequently appeared at charitable entertainments and students' concerts. The frequency with which I used to take part in such enterprises led to my spending an evening once with Dalsky in a very odd fashion. We were invited to appear at a concert somewhere or other, but no carriage was sent for us. We determined to go there ourselves without waiting any longer. We did not know where the concert was being held, however, and therefore went to the first hall we could think of and asked the manager of a concert which was being given there, whether we were not taking part in it.

"No," we were told. "We are sorry to say you are not participating, but if you would care to do so . . ."

We took off our overcoats, sang our songs, and went on to the next place. Once more we failed to find the right concert hall where we were awaited. However, I sang again there, and Dalsky recited. In this manner we appeared, not without pleasure both for ourselves and for the public, at no less than four different concert halls, but without succeeding in getting to the function to which we had been invited.

I was terribly provincial and clumsy in my ways. V. V. Andreiev zealously and very skilfully strove to remodel my education, persuading me to cut short my hair, which I wore long in the manner affected by some singers in Russia, teaching me how to dress properly, and in every way looking after me. I stood very much in need of his kind offices, for all sorts of queer incidents used to befall me. One day, for instance, I was invited to afternoon tea at a certain very lordly mansion. I put on the dress coat given me by Usatov, polished up my boots, and bravely made my appearance in my host's drawing-room. Next to me, when we sat down to tea, were several very merry and witty young ladies, while I was dreadfully backward and modest. All at once I felt that some one was tenderly and methodically pressing my foot.

"Heavens!" thought I. "Which of these ladies is pressing my foot?"

Naturally, I did not venture to move my foot, and was dreadfully eager to look under the table. Finally, I could bear it no longer. Jumping up from the table, I said I must go at once. While I was bowing my farewells, my eyes fell upon my shoes and I suddenly noticed that one of my boots shone dazzlingly, while the other had turned a rusty colour and was damp. At that moment a St. Bernard dog emerged from underneath the table, licking its chops, which were smeared with blacking. My disillusionment was great and I laughed wildly as I walked home in boots of two different shades. Andreiev told me afterwards that one did not go to afternoon tea in a dress coat and that I ought to have worn patent-leather boots with it, in any event.

*   *   *   *   *

The contract which I signed with the administration of the Imperial Theatres stated that I was entitled to make three appearances and if I did not give satisfaction on these occasions the contract would not be ratified. I forthwith ordered visiting cards with the imprint, "Artist of the Imperial Theatres," a designation which much flattered my self-esteem and of which I was very proud.

My first appearance was in "Faust." I already had my own ideas about playing Mephistopheles, but those in authority ordered me to wear the costume of tradition, and my make-up, which I had carried out according to my own ideas and which differed from that established by custom, excited laughter and misunderstanding. This attitude embarrassed me and cooled my enthusiasm, with the result that I don't think I sang Mephistopheles very well on that occasion.

Afterwards I was told to sing Zuniga in "Carmen." I emphasised the comedy of the character, and produced a better impression by my performance.

The stage manager asked me if I did not know the rôle of Russlan, and told me that the administration would take particular note of the way in which I performed it. At that time I had already acquired something of the self-confidence, bordering on audacity, which appears to be a characteristic of all young artists. I had already experienced a considerable degree of success at the Panaevsky theatre

A PICTURE TAKEN DURING MY FIRST SEASON AS ARTIST OF THE IMPERIAL
THEATRES

and at charitable concerts, and had grown accustomed to receiving bouquets from feminine admirers, and often heard my name pronounced behind my back in that special sort of whisper which gives one a peculiar tingle of emotion. The praise of my friends on the stage, and favourable notices in the press, combined to turn my head, and I already regarded myself as a distinguished artist.

Knowing how quickly I could learn a part, I told the stage manager that in three weeks I could learn not one, but two operatic rôles like Russlan, if required.

"Very well; learn it," he requested me.

I forthwith found an accompanist and learned the rôle, as I thought, after three weeks of hasty study. The day of the performance arrived. Napravnik was conducting the orchestra. I put on the costume of a Russian warrior of early times, padding myself out to increase my girth, stuck on a red beard, and went on to the stage. From the very first note I felt that I was singing badly and that I was very like those knights who dance quadrilles and lancers in Russian merchants' houses during the Christmas holidays. When the consciousness of this came to me fully, I lost my head, and although I industriously flourished my arms about and made strange grimaces, that did not help me out. The conductor made faces at me and whispered to me:

"Shsh! . . ."

Next day there were notices in the newspapers saying that a young artist by the name of Chaliapine had sung Russlan very badly. The administration was censured for having entrusted such a rôle as that of Russlan to an ignorant young nobody, after the great Melnikov had created it. Many other bitter truths were written about me. Thank goodness, that humiliation occurred at the very beginning of my career as a singer! It did me good by sobering me and compelling me to think seriously about myself and the profession I was engaged in. It stripped from me the impudence and excessive self-confidence with which I was infected.

A fresh rehearsal was appointed, and I was given the rôle of Russlan to sing once more. I sang rather better, but trembled inwardly with fright. My heart seemed to stop beating and I could scarcely breathe.

The three appearances were over. I was retained on the payroll of the theatre, and many varied rôles were entrusted to me. I took my scores with me, and went for the summer to Pavlovsk, a fashionable summer-villa neighbourhood not far from Petrograd, where I had the companionship of Wolf Israel, the 'cellist of the Mariensky theatre, who was of the same age as myself. While at Pavlovsk I went every day to Taskin, who was a good musician and accompanist, besides being a very agreeable companion. I studied my rôles with Taskin's aid as accompanist, and for the rest lived quietly, walking in the great park of the grand dukes, fishing and meditating on the manner in which various rôles should be acted.

My friends and acquaintances unanimously told me:

"You must work! You have a good voice, but you don't work enough."

I did not comprehend very clearly what they meant by "work." I supposed that I ought to sing vocal exercises as frequently as possible, and did so, but my friends continued to repeat:

"You must work!"

But no one could explain to me in a comprehensive way what to do and how I ought to "work."

The operatic season began, but even then I did not have to do any "work." I was not given an opportunity to sing. I sang only "Russlan," and thereafter did nothing for some time. Then I several times took the part of the Count in

Cimaroso's beautiful old opera, "The Secret Marriage."
Also I played Zuniga in "Carmen." And that was all!
My enforced inactivity upset me very much, and I could
console myself only by singing at charitable concerts.

These concerts, however, necessitated a clean white shirt
on almost every occasion. I was receiving two hundred
rubles a month, but as, while engaged at the Panaevsky
theatre, I had signed every document that was put before me
and would even have signed my own death warrant without
looking at it, I found myself pursued by various persons
for recovery of all the debts incurred by the artists who
coöperated in the Panaevsky partnership. Thus, as soon as
I joined the Imperial Theatres, summonses, warrants of
execution, and other strictly legal documents simply poured
into the box office, addressed to me. It was sought to recover from me sums of 600 rubles, 716 rubles, 1,000
rubles, and finally even 5,000 rubles. As I did not go near
the courts, being afraid of judicial institutions, the courts
gave judgment in my absence and always against me.

The management of the theatre was obliged to deduct
one half of my salary to pay off these debts, and I got only
one hundred rubles a month. It was very hard to live on
the money. Probably I should have continued for at least
sixteen years paying off these debts, of which I knew nothing
at all, if the well-known Petrograd lawyer, Mr. M. F.
Wolkenstein, had not taken up the cudgels on my behalf.
I give him my power of attorney and, without taking a cent
of money, he won all my suits and thus freed me from the
necessity of working for other people's benefit.

My situation at the theatre went from bad to worse. If
any member of the council of the theatre proposed to en-
trust a rôle to me, a majority of votes rejected the proposal.
Several Czechs (for in the Imperial Theatres there were
many Czecho-Slovakians) and others even said outright

that it would be a "downright disgrace" to give a rôle to Chaliapine.   To some extent I had merited that such an attitude should be taken by having sung Russlan so badly. Still, it seemed to me to be unjust.   If I acted badly, then I ought to be taught to act better!   But they taught me badly, too.

Very likely I was clumsy on the stage.   Perhaps my gestures were not adapted to the rhythm of the music, but I felt sure that I knew and grasped the meaning of the Russian language better and more profoundly than Czechs or other foreigners.   Meanwhile, the stage manager Pale-chek, a Czech, used to tell me how I ought to sing Russian words, while himself making the most ridiculous errors of grammar and pronunciation.

Besides all that, Dalsky, in looking over the *répertoire* announced for the week, remarked to me:

"You ought to have your name in the *répertoire* at least twice a week.   If an artist is not included in the *répertoire*, it means that the theatre does not need him."

He pointed out to me:

"Look at the *répertoire* of the Alexandrinsky theatre. . . . Monday, 'Hamlet,' Dalsky plays; Wednesday, 'Bie-lugin's Wedding,' Dalsky again; Friday, 'Ruy Blas,' once more Dalsky.   Just compare it with the Mariensky theatre: 'Russalka,' Kariakin sings, and not Chaliapine; 'Rognieda,' Chernov is singing, but again not Chaliapine."

These comments greatly disturbed me.

"But what can I do?" I said to my friend.   "They don't give me an opportunity to appear!"

"Well, then, leave the place.   Give up your appoint-ment!"

It was easy to say "Leave," but where could I go?   In sorrowful meditation I went to Leiner's restaurant.   The frequency of my visits to Leiner's gave rise to a popular legend that I was never sober. The longer the season went on, the more painful and difficult I felt my situation to be. The rehearsals were especially burdensome to me, for it seemed as though everybody present, the stage manager, the prompter, the members of the chorus, and even the carpenters, combined to teach me how to do my work.

V. V. Andreiev took my ill success to heart quite especially, and did all he could to be of use to me by increasing my circle of acquaintances amongst those who could really help me to learn.

One day he introduced me to Tertius Philippov, Chancellor of the Empire and the Tsar's right hand. He was also a personage of importance in the world of art, a friend of the celebrated playright Ostrovsky, devoted heart and soul to Moussorgsky and an admirer of everything that showed originality and character. At Philippov's house I saw the celebrated story-teller Orina Fedosova. She created an impression on my mind which I have never forgotten. I had heard plenty of anecdotes, old-time songs and legends, before I met Fedosova, but it was her wonderful power of vividly reproducing the colour and atmosphere of the old traditional Russian "unwritten literature," handed down from the past, that made me comprehend all at once the profundity and beauty of our national heritage of fable. The little bent old woman with the merry childlike face used to relate the old stories of the Snake Gorynych, of Dobrinia and his gallant adventures, of his mother, and of love, with inimitable beauty. The fable seemed to be reborn before my very eyes, and Fedosova herself was in her way as marvellous as a legend.

When we sat down to supper, Ivan F. Gorbunov began to talk, and his talent surprised me no less than that of Fedosova. I had never before experienced, as I did then, how it was possible with two or three words, by proper intonation and mimicry, to bring before the eyes of one's hearers an entire picture. Listening to Gorbunov's thumb-nail sketches of real life incidents, I was conscious, not without wonderment, that he magically set before me all that was most characteristic in the life of Buzuluk, Samara, Astrakhan, and all the other towns and hamlets of the Russian Empire which I had seen in my wanderings and from which I had acquired a multitude of chaotic impressions, which had settled down on my spirit with an effect of boredom, like a grey cloud of dust.

I sang several songs and also the trio, "A golden cloudlet slept" ("*Nochevala tuchka zolotaya*"), with Kariakin and some one else. In singing the trio, Kariakin pronounced the word *tikhonko* (quietly) so loudly, that the glass in the windows shook! Philippov was a very gracious host to me that evening.

I went on another occasion to Philippov's to hear a marvellous boy, a virtuoso of the pianoforte. He was a meagre, slender, and, so to say, not very noticeable child, but when he sat down at the piano and began to play he fairly made me look around in astonishment and noncomprehension, such were the force and tenderness of the sounds which fell on my ears. It seemed as though some magician were exhibiting a masterly piece of sleight of hand.

This marvellous boy was none other than Josef Hofmann.

The more I saw of talented people, the more I felt that all I knew was the merest trifle, and that I had much, very much, to learn. But how to learn, and what, exactly?

In conversation with Dalsky I told him more than once that the operatic art to which I dedicated my services was incomprehensible to me and did not satisfy me. I regretted that I was not an actor on the dramatic stage, for it seemed to me that singing could not give expression to all that could be said in dramatic speech. Dalsky, of course, quite agreed with these views of mine, and the thought began to obtrude itself insistently on my mind: Was it not possible to unite the opera and the drama in one?

At the end of the season the stage manager Kondratiev told me that I was to sing the rôle of the Miller in "Russalka."

"I don't think that rôle is suited to me," I said, recollecting how coldly the public of Tiflis had received my performance of the part.

Kondratiev told me I was a fool, and commanded me to prepare for the performance, which was to be a Sunday matinée. While I was studying the rôle of the Miller, Dalsky asked me to read over to him the aria which the Miller sings when first coming on the stage. I did so.

"It seems to me," said Dalsky, "that you have a wrong idea of the Miller's character. He is not an agile, sturdy young countryman, but a dignified, respectable peasant in middle life."

I at once understood my error. In Tiflis I had acted the Miller as a lively little old man.

On the Sunday my singing of the Miller was rewarded with great success—my first and only successful performance in all that season. I was much applauded, and received a number of wreaths from the audience; but amongst my comrades on the boards my success passed unnoticed. Nobody congratulated me; no one even said so much as a single kind word. When I went behind the scenes with a wreath in my hands, the stage manager turned aside from me and began to whistle indifferently, with an air as though it all did not concern him in the least.

Quite apart from my lack of success, I hated going to the theatre on account of the attitude of the officials of the management. I felt that an artist ought to be a free and independent person, and that he was so in reality. But at the Imperial Theatres, when the director appeared behind the scenes, the artists drew themselves up before him like so many soldiers and grasped with an ingratitiating smile the two fingers which he condescendingly extended to them in greeting. It must not be forgotten that I am speaking of the Imperial Theatres of my youth, of 1895. Hitherto I had seen such relations only in government offices. They seemed to me to be out of place in the theatre. Once the stage manager severely rebuked me for not having made a formal visit to the director on New Year's Day. The absence of my name from his visitor's book had been noticed and commented on. It seemed to me to be humiliating to show one's respect to the director through the intermediary of a hall porter; and indeed, I don't think I was aware of the existence of such a custom. There were many other little things which weighed on my spirits. I ceased to be proud of being an artist of the Imperial Theatres.

I recall only one pleasant impression during the whole season, namely, making the acquaintance of the composer Rimsky-Korsakov, when we were preparing "The Night Before Christmas" for a performance. I looked with vast interest on the taciturn, meditative composer, whose eyes were concealed behind double glasses. Apparently the general attitude observed towards him was in no way better than towards an unimportant person like myself. I recollect how unceremoniously entire pages were struck out of the score of his opera, how he knitted his brows and protested, while with stony insistence it was argued that if the opera were not cut it would appear to the public to be tediously lengthy.

Perhaps those who wished to shorten it were right, for it

THE MAD MILLER IN "RUSSALKA"

frequently happened that an interesting opera and beautiful music failed to please the public, which merely said:

"How boring! Russian composers always create such tedium!"

The public was not pleased if an opera did not contain arias such as, for instance, "The Golden Calf" in "Faust."

"Trovatore" was the sort of opera that was sure of a welcome.

Altogether it did not seem to me that Russian music was held in much esteem.

I was desirous on one occasion of singing Moussorgsky's "Trepàk" at a concert. I had a great liking for it. At a rehearsal at the house of the artiste who was arranging the concert I met a well-known musical critic of the day. He was to play accompaniments at the concert.

"Why are you going to sing 'Trepàk'?" he asked me.

"Because I like it very much."

"But, really, it's frightful rubbish," he said kindly.

"I shall sing it, all the same. . . ."

"Well, that's your affair. Sing it, then," he said, shrugging his shoulders. "Give me the music, so that I can have a good look over it at home."

I gave him the music, but, not being very hopeful that he could play the accompaniment well for a work which he criticised so severely and unjustly, I asked my friend Dlussky, an accompanist, to play for me at the concert. I was told that the critic was very much annoyed at this action of mine.

However, when I sang "Trepàk" at the concert it became clear to me that the public does not care for such compositions.

Later on, when I came to Petrograd with Mamontov's opera company, I sang at concerts many songs over the study of which I had laboured a good deal, and the criticisms were very severe both on them and on me.

* * * * *

In the middle of Poushkin Street, Petrograd, was a so-called "square" where stood the monument to our great Poushkin. The small figure in a little surtout stood on a square pedestal and seemed both comic and awkward.

Just opposite, was a huge building that resembled a storage warehouse. In spite of the fact that it bore the name "Palais Royal," this building was in reality a very second-class hotel, which served as a refuge for the artistic Bohemians of Petrograd. In my time, this refuge was very dirty and the only pleasant thing about it—besides the people who lived there—was the staircase. Its shallow steps were easy to climb even to the fifth floor, where I lived in a dismal little room such as could be found only in a country hotel. The heavy window curtains were faded with the passage of years, and harboured a great deal of dust, not to mention fleas, flies, and other insects. Tipsy people, men and women, were to be met in the corridors at all hours of the night. Noisy disputes were, however, a rarity. On the whole, life in the Palais Royal was both interesting and jolly. Dalsky occupied a room on the same corridor as myself. Actors and admirers of both sexes were continually calling on him. He loved to hold forth amongst them by the hour, appearing to know something about every conceivable subject, and discussing it boldly and freely, no matter what it was. I used to listen to his conversation very attentively.

Gulevitch, an old man who had been an actor and who lived in a charitable institution like the Actor's Fund Home in America, often looked in on us. He was without means and wore shabby clothes, but he had a peculiar wit of his own.

He used to divert us with astonishing tales drawn from his own imagination, about the doings of the popes of Rome after death; for instance, how Piux IX wanted to take a walk along the Milky Way, and about what goes on in the infernal regions, in heaven, or at the bottom of the sea.

During Holy Week Gulevitch told me:

"Of course we in the 'Refuge' are also going to celebrate Easter, but I shall come to spend the evening with you."

He arrived on the Saturday evening with a number of little bundles in his arms. I was very pleased, as I thought he had brought a supply of Eastertide dainties and drinkables with which to break our fast, and rejoiced all the more as I had not a kopek in my pocket. It turned out, however, that he had only brought a dozen or so of paper lanterns and candle ends.

"There," said he, "I spent the whole week making them myself! Let's hang them up, and at midnight we will light them. We shall have illuminations!"

When I told him that the lanterns were all very well, but we had nothing to break our fast with, the old fellow was very downcast. Unfortunately, there was no one in the house whom I knew. Dalsky and other acquaintances had gone out in various directions to celebrate the evening at the houses of their friends. We were very dismal.

All at once Gulevitch looked at the ikon which hung in the corner of the room, mounted on a chair and took it down, placing it outside in the corridor with the words:

"When actors have got the blues, they don't wish you to be sorrowful with them."

He put the ikon on the window sill in the corridor, face towards the glass.

Just then a man in livery came up the stairs and said:

"Are you Mr. Chaliapine? Madam So-and-so begs your company to supper with her!"

This was a very pleasant lady of high rank. Andreiev had introduced me to her, and I frequently sang in her drawing-room. I set out at once, after borrowing an over-coat from the porter in the corridor, for one of my neigh-bours had pawned my own coat or sold it to buy drink. There were many guests assembled in my hostess's dining room. We ate, drank, and were very merry, but I could not help thinking of old Gulevitch, and the recollection made me feel embarrassed and unhappy. I went to the hostess and whispered to her that I was anxious to get away, as an old man was sitting waiting for me at home. Would she not perhaps be so kind as to give me some trifles for him?

She received my request very simply and kindly, told her servants to fill a basket full of good things of every descrip-tion, and gave me some money, and in half an hour I was back once more at the Palais Royal, where Gulevitch was sitting alone and smoothing out his moustaches with moist-ened fingers and a melancholy air.

"Deuce take it!" said he, unpacking the basket. "Why, there is not only vodka, but even champagne here!"

He darted into the corridor and brought back the ikon, hung it up in its place once more, and said in explanation:

"People make holiday in company, but when they are tedious they are better in solitude!"

We welcomed Easter in splendid style, but when I awoke the next morning I saw Gulevitch lying on the couch all doubled up and groaning.

"What's the matter?" I enquired.

"Lord knows! It was not with good will that they gave you everything we have been eating! I am very sick. . . ."

All at once I noticed that a bottle in which I kept a gargle for my throat was empty.

"Hullo!" said I. "What has become of my gargle?"

"Was that a gargle?" asked Gulevitch, with raised eyebrows.

"Of course it was!"

"Hm. . . . Now I understand. To tell you the truth, I drank it," confessed the old man, pulling at his moustaches.

My "domestic" life in the Palais Royal was full of such laughable and melancholy, half-farcical incidents, while behind the scenes at the theatre I felt myself to be more and more a stranger. I had no friendly comradeships with the other artists, and in fact I have never observed any such on the boards of the state theatre.

I felt a sensation of emptiness, of something lost. It seemed as though, while advancing along a beautiful broad highway, I had suddenly came to a crossroad and knew not which way to go. I needed something, but what I did not know.

The season closed. I received some rôles for study in preparation for the next season, and wondered where I should go for the summer. My friend the barytone Sokolov proposed a visit to the All-Russian Exhibition at Nijny Novgorod. He described to me with much enthusiasm an opera company which was to appear there, spoke of the problems with which it would have to deal, and awakened my interest. I determined to go to Nijny. There I soon succeeded in securing an engagement.

Till then I had not seen anything of the Volga above Kazan. The special character of its beauty, the walls and towers of its ancient Kremlin, the wide expanse of water and meadowland which it overlooks, all combined to charm me with their novelty. I speedily fell into a contented and enjoyable frame of mind, as I always do when I am near the Volga or voyaging on its broad surface.

I engaged a room in the house of an old lady on the Kovalikha Street, and then set out to see the theatre, which was new, clean, and had just been completed. Rehearsals began. I made acquaintance with the other artists of the company, and good, comradely relations at once came into being between us. Immediately I noticed that in private opera companies the relations of the artists among themselves were always simpler and more sincere than in the Imperial Theatres.

Amongst the artists was Kruglov, the barytone, who had been one of my demigods when I used to go to the theatre at Kazan as a boy.

I very soon learned that the enterprise belonged not to Madame Winter, whom I had understood to be the proprietress, but to Savva Ivanovitch Mamontov, who was really supplying the funds. I had heard many interesting details about Mamontov when I was in Tiflis, from Conductor Truffi. I knew him to be a "Mæcenas," one of the greatest in Moscow, and a man of profoundly artistic tastes. Mamontov, however, was not yet at Nijny.

Madame Winter used to have interesting evenings at her house after the play, to which all the members of our opera company were welcomed. I made myself a regular showman at these parties, telling stories and anecdotes founded on my own experiences. I had plenty to tell, too. My tales soon won me the attention and sympathy of my companions, and I felt at my best in their company. I dare to say that I held the interest of my audience, for in my two years in Petrograd I had been under the influence of Gorbunov and others, which had taught me much.

When dining one day at Madame Winter's, I saw at table a thick-set full-bodied man with a very striking head of the Mongolian type, whose lively eyes and energetic movements attracted my attention. It was Mamontov. He looked at me with a severe expression, but did not speak to me, and continued his conversation with a young man who wore a little chin beard after the Henri IV fashion. This was K. A. Korovin, the painter.

It is a difficult matter to pronounce judgment, with thoroughness and complete knowledge, upon any subject. But as an observant traveller through the world I think I may be permitted to express a modest opinion upon art lovers. Of course, I wish to speak of the rich lover of art, for the impecunious worshippers at this shrine can help only by exercising their own talents or by crying "Bravo!" in a loud voice to some already established celebrity.

The rich lover of art is usually shy. He often has a particularly small voice, and therefore is totally incapable of shouting "Bravo!" but condemned to figure, in silence, as a Mæcenas. As a son of my country I must say that the Russian Mæcenas is of a totally different colour from those of other countries.

The Russian Mæcenas, I have observed, loves art not alone that he may be deluged with publicity, that, through the press the public may gain false impressions about him. He is a protector of art in the fullest sense and he loves it with his heart and soul. We have had Tretiakov, who founded the Musée des Beaux Arts at Moscow; Morosov, who supported the Moscow Art Theatre, and many others, too numerous to mention for fear of boring my readers.

But I cannot refrain from a word, *en passant*, about Mamontov. He not only gave his money to help rebuild a certain form of art, but actually cried with joy or sorrow over his enterprises. He loved music very much, but he never had an organ in his bedroom, he never drank his morning coffee to an accompaniment of Chopin's *Funeral March*, played by a poor wretch who earned the merest trifle each week for this privilege! Mamontov attended symphony concerts and went to rehearsals of opera at ten o'clock in the morning. During intermissions he was to be found munching a bit of salami as he discussed the beauties of Rimsky-Korsakov's "Sadko," some passage of Wagner, or new problems in theatrical life. How good he was, this Russian Mæcenas, and what a pleasure for me to remember this exceptional man!

Of course, everyone should be grateful to a Mæcenas because he is occupied with the cause of art. Therefore I say "Thank you!" to all Mæcenases, but keep for myself the pleasure of embracing my own dear Mæcenas— Mamontov!

As was my habit, I began to joke and tell stories with my usual freedom. Very soon everyone was laughing, Mamontov with the rest, his laughter sounding as eager and youthful as any in the room. With Mamontov, Korovin and Melnikov, the latter the son of the well-known artist, our pleasant company grew still more agreeable and lively.

*   *   *   *   *

Before long a ballet troupe arrived in Nijny from Italy. I remember, as though it were only just now, what a wonderful merry uproar and din the Italians brought with them into our theatre. Everything about them, every movement, intonation, and gesture, was so sharply differentiated from all that I had seen hitherto! It was altogether new to me. This crowd of astonishingly vivid people came straight to the theatre from the railway station, bringing with them trunks, boxes, and bags. Not one of them understood a word of Russian, and they were all like so many children. It seemed to me that my temperament was most similar to theirs. Like them, I could hold forth at the top of my voice, laugh, and flourish my arms about inexhaustibly. I therefore undertook the duty of finding them lodgings. I announced my intention to them by means of a variety of eloquent gestures. They at once surrounded me and began to shout, as though they were angry and were "giving me a piece of their minds." Of course it was only their manner of talking which gave one that impression.

We set off to scour the town in search of quarters for them, climbing up to attic chambers and descending into cellars. Everywhere the Italians cried:

"Caro! Caro!"

They tore their hair, snorted, laughed, and, as far as I could judge, were extremely dissatisfied with everything. I, of course, like a true Russian, endeavoured to persuade them to "put up with the unavoidable," and somehow or other succeeded in finally accommodating them all with lodgings.

Mamontov began to be present more and more frequently in the theatre and behind the scenes, as our performances went on. He never told me I had played well or badly, but it was noticeable that he began to pay more attention to me, and was more courteous; I had almost said kinder. I ought to have mentioned that I was a very definite success at Nijny.

While walking one day with me on the bank overlooking the river Volga, Mamontov began to enquire what I intended doing in the future. I said that I should continue to fulfil my engagement in the Imperial Theatres, although I was encountering great difficulties there. He made no comment, but began to talk about his affairs at the Exhibition, saying that some one or other did not understand him.

"They are queer people," said he.

I on my part did not understand what he was talking about. On another occasion he said to me:

"Let us go to the Exhibition!"

I knew that Mamontov had been the builder of a railway, and therefore supposed that he was exhibiting machinery or railway cars. Great was my surprise when he brought me to a large wooden structure on the walls of which two enormous canvases were stretched, one facing the other.

One picture depicted two legendary or fabulous personages, Mikula Selianinovitch and the "Volga-Bogatyr." It was painted in a very strange way, all in cubes of various colours, which made it appear very gaudy and, as it were, incoherent. Hitherto I had seen only pictures carefully painted in elegant colouring, recalling the suave music of Italian operas. But here there was a perfect riot of colours.

Evidently, however, Mamontov thought very highly of this picture. He gazed on it with obvious pleasure, and remarked:

"Horosho!" ("Good!"), in his emphatic way.

"Why is it good?" I enquired.

"You will understand later on, old man. You are only a boy. . . ."

He told me the subject of the other picture, which was Rostand's "La Princesse Lointaine." Afterwards, on our way back to the town, he told me with much warmth how unjust was the attitude of the jury of the artistic section of the Exhibition to Wrubel, the painter of these strange pictures, and said that the members of the jury were no better than house painters.

My interest was aroused, and in my leisure hours I paid repeated visits to the art section of the Exhibition and the Wrubel pavilion, which was erected outside the Exhibition grounds. I very soon found that the pictures which had received the approval of the jury bored me, while those of Wrubel, which they had rejected, pleased me more and more. It appeared to me that the difference between his pictures and those which had been admitted to the Exhibition was precisely that which exists between the music of Moussorgsky's "Boris" and that of Verdi's "Trovatore" or Puccini's "Madame Butterfly."

The operatic season went on brightly, and I was altogether content. Our theatre was animated by a joyous tire-
less energy. I could not but be downcast, however, sometimes, when I reflected that it would soon all be over and
I should have to recommence the tedious round of rehearsals
in the state theatre, and participate in performances which
were like so many school examinations. I was all the
sadder at the prospect, because Mamontov, Korovin, and
all the artists of Madame Winter's company had become
dear friends and necessary to me.

However, one day when walking about Nijny, Mamontov proposed that I should go to Moscow and remain with
the company. I was overjoyed at his offer, until I remembered my contract with the Imperial Theatres threatened
me with a fine of 3,600 rubles.

"I could give you six thousand rubles a year and a contract
for three years," said Mamontov. "Think it over!"

Amongst the Italian *ballerinas* there was one with whom
I was immensely taken. She danced wonderfully, better
than any of the dancers of the Imperial Theatres, as I
thought. She was always sad and evidently did not feel at
home in Russia. I could understand her melancholy, for
I had myself felt like a foreigner in Baku, Tiflis, yes, and
even in Petrograd. At rehearsals I used to approach this
ballerina and say to her all the Italian words I knew:

"*Allegro andante religioso moderato.*"

She could not help smiling, but very soon her face was
again overcast with an air of sadness.

It happened one evening that I had supper with her and
two of her friends in a restaurant after our performance.
It was a marvellous moonlight night. I wanted to say to
the young ladies that it was a sin to sleep on such a night,
but, as I did not know the Italian word for "sin," I began
to explain my thought more or less as follows:

"Faust, Margarita. Do you understand? Bim-bom-bom. *Church-chiesa. .Christos non Margarita. .Christos non Margarita.*"

"*Perche Christos, non Margarita?*" She questioned.

Then, after thinking it over, she said, laughingly:

"*Margarita peccata.*"

"Aha! *Peccata.*" At last I had got hold of the word I wanted.

After prolonged efforts she succeeded in interpreting my remark:

"*La notta a cosi bella, que dormire e peccata.*"

Our conversations in Russo-Italian afforded us considerable entertainment.

Very soon Tornaghi, the girl whom I liked so much, fell ill. I did my best to look after her, bringing her chicken broth and wine, and in the end I persuaded her to remove to the house in which I lived, which enabled me to care for her more easily. She told me about her beautiful native land, its sunshine and its flowers. I soon gathered her meaning even when I could not understand her words precisely.

I think I must have remarked once in Mamontov's presence that if I knew Italian I would marry Tornaghi; for very soon afterwards I learned that Mamontov had extended the *ballerina's* contract.

Nevertheless, I had to return to Petrograd, resume my life in the Palais Royal, and attend rehearsals at the Imperial Theatres. It was autumn, misty and rainy. Petrograd with its electric lights was not so attractive to me as it had been.

At the beginning of the season I was given the rôle of Prince Vladimir in Serov's opera, "Rognieda," and at rehearsals they were constantly telling me that Melnikov used to play the part wonderfully, while I was an utter failure in it. People showed me how Melnikov walked when on the stage, how he used his hands and arms, but evidently Melnikov was not at all like me, and as for my attempts to imitate him, well, honestly, the results were curious! I felt that the personality which I attributed to Prince Vladimir could not be exhibited with the gestures and movements which the stage manager required of me. The rôle seemed to lose in character, and I only succeeded in performing it conscientiously from a musical point of view. I had quite a number of unpleasant passages with Napravnik with regard to the music. I understood later on, however, that Napravnik was right in his pedantic insistence on a strictly rhythmical performance of the rôles, and I know that my own attitude since then to rhythm is due to the lessons impressed upon me by that great musician.

Some three weeks after the commencement of the season Tornaghi arrived, and did her best to persuade me to go to Moscow to join Mamontov. With many regrets I refused, but I soon fell a prey to such melancholy that I changed my mind, followed her back to Moscow, and on the evening of my arrival was already sitting amongst other artists in Madame Winter's box. My friends welcomed me like a brother. The theatre was dull that evening and the audience was small.

At supper at Testov's restaurant after the opera, Mamontov again asked me to join his company. I was worried by the thought of the impending fine for two seasons. Finally, Mamontov said he would pay me 7,200 rubles a year and we would share the fine between us, each of us paying 3,600 rubles.

I agreed to this, and thus found myself once more a member of Mamontov's company. The first performance of "A Life for the Tsar" gave me much food for uneasiness, as

I feared that I might fail to justify the confidence reposed in me by my colleagues and the hopes of the *entrepreneur*.

Next day, however, the theatrical critic, S. Kruglikov, who enjoyed great repute at that time, wrote in his account of the performance:

"A very interesting artist has appeared at the Solodovni-kov theatre. His performance of the rôle of Susanin was very new and original. The artist received much applause from an audience which, unfortunately, was not very numerous."

The comment had its effect. The audience was larger at every successive performance of "A Life for the Tsar."

I had to sing Mephistopheles in "Faust." I told Mamon-tov that I was not satisfied with the rôle of Mephistopheles as I had hitherto played it, and that I imagined the rôle quite differently, with a very different costume and make-up. I wished to depart from the theatrical tradition which prevailed.

"Please," said Mamontov, "what exactly do you want to do?"

I explained my ideas to him. We then went to Avanzo's, the art dealer's, and looked through all the pictures of Mephistopheles he had. I finally made a sketch combining suggestions from the pictures I had seen with my own idea. On the day of the performance I went early to the theatre, spent a long time in making up, and in the end felt that I had realised the effect I wanted.

When I went on to the stage I felt myself quite another man and was conscious of greater freedom in my movements and the possibility of greater force and beauty in my acting. It seemed I was a success. The critic Kruglikov wrote next day:

"Yesterday's Mephistopheles, as played by Chaliapine,

was perhaps not perfect, but it was at all events so interesting that henceforward I shall not omit to be present at any performance in which this artist takes part."

The tone of the criticism was serious and in no way resembled the usual comments on theatrical performances.

Mamontov told me:

"Fedenka, you may do whatever you wish in this theatre! If you want costumes, say so, and you shall have them. If you wish a new opera to be staged, we will do it!"

Everything conspired to put me in holiday mood, and for the first time in my career I felt that I was free, strong, and able to overcome all difficulties.

*   *   *   *   *

I have already said that the opera as I found it did not satisfy me. In fact, I must say that opera, today, does not satisfy me much more. I could see that in "Russalka" Dargomijsky had obviously given a dramatic character to certain phrases and seemed to have striven to combine the opera with drama, while on the other hand singers and stage managers always emphasise the lyrical portions of an opera to the disadvantage of the dramatic content, and thereby render the opera as a whole spiritless and feeble.

Dalsky used to speak almost contemptuously of opera, saying that Shakespeare's plays, for instance, could not be converted into opera. I did not think he was right. Why must it be so?

At the same time I could not but see how different the operas of Rimsky-Korsakov were from "Rigoletto," "Traviata," "Fra Diavolo," and even from "Faust." I could not, however, precisely define to myself what was needed, and I felt that I was likely to fall between two chairs.

Now that Mamontov had accorded me the right to work freely, I began to do so with a view to perfecting all the rôles of my *répertoire*: Susanin, the Miller, Mephistopheles, etc.

No one hindered me or rapped me over the knuckles for not using the accepted gestures. No one even tried to tell me how Petrov or Melnikov had been accustomed to do this or that. It was as though chains had fallen from my spirit.

The circle of my acquaintance amongst painters gradually widened. Polienov came behind the scenes to me one day and kindly drew me a sketch for the costume of Mephistopheles, correcting some errors in the attire I wore. Serov, Wrubel, Victor Vasnetsov, Yakunchikova, and Archipov were amongst the painters whom I met at the theatre and at Mamontov's house. I adored Wrubel, Korovin, and Serov.

At first they seemed to me very much like other people, but I soon began to see that there was some special quality in each and all of them. They talked briefly and, so to say, in sudden outbursts of communicativeness, and made use of expressions which were new to me.

I heard Serov say to Korovin, for instance: "I like your leaden hue on the horizon and that . . ."

Placing his thumb and index finger together, he drew a contour in the air, and without seeing the picture which was being discussed I comprehended that he was speaking of fir trees. I was surprised by the power some of these people had of giving an exact idea of form and content with a few words and two or three gestures.

Serov, in particular, was a master of the art of bringing a picture before one's eyes by means of gestures and one or two words. He was a dry-looking man of somewhat forbidding aspect, and I was at first inclined to be intimidated by his looks, but I soon found that he was a humourist, very jolly and extremely sincere, not to say candid. He could say sharp things at times, but one always felt that his attitude was well meaning. He was talking one day about the drivers of fast-trotting horses, or so-called *likhatchi*, who used to stand facing the Passion Monastery in Moscow. The thick-set Serov, sitting on his chair, could mimic with the greatest vividness a sleigh driver sitting on his sleigh, and reproduced quite wonderfully the tone and manner of a *likhatch* inviting a prospective client to engage his services.

"Would you like a drive?   Six rubles, your honor!"

On another occasion, when showing Korovin his studies of wattle and willows, he pointed to a fan of greyish spots and lamented:

"I was not successful with that. I wanted to draw sparrows just rising from the ground, you know, with their wings aflutter!"

He made a queer gesture with his fingers, and I understood at once that he really had not succeeded in depicting what he wanted to in his picture.

I was wonderfully struck by the adroitness with which the painters could, as it were, seize on a bit of real life. Serov reminded me of I. F. Gorbunov, who by means of a single phrase and appropriate mimicry could depict an entire choir with a tipsy choirmaster. Profiting by my observation of them, I endeavoured both in everyday life and on the stage to be expressive and plastic. My *répertoire* began to seem played out and uninteresting, although I continued to work and to try to introduce into each rôle something new. I knew that Rimsky-Korsakov had an opera, "The Maid of Pskov" (*"Pskovitianka"*), but when I proposed staging it, in order to play the rôle of Ivan the Terrible, everyone in the theatre, and even Mamontov himself, was very sceptical with regard to it. However, Mamontov did not protest against my choice, which was fortunate for myself. I found that I had hit on the very thing that would enable me to unite lyrical song with the drama.

When I began to study the opera attentively, however, it rather alarmed me, I began to fear that it was too difficult, indeed altogether beyond my powers, and that it would also probably not produce any impression on the public. The rôle in the opera which I proposed to take contained not a single aria, duet, or trio; in fact, nothing of what is required by tradition. At that time I had not such a splendid teacher as V. I. Kluchevsky, with whose assistance I studied the rôle of Boris Godounov. I had to make use of the advice of the painters whose acquaintance I had made. They explained to me as much as they could, and brought me to some understanding of the epoch and the character of the Terrible Tsar.

I was very much upset when I came to act as stage manager of the opera, and found myself becoming disagreeably convinced that I was not making a success of the part of Ivan the Terrible.

I knew that Ivan the Terrible was a bigot, and therefore pronounced quietly, meekly, and yet malignantly the words, "Shall I enter, or no?" which he speaks on the threshold of Tokmakov's Palace, and with which the drama begins. I continued the rôle in similar tones. An unbelievable tedium invaded the stage, and was felt both by myself and by all the company. Matters were no better at the second rehearsal. Finally I tore up my music, broke something or other, rushed into my dressing room, and there fairly wept with despair. Mamontov followed me, patted my shoulder, and counselled me in friendly fashion:

"Don't get in such a nervous state, Fedenka! Pull yourself together, scold your colleagues a little, and also pronounce the first phrase a little more emphatically!"

I at once understood my mistake. True, Ivan was a bigot,

but none the less he was the Terrible Tsar. I returned to the stage, changed the tone of the rôle, and felt that I had found the right accents. Everything grew animated at once. The actors, responding to my "threatening" tones, also changed their attitude to their own parts. So you see, my dear readers, the importance of giving just the right intonation.

To know what Ivan the Terrible was like I visited the Tretiakov Gallery to look at the pictures of Schwartz and Riepin, and Antokolsky's statue. I was not satisfied. Some one told me, however, that the engineer Tchokolov had a portrait of Ivan the Terrible by V. Vasnetsov. I don't think this portrait is even now known to the general public. In it the face of the Terrible Tsar is about three-quarters life size. The gaze of the fiery dark eyes is directed away from the spectator.

Combining what I had learned from Riepin, Vasnetsov and Schwartz, I made myself up fairly satisfactorily, and presented what I thought to be a fairly truthful portrait of the Tsar.

Since ours was the first production of the opera, the public knew little or nothing about the work. Naturally, when I appeared on the stage on horseback in my first scene everyone expected me to sing. But the curtain fell without anyone singing a word. In spite of the noncomprehension caused by this dumb scene, the audience applauded heartily, so that the curtain had to be raised several times.

"The Maid of Pskov" was a decisive success and was staged fifteen times during the season, always before full houses. Mamontov was delighted with the success of the opera. Before our productions of Russian opera he had given most of his admiration and attention to Italian works, but after we had together staged several Russian operas he began to see the importance of our national opera.

In the earlier day the most celebrated foreign singers sang for him—Mazzini, Tamagno, Van Zandt, and others.

I have heard many people say that Mazzini was a splendid singer, but one ought to listen to him with one's back turned, as it did not do to look at him. Personally, I don't think this is just. He was vocally so richly endowed that sometimes he permitted himself indifferent acting. He sang like an archangel sent from heaven above to ennoble his hearers. I never heard anyone else sing like him. And I assure you he could act just as magnificently! I have seen him in "La Favorita." It seemed at first as though he did not wish to act. Badly dressed in inferior tights and a queer old costume, he frolicked about the stage like a boy, but suddenly in the last act, when he is wounded and dying, he began to act so wonderfully that not only I, but even such an experienced dramatic artist as Dalsky, was surprised and touched by the power of his acting. Oh, my dear friends, I am sorry for those of you who never heard the tenor Angelo Mazzini!

* * * * *

In the spring of 1897 I realised a dream I had long cherished. I went abroad.

Already at Warsaw I noticed the sharp contrast with all that I had seen hitherto in Russia. Naturally, cab drivers are everywhere almost alike in their addiction to bad language. Policemen in Poland were also no different from those in Moscow. But nevertheless everything bore the stamp of a different life, other manners and customs. The change seemed to wake me up and gave me a pleasant feeling of animation. The train from Warsaw westwards rushed on with such enhanced speed that I every moment thought it

IVAN THE TERRIBLE IN "PSKOVITIANKA"

must leave the rails, and came out repeatedly on to the platform at the end of the car, with the idea of jumping off in the event of a catastrophe. The platform afforded me, moreover, a better view of the novel, densely populated country, the fields of which were so unlike Russian fields. The crops grew thick and luxuriant; one saw the loving care of the farmer for his land. Amidst the fields were stone-built barns and farm buildings with tiled roofs; here and there rose the smoke of factory chimneys.

As we passed through Vienna, the city appeared to me to cover an almost immeasurable expanse of ground. As our train stood in the station for a few moments my heart beat wildly. We were on holy ground, in the sacred city where Beethoven, Schubert and Mozart had lived, thought and created! My fleeting impression of the Austrian capital was succeeded by landscapes such as I had seen only in pictures and the reality of which seemed to me more wonderful than any painting. Mountains, suspension bridges, fabulous castles, rocky ascents, flew by, and everywhere the same wonderful order and care appeared to reign.

I got no sleep until we reached Paris, after a journey of three nights and two days, every moment of which gave me the feeling that I was, so to say, entering deeper and deeper into a fairy tale. We passed through Belgium by night, and the lights of factories and the red glare in the dark heavens furnished me with impressions of enchanting novelty.

At length I was in Paris! The bustle of the crowded terminal and its busy approaches fairly took my breath away. Jostled by vivacious Frenchmen, and already feeling the infection of a new gaiety of spirit, I collected my luggage, engaged a fiacre, and drove to the address given me by Melnikov, No. 40, rue Copernic.

It was six o'clock in the morning. The great grey houses, the boulevards, the churches—all I saw seemed pleasantly

familiar, as thought I had been there before. I was reminded of the novels of Gaboriau and Terrail, which I had
read as a boy.

Men in blue blouses and aprons were watering the streets
and sweeping the pavements with brushes, as sailers do the
deck of a ship. If only they could be made to clean Moscow! or better still, Astrakhan! I thought.

My fiacre stopped before a small two-storied house in the
rue Copernic. A man in a white apron answered my ring
and began to speak to me in French. What an oddity! I
explained to him with much precision, and with the aid of
arms and legs and every sort of mimicry, that it was absolutely useless to talk French to me and that I wanted to
see Melnikov. A pleasant old lady with nicely combed
hair, simply and cleanly dressed, appeared. I noticed that
her hair was held in place by a net, which seemed to me a
very neat and novel fashion.

I asked her, in Russian, which was Melnikov's room.
She understood what I wanted, and showed me a door, on
which I immediately drummed with my fists, shouting to
my friend:

"Enough of sleeping! You ought to be ashamed to sleep
so long in Paris!"

The door opened and, overjoyed at being in Paris and
able to speak Russian, I burst into song. My friends hastened to impose silence upon me, saying that everyone in
the *pension* was asleep and that it was not proper to make
a great deal of noise. I washed and changed, and drank
some coffee, all in great haste. I was bubbling over with
gaiety, and eager to be out of doors again. My friends
restrained me, saying that they would take me out for a
walk after breakfast.

I looked about me. The room seemed to be furnished
with a great deal of comfort. Everything in it was clean

and handsome. Over the fireplace was a gilt-framed mirror, and the mantelpiece was ornamented with a number of statuettes. I imagined that such cleanliness and simplicity must be expensive, and my surprise was the greater when I learned that the cost of the room, including breakfast, dinner, wine, coffee and tea, was only eleven francs. The food, I thought, must necessarily be bad, but the breakfast which I shared was excellent in quality. I fell into a condition of bovine satisfaction.

There were ten people at breakfast: five Russian friends of mine, an estimable, cheery old abbé, a teacher of singing, a journalist, a young Greek, and lastly a very beautiful young Greek lady named Calliope. I drank two glasses of wine and would have drunk a third, but feared that I should be exceeding the privileges of a guest. My friends told me, however, that I might drink as much wine as I chose, and the hostess, overhearing our conversation, added that it would give her nothing but pleasure if I did.

How kind that seemed!

After breakfast I was taken to see the Eiffel Tower. I climbed to the topmost platform and gazed thence for a long time with a species of awe on the mighty metropolis. I was surprised to encounter very few Frenchmen on the Tower, and reflected that use must have accustomed them so much to the wonderful structure that they no longer took any interest in it.

My friends told me that the Tower was but a trifle and that there were many beautiful things in Paris compared with which it was of no account.

I understood them when I had seen a little more of the city and had visited the Louvre. I wandered for hours through the museum, intoxicated by the sight of so many treasures, and returned to it whenever I had any time to spare. The Louvre and, indeed, Paris as a whole, enchanted me, and I liked the Parisians, especially the abbé in our *pension*.

The abbé was a very lovable, good-natured old man, who drank wine without ever becoming intoxicated, shared in the jests directed at his spiritual dignity, and was simple and sincere in all his behaviour. Still he never ceased to be conscious of his own worth as a man. This same feeling of one's own worth as an individual was a characteristic which I noticed in all Parisians, even the cab drivers and household servants.

After a month spent in Paris, I went to Dieppe, where my friends were studying with a feminine singing teacher. I also had to study the part of Holofernes in "Judith." There was not a room available for me in the house, except an attic, which was placed at my disposal if I cared to occupy it. It was very clean, although it had been used as a store-room for disused and broken furniture. A good bed was set up for me in the attic, and altogether I was made very comfortable. The summer weather ensured me against feeling cold.

I noticed that everywhere in France even the servants had very good beds. My hostess explained that since a man spends one-third of his life in bed, he ought to make himself comfortable there, for to work well one must rest well. I thought the observation a very apt one.

An excellent orchestra played at a restaurant overlooking the sea, where *chansonniers* also sang. Unfortunately for me, there was also the game of Petits Chevaux, which was the cause of my staking five francs as a trial, and at which I speedily lost all my money! Mamontov, who was in Paris at the time, scolded me, gave me some more money, and paternally forbade me to play Petits Chevaux any more.

My parting with the world "abroad" was even kindlier than my reception. A very agreeable young pianist was studying singing with the teacher in whose house I stayed. When I studied "Judith" she was kind enough to accompany me, and in spite of my urging would never accept any remuneration for her work. She wished to learn to ride a bicycle, and I took pleasure in teaching her in grateful return for the help she gave me, running round the town square of Dieppe to assist her until she had learned to balance. I knew only a very few French phrases, and we understood one another but slightly, with the aid of much gesticulation and a great deal of laughter. The evening before leaving for Russia I went up early to my attic, in order to get a good night's rest. At daybreak I was awakened by some one kissing me. When I opened my eyes I saw that it was my young accompanist. Her caress aroused in me complex feelings which I should have difficulty in defining precisely. I was surprised, and touched almost to tears, and strangely glad. We had never spoken to one another of love, and indeed could not do so. I had not "courted" her and had never observed any inclination to sentiment on her part. I could not even ask her the reason for her action, but I was sure that it was due to nothing but feelings of humanity and feminine tenderness. I never met her again, and left France with a strange and yet joyous feeling, as though I had received the embrace of some new existence, to which I had hitherto been a stranger.

* * * * *

In the summer of 1898 I was invited by Madame T. S. Lubatovitch, a *protégée* of Mamontov's, to visit her country house in the Yaroslavl government. There, with S. V. Rachmaninov, who was at that time conductor of Mamontov's opera company, I occupied myself with the study of "Boris Godounov." Rachmaninov had finished at the Conservatoire only a few years earlier. He was a lively, jolly, sociable man. An excellent artist and a splendid musician, he taught me the elementary principles of music and even something of harmony, and altogether endeavoured to educate me on the technical side of music.

I liked " Boris Godounov" so much that, not content with studying my own rôle, I sang the entire opera in all its parts, both male and female, from beginning to end. When I understood the usefulness of such a complete knowledge of an opera, I began to study in the same way all the others—that is to say, studying the opera as a whole, not omitting even those which I had been accustomed to sing before.

The more I learned of Moussorgsky's opera the clearer it became to me that even Shakespeare's plays could be worthily treated in that way. Much depends on the author of the opera. When I learned Moussorgsky's life story I was greatly surprised, even awed, to find that the possessor of such a magnificent and original talent passed his life in poverty and died in an ill-kept hospital from the effects of drink! Afterwards I learned that he was not the first Russian of talent to die in such a way, and saw for myself that, to our shame, Moussorgsky was not the last, either, to come to such an end.

While studying "Boris Godounov" from the musical point of view, I wished to learn something of the character in history. I read Poushkin and Karamsin, but this was not sufficient. I then asked friends to introduce me to V. I. Kluchevsky, the celebrated professor of history at the University of Moscow, who was then residing at a summer villa in the government of Yaroslavl.

I went to see the old man, who welcomed me hospitably and gave me tea, saying that he had seen me in "The Maid of Pskov" and that he liked the manner in which I depicted Ivan the Terrible. When I asked him to tell me something about Boris Godounov, he proposed that we should go for a walk in the woods. I shall never forget that walk amongst the lofty pine trees on the sand and pine needles. The little old man with his hair clipped in a countrified way and wearing a little grey beard, walked beside me, with spectacles on nose, looking up occasionally with his little, restless, clever eyes. Stopping every few paces, he related to me in a low, almost stealthy voice, as though he had been an eyewitness of events, dialogues between Shouisky and Godounov, telling me about Varlaam, and Misail, as though he had known them personally, and describing the fascination of the Pretender. He talked a great deal, and always so wonderfully vividly that I seemed to see before me the people he described. I was particularly impressed by the dialogues between Shouisky and Boris Godounov as related by Kluchevsky. He told them so artistically that when I heard the words of Shouisky from his lips I involuntarily reflected:

"What a pity Kluchevsky cannot sing, or he could have played Prince Vassily (Shouisky) with me!"

The figure of Tsar Boris arose before me, powerful and interesting, from the stories of the historian. I listened and felt sincere sorrow for the Tsar who possessed such wonderful power of will and mind, who wished to do so much good for Russia, and only succeeded in creating the law which bound the serf to his master. Kluchevsky particularly emphasized the loneliness of Godounov, his alert mind, and his longing to bring enlightenment into the country. It seemed to me at certain moments that Vassily Shouisky had risen from his grave and was acknowledging his error, and that he had destroyed Godounov in vain!

I spent the night at Kluchevsky's, thanked him for his teaching next morning, and said good-bye to the wonderful old man, and his dear, good family. Afterwards I very often made good use of his advice and the instruction I had derived from our conversation.

During that summer of 1898, while I was staying at Madame Lubatovitch's summer villa, I married the *ballerina* Tornaghi at the little village church. After the wedding we held a ridiculous sort of banquet, sitting Turkish fashion on the floor on carpets and cushions, and frolicking like a lot of little children. There was nothing of all that is considered indispensable at weddings, no richly adorned table with a multitude of dainties, no eloquent toasts, only a great quantity of field flowers, and a good deal of wine.

At six o'clock next morning there was a fiendish uproar outside my window, caused by Mamontov and a crowd of my friends playing on stove lids and other ironware, tin buckets, and ear-piercing whistles. It rather reminded me of the Sukonnaya Sloboda.

"Why are you dozing still?" shouted Mamontov. "People don't come to the country to sleep. Get up. We are going to the woods for mushrooms."

And the concert recommenced with howls, whistlings, and deafening din. Rachmaninov acted as conductor of this witches' festival.

Shortly afterwards I was to experience the actual feelings of a murderer! By a horrible mistake I killed one of Madame Lubatovitch's little dogs. She had two fox terriers and a little pug called Filka, her favorite. One day I was walking through the woods with the three dogs, throwing sticks to the fox terriers, which they ran after excitedly and brought back to me to be thrown again. They seemed to be enjoying this game hugely. Suddenly—a tragedy! A stick not intended for her hit the little pug on the nose. She gave one yelp of pain and instantly fell dead. My heart stopped beating for a moment and I felt

myself turning pale. Trembling with horror, I stooped
down, picked up the little body and fled into the deepest part
of the woods, where I dug a grave for the dead with my
hands, tearing my nails in the process.

Feeling frightfully ashamed before the two fox terriers
and doubly distressed both by the horrible accident and the
fact that I knew the loss of her pet would grieve Madame
Lubatovitch deeply, I took the longest way back. But when
I reached the house I managed to wear a look of complete
innocence.

Within five minutes Madame Lubatovitch began to worry.

"Where is Filka?" she asked.

"She was with you, wasn't she?" some one else interrupted.

"Yes, but she ran away," I lied.

Filka was searched for everywhere. I, too, joined in looking for the little dog. Naturally she was not to be found.
Then everyone forgot about her.

But for me there was no peace. I kept thinking that
Madame Lubatovitch really knew all about the accident
and kept looking at me with reproachful and expectant eyes.
At any moment, it seemed, she might exclaim:

"Confess, villain!"

I even saw poor little Filka in my dreams!

But it was not until two years later that, meeting Madame
Lubatovitch, I confessed my crime to her. She shook her
head regretfully and forgave me.

Perhaps this incident may not seem very interesting, but
I cannot refrain from relating it because to this day I feel
the weight of this involuntary crime upon my conscience
and now, perhaps, having made public confession, I may
feel some relief.

*   *   *   *   *

Soon after we were married we took an apartment and went about eagerly buying furniture. When this was all in place—beds, bureaus, tables, mirrors, sofas, chairs, even a gold chair!—I kept looking at these possessions with a strange feeling that they could not possibly be mine!

"All these things cannot belong to me!" I exclaimed incredulously. "One fine day some one will come and take them away!"

Of course, I was joking but, strangely enough, that day came!

* * * * *

The season began with rehearsals of "Boris Godounov." I saw at once that my companions had an incorrect idea of their rôles. The training appropriate to the school of opera which existed then and still exists today did not serve to meet the demands of works such as Moussorgsky's opera. The contrast between the established school and the newer type of opera was also evident in "The Maid of Pskov." Of course, I myself am a child of the old school of singing, as are all the singers of the present time. In that school one learned how to produce tones on syllables, how to vocalise, but not how to sing and opera.

In the new products of opera like the works of Rimsky-Korsakov and especially Moussorgsky the old school of singing appeared—if I may use the expression—very shabbily dressed, for the reason that the new Russian operas presented special problems to singers. The vocalism and high C's that issued freely from tenors' throats were of very little importance in connection with these operas, for the beauty of both text and music was so impressive that high C's and such traditional arias as "Di quella pira" seemed poverty-stricken in comparison.

Traditions, by the way, create cemeteries, and the gravestones in these cemeteries are far more enduring in the scheme of human existence than the skyscrapers that I have seen in America. A great deal of moss has grown over the gravestones in these eternal cemeteries. It is young and green. But when this moss will succeeed in devouring the stones—who shall say?

At the rehearsals of the opera, the words of which are taken from Poushkin and Karamsin, the deficiencies of those trained in the old operatic school were especially evident. It was difficult to act when one did not receive responses from one's confrère in tones corresponding to the action of the drama. I was particularly disappointed with Shouisky, although the rôle was sung by Monsieur Sha . . . one of the best-trained artists of the day. Listening to him, I could not help reflecting:

"Oh, if only Kluchevsky could take the rôle!"

The decorations, the stage properties, the orchestra, and the chorus were all satisfactory in Mamontov's theatre, but I was obliged to admit to myself that "Boris Godounov" could be immeasurably better staged on the boards of the Imperial Theatres, with their abundant means.

The day of the public performance arrived. After the success of "The Maid of Pskov" I had become an extremely popular artist in Moscow. The public seemed more than willing to attend performances in which I was to take part.

"Boris" met at first with a cold and languid reception. I was somewhat alarmed; but the hallucination scene produced a very strong impression and the opera ended in triumph.

It seemed strange to me that "Boris Godounov" had not produced such an impression at previous performances; for the opera is written in a very powerful and beautiful style, worthy even of Shakespeare. At succeeding performances the public were more sensitive to the music, and yielded to its beauties from the very first act.

I noticed that I seldom seemed to succeed with a rôle from the very first. No matter how much I worked, still the chief part of the work was done only during public performance, and my understanding of the rôle deepened and widened with each new presentation. The rôle of Ivan the Terrible was the only one which I felt I had mastered from the beginning. But even this rôle, as had the others, grew more significant and important the oftener I acted it.

During the following season we staged "Khovanstchina." I did not quite grasp the rôle of Dosiphei. I applied once more to Kluchevsky, and he very kindly told me with much detail and vivid description about Prince Mwishetsky, the Streltzy, and the Tsarevna Sophia.

At first we feared that we would not be permitted to stage the opera. There are scenes in it which remind one of ecclesiastical ceremonies. However, the authorities allowed it to be played.

The first performance was successful, but I cannot say that the opera created such an impression on the audience as "Boris" and "The Maid of Pskov." The audience listened attentively, but without enthusiasm. I thought that Moscow in particular should have welcomed "Khovanstchina."

I think it was during the third performance, when I was singing, "Sisters, observe the Lord's command! In the name of the power of the Almighty . . ." when a Muscovite voice resounded indignantly from the gallery:

"That's enough about the Almighty! You ought to be ashamed!"

Everyone was frightened, thinking that after such an incident the opera would have to be taken off, but fortunately the voice of the censor in the gallery did not reach the ears of the authorities.

Mamontov began to take more and more interest in Russian music. We staged "A May Night," "The Tsar's Bride," and "Sadko," which had only just been written by Rimsky-Korsakov. Mamontov began to take an active part in the staging, himself inventing various novelties, and although they sometimes appeared out of place, in the end it always turned out that he was right. His artistic intuition did not deceive him. For instance, in "Sadko," the decorations for which were designed by Korovin, who painted a wonderful picture of the sea bottom, Mamontov introduced a serpentine dance, which has been played so much in *cafés chantants* that it would seem there is no place for it in serious opera. But the *ballerinas* were given splendid costumes, and the serpentine dance at the bottom of the sea produced a wonderful effect, by special lighting which suggested the undulations of the waves.

I did not participate in the first public performance of the opera, but as the artist who sang the Viking Guest was not equal to the part, it was entrusted to me at the second performance.

I remember when I dressed myself as a viking in accordance with Serov's drawing, the painter himself burst into my dressing room, greatly excited. All the painters were greatly attracted by "Sadko" and behaved as though the performance of the opera were their own festivity.

"Excellent!" said Serov. "Only your arms look too effeminate!"

I emphasised the muscles of my arms with colour, and thus made them look powerful and rounded. The painters were well pleased with the effect, and praised me. Their praise was more agreeable to me than even the applause of the public.

The more I acted Boris Godounov, Ivan the Terrible, Dosiphei, the Viking Guest and the Mayor in "A May Night," the surer I became that an operatic artist must not only sing, but must act his part as an actor does in the drama.

In opera one should sing as one speaks. I afterwards observed that those artists who attempted to imitate me did not understand this.

Just at the time when all this became clear to me, the occasion arose for playing Salieri, a much more complicated and difficult task than any that had preceded it, for the rôle was all in a sort of musical recitation. I was much attracted by this entirely new problem, and knowing that Rachmaninov could explain and elucidate all my difficulties, I went to him. He is a wonderful, magnificent artist!

All the musical movements are indicated by the composer of "Mozart and Salieri" by means of the usual terms—allegro, moderato, andante, etc.—but it was not always possible to observe these indications in practice. I sometimes proposed to Rachmaninov to make changes in these indications, and he used to tell me where it was possible to do so and where it was out of the question.

Without infringing on the composer's intentions, we found a method of performance which boldly rounded out the tragical figure of Salieri. Mozart was sung by S., an artist who always gave the most loving care to his rôles. I began the performance with great emotion, conscious that Salieri must show the public that it was possible to unite the opera with the drama. But, no matter how much effort and emotion I devoted to my rôle, the audience remained indifferent and cold.

I was greatly disappointed. However, my painter friends encouraged me. Wrubel came behind the scenes and said with emotion:

"It is magnificent!"

I knew that Wrubel, like Serov and Korovin, did not idly compliment one; they all took a serious comradely interest in my work, and had more than once criticised me very severely. I believed what they said and saw that they were all sincerely delighted with Salieri. Theirs was to me the highest court.

After the presentation of "Mozart and Salieri" I was convinced that such an opera was a renaissance. Perhaps it is true, as many people say, that Rimsky-Korsakov's composition is not on the same high level as Poushkin's text, but I was convinced, nevertheless, that it was an entirely new departure in scenic art, successfully uniting music with the psychological drama.

One Easter, Mamontov's opera company went to Petrograd to appear at the theatre of the Conservatoire, which is bad for artists in an acoustic sense, and also for the audience. It consists of a long corridor with a small stage at one end. There was no room to turn round on the stage, and such scenes as the entry of Ivan the Terrible or the first act of "Boris Godounov" did not turn out very well on it. Nevertheless, the performances went on with great and continually increasing success.

On one occasion, after my scene with Tokmakov, the Boyar in "The Maid of Pskov," I was sitting in my dressing room when I heard on the other side of the door a thunderously loud, animated voice:

"Show him to us, for goodness' sake! Where is he?"

In the doorway appeared a gigantic figure with a long greyish-white beard, large features, and the eyes of a young man.

"Well, little brother, you have surprised us!" he cried. "Good evening. I have even forgotten to say good evening! Let's get acquainted with you! I live here in Petrograd, but I have been in Moscow and abroad, too, and I have heard Petrov and Melnikov, but certainly I never listened to anything so wonderful! No, indeed! I owe you my thanks!"

He talked thunderously, in a very animated fashion, while

behind him stood some one else, in black, with a thin, dark, arresting face.

"We came together. I could not come alone to tell you all I felt. It was easier in company. This is Antokolsky, who has made a statue of Ivan the Terrible. I am Vladimir Stassov."

I fairly gasped. I was delighted to meet the celebrated director of the St. Petersburg Public Library, himself a distinguished critic and writer on the fine arts, founder of the famous Koutchka—the group known as "The Five," which included Cui, Balakirev, Borodin, Moussorgsky, and Rimsky-Korsakov. Stassov was also the friend of Turgeniev, Nekrassov, Dostoevsky, both the Tolstoys. I was silent from pure embarrassment.

"You are quite young still," he went on. "How old are you—fifteen? Where do you come from? Tell us something about yourself."

I told him something or other. He embraced me with emotion and went out with tears in his eyes. Antokolsky also praised me with sincerity. They went away together, leaving me charmed by their enthusiasm.

Next day I went to see Stassov at the Public Library and to behold once more his youthful eyes and listen to his thunderous words of greeting.

"Well, little father, good morning! I am very pleased to see you. Thank you! You know, I haven't been able to sleep all night with thinking over your acting. It is true the opera has been played here before, but badly! What a man Rimsky-Korsakov is! He can do great things, but not everyone understands him. Sit down! No, here, in this armchair!"

He undid some cords which were bound across the arms of the chair to prevent anyone from using it, and explained:

"This is where Gogol and Turgeniev have sat!"

I was embarrassed, and remained standing hesitantly.

"No, no! Sit down!" he said. "It does not matter that you are young still!"

The man fairly seemed to hug me, metaphorically speaking. It is rare for anyone to confer such happiness and so generously as did he.

He asked me about my artistic career, scolded about the Imperial Theatres, calling them "cemeteries," praised me for leaving them in spite of the fine.

"What does money matter, after all? You will have plenty of money! It is always so. At first one has no money, and afterwards it turns up. Money is dirt! Mamontov is a clever fellow. What things he does! Yet formerly he went in only for trifles, such as Italian opera! Rimsky-Korsakov has done great things, too! How glad I am! Russian art is a great power! Of course they don't understand it in the Imperial Theatres: it is more like being in a government department there. But never mind. There have to be people of every sort in the world, and things will be better later on. That is the meaning of everything."

He stroked his beard, flourished his arms, talked in his loud tones, full of untamed energy and militant ardour and endless Russian good nature.

Stassov became a constant frequenter of our theatre. When responding to calls from the audience I often saw him standing like a tower and clapping his great palms together. If he was not contented with anything he did not hesitate to voice his disapproval loudly.

An article appeared in the *Novoye Vremya* which endeavoured to show that "The Maid of Pskov" was an inferior opera and that Ivan the Terrible, as depicted by Chaliapine, was also worthless. I read the article and saw with regret that it was written with special journalistic logic.

"The author must be a very able man," I thought sadly.

I felt like a fly in October. When I went to see Stassov at the Library, however, he met me with a militant outburst:

"I know all about it. I have read the article. It is rubbish! Don't pay any attenion to it. The man who wrote it would write about anything in the same style. He is like a camel: no matter what you offer him, be it a bundle of hay or an orange, he only turns away in disgust. I will answer him!"

Next day in the *Novosti* there was an article by Stassov, headed "As blind as a hen," in which he savagely tore to tatters all the assertions of the critic of the *Novoye Vremya*. Whenever I have been in a difficult situation in life and wanted good advice, after that, I went to Stassov as to a father. I sometimes even came on purpose from Moscow to talk to him, and it has never happened that he did not help me.

He liked Salieri very much. In speaking enthusiastically about that opera, he told me:

"You know there is another wonderful opera you ought to play in—'The Stone Guest' of Dargomijsky! It is a magnificent composition. You certainly ought to stage it!"

When I looked through Dargomijsky's opera, based on Poushkin's "Don Juan," I saw that very fine artists indeed would be necessary for the parts of Laura and Don Juan. Ordinary performers would only spoil the opera. I did not wish to disappoint Stassov, however, so learned the whole of it and offered to sing the entire opera with all its rôles, by myself, for him. He was very much pleased. Shortly afterwards there was an evening party at Rimsky-Korsakov's, at which, besides the host and Stassov, the brothers Blumenfeld were present, also Cesar Cui, Wrubel and his wife, and many others. I sang the whole of "The Stone Guest," also "Rayeshnik" ("The Showman"), Moussorgsky's satire "The

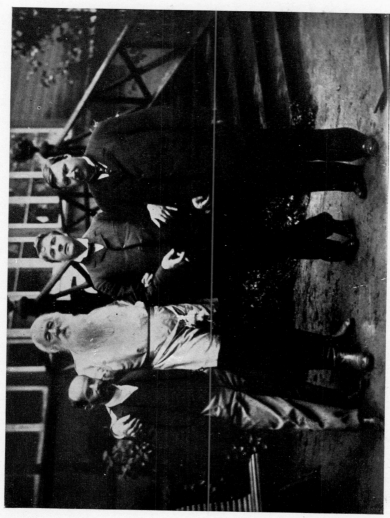

LEFT TO RIGHT: GINSBURG, SCULPTOR; STASSOV; CHALIAPINE; GLAZOUNOV, COMPOSER, AT STASSOV'S COUNTRY HOME, PARGALOVO

Song of the Flea," "The Seminarist," and many of his other compositions. It was a very jolly evening!

After supper we sang Borodin's "Serenade of Four Cavaliers to One Lady," in which Rimsky-Korsakov took the first bass part, I the second, Blumenfeld the first tenor, and Cesar Cui second tenor. The result was extremely amusing.

Rimsky-Korsakov, with his grey beard and his double spectacles, was especially good. He was just as serious and unsmiling with regard to this musical jest as he was when listening to "The Stone Guest."

"Ah, how I l-o-v-e you-oo-oo!" he gloomily chanted, and cheerful, old Cui sweetly repeated the phrase:

"Ah, how I l-o-v-e you-oo-oo!"

and we all sang, hardly able to restrain our mirth:

"Ah, how we love you!"

The joyous, grey-bearded giant Stassov was noisier and more delighted than anyone. It did not seem at all like a staid company of people well known to the whole of cultivated Russia, but more like a students' evening party. All these good people seemed as young as I was, and I felt wonderfully gay and at my ease amongst them. I shall never forget that evening!

Stassov very much regretted that "The Stone Guest" could not be staged, but agreed with me that I had no one to sing the rôles of Laura and Don Juan as they should be sung.

"But if artists turn up who are capable of taking the rôles, we will stage the opera. Give me your word?" said he.

I promised him that I would, but unfortunately, I have never yet been able to play "The Stone Guest" on the stage. Whenever he encountered me Stassov used to remind me:

"You owe us something, Feodor Ivanovitch!"

But he died without seeing it on the stage.

Wonderful man! I remember falling slightly sick during

the season. Unexpectedly Stassov came up to the fourth floor where I lived. He was seventy years of age. I was quite astonished.

"How could you climb up such a tower, Vladimir Vassilievitch?" I said to him.

"Well, I was on my way home and thought that I would look you up, as I knew you were sick. It's on my way!"

He lived at Peskí, and I resided on Kolokolnaia Street. That is about the same as saying that a person called at Astrakhan on the way from Kiev to Moscow. He stopped a long time, talking about the museums abroad, the Milan theatre, La Scala, the Escorial, and Madrid, and his friends in England.

"You must really go to England, young man. They don't know of these things there. They are a wonderful people, the English! But they haven't any music! They have no 'Maid of Pskov,' nor 'Boris.' You must play Ivan the Terrible for them. By all means go to England."

"But I don't know the language!"

"That's a trifle. Act in your own language; they will understand. You don't need to know any languages! You are already understood."

This unusual man loved Russian art and believed profoundly in its power.

Later, when I was in England with the Russian opera and sang in the Russian tongue, I thought with tears in my eyes of my dear Stassov and I hoped that those who saw and heard me at Drury Lane felt as he had:

"Chaliapine, you don't need to know any languages! You are already understood!"

CHAPTER SEVEN

*My Return to the Imperial Theatres—First
Appearance in "Mefistofele" at La Scala,
Milan—Italian Audiences—Meetings with
Arrigo Boito and Angelo Mazzini.*

MY STAGE successes were noted by the direction of
the Imperial Theatres. Just at that time Colonel
Teliakovsky, a former cavalry officer, had been made manager of the Moscow Imperial Theatres.

I became acquainted with him soon after he took up his
post, and he aroused my warmest sympathies. It was evident
to me that here was a man who really wished to comprehend
and love art, and who was ready to dedicate his services to it
with all the devotion of a chivalrous nature. Somehow or
other, I found myself talking to him of my dreams, of opera
as I should like it to be. The outcome of our discussions was
that he proposed that I should sign a contract once more with
the Imperial Theatres.

My contract with Mamontov was drawing to an end. The
idea of again appearing in the Imperial Theatres, under the
management of a new chief who was willing to fall in with
the wishes of the artists, was agreeable to me, for I knew
what incomparably greater opportunities for wide artistic
activity, what possibilites for the appropriate staging of
opera, the Imperial Theatres could afford. Furthermore,
Teliakovsky told me:

"By degrees we will do everything that you think necessary."

I signed a contract for three years which stipulated a salary
of nine, ten, and eleven thousand rubles for the first, second,

and third years, respectively, with a fine of 15,000 rubles in the event of failure to fulfil the full period of the engagement.

When the private opera season reopened, however, I felt a keen regret for my old comrades and especially for Mamontov. I quite resolved to remain with them, but Teliakovsky told me that I could not do so unless I paid the fine. I reflected that, though I might find some means of paying the fine, there was still the possibility that I might be exiled for my capriciousness, or even prohibited from singing altogether. For Russian laws included the unexpected.

None the less, I endeavoured to find some one amongst my well-to-do acquaintances who would advance the 15,000 rubles. They were all very courteous, but, sad to say, did not appear to have any money available for the purpose—not one of them! Somehow, they all seemed to have grown poor suddenly. With sorrow in my heart, I said farewell to the private operatic stage.

No doubt my readers have noticed the sadness I often feel regarding the deficiencies of my native country, but I do not wish to give the impression that in my country there are only defects, nothing in which one may take satisfaction. There is, for example, the theatre—my real home.

Those who have never been in Russia cannot possibly imagine what a magnificent institution were the Russian Imperial Theatres and their schools. It is true that both artists and theatres were born of the caprices of aristocrats, owners of land and serfs, but, through these same aristocrats and serf owners the theatre was established as an intellectual recreation by the artists. Nowhere in the world, except perhaps in France under Louis XIV or during the Empire, was the theatre so pampered and caressed. The care bestowed upon them and the good will of the Tsars placed the Russian Imperial Theatres in an extraordinary position.

Hotheads of the populace recently said that the theatre with its high prices is a bourgeois amusement. I frankly state that this is not true. Being Imperial, the theatres were also for the people. Having been in their service and having travelled all over the world, I have never found any stage that could be compared with them from the artistic point of view. The beauty of their productions of drama, opera, and ballet inspired many great musicians, and it is common knowledge that they produced not only exceptional composers, but great and serious dramatists.

The traditions of the Russian Imperial Theatres were so powerful that not even revolution could crush them, and so, during the great revolutionary conflagration, the Russian stage stood like a knight in indestructible armor, ready to meet any and every enemy. Today this handsome and gracious figure still firmly stands its ground, smiling a welcome to new artists, new writers, and new composers.

My first re-appearance on the Imperial stage took place in "Faust." The public received me with much warmth. I was presented with a garland and a parchment shield bearing the inscription, "With your shield or upon it."

I think I have said already that I had been urged even before then to appear on the boards of the Imperial Theatres. Their financial wealth provided great possibilities for the attainment of the aims I had in view. Splendid scenery and costumes could be arranged, and I foresaw that perhaps it would even be possible to found a new school of operatic art. When I disclosed my ideas to Teliakovsky, he appeared to agree with me, and promised that during the following season we should begin to do various things. During the first season it would be necessary to put up with what we had. "Boris Godounov," therefore, was staged with the decorations which already existed, but I was allowed to order the costumes in accordance with my own taste and choice.

The artists, however, continued as before to be subject to the direction of official personages who knew little of the demands of art, its cultural influence and power.

In the private opera I had grown accustomed to feeling that I was free and the master of my own work, its guiding spirit. In the Imperial Theatres, too, I wished to draw a line between the officials and the artists. When, therefore, on one occasion I noticed an official giving orders on the stage and shouting at the artists as though they were soldiers or servants, I requested him pretty straightforwardly to leave the stage as soon as he liked, and not to interfere with the artists. He went away very much surprised and somewhat intimidated, and I told my fellow actors that, naturally, we must respect the officials as people who were necessary to prevent disorder, but that there was no room for them on the stage, where their rôle was to be as little in the way and to attract as little attention as possible. When we needed them we should always be able to find them in the office; but in the theatre and on the stage we must be the masters. The artists were pleased by my remarks. Some of them even thought my action savoured of the heroic, and expressed their gratitude to me for attempting to free them from the yoke of officialdom. Our family of actors began to lead a more harmonious existence. The officials came upon the stage only in cases of real necessity. Teliakovsky himself confirmed my action by saying that the officials must exist for the artists, and not the artists for the officials.

But very soon everything began to relapse into the old conditions. The artists themselves soon began to tell the officials that, of course, Chaliapine was right from one point of view, but on the other hand changes ought not to be made all at once, in so drastic a form.

"And altogether, you know, he isn't tactful!" they said.

"We did not say anything at the time, but you understand. . . ." And so on.

The officials understood well enough that the artists wanted to "bring a goose to their back door," as we say in Russia, and it soon began to be the more or less general opinion that I was an arrogant, conceited, capricious despot and a rude, loutish fellow. I won't deny that it is often my inclination to be rude to those who are rude to me. Not everyone is capable of complacently offering his back to the cudgels.

Rumours of my unbearable character spread outside, amongst the general public, who, as the saying goes, would rather sit in judgment on some one than eat!

The legend about my drunken habits grew, too. It was reported that in the privacy of my home I used to knock people about with the samovar or any other heavy article that came handy. On one occasion I sang Mephistopheles' serenade while seated on the steps of Margarita's porch, instead of standing as usual. After that it was currently reported that Chaliapine sang the opera in a state of blind intoxication, so drunk, in fact, that he could not stand and had to sing lying down.

These were all trifles, of course; but so is a gnat a trifle. Still, if about six hundred gnats begin to bite you, you won't think life altogether a holiday.

I had been accustomed since early youth to spend my free hours in cafés and restaurants, and it was perfectly natural that I should continue to derive pleasure from the time I spent in such places; not because I loved getting drunk, but because I always found that in this atmosphere people were more interesting, gayer, and less constrained than in their own homes.

Even as a choir boy I used to spend the interval between the first and second liturgies of the morning in an inn which boasted a machine for the production of music by mechanical means. I used to love watching the little sticks which, actuated by an invisible force, beat upon a drum, and even the squeaking of the machinery when it was being wound up gave me pleasure. Besides that, there used to be dignified people sitting in the inn and talking about their business affairs with an important air, gravely pronouncing words that were quite unfamiliar and that I never heard at home. They were skin dressers, lumber dealers, workmen of various trades, all of them very interesting and uncommon in my eyes.

Ludicrous incidents used to occur in restaurants to which I repaired after playing Mephistopheles or the High Priest in "Lakmé." Some naïve, well-intentioned person, seeing me in everyday dress and looking like anyone else, would exclaim with enthusiasm:

"What a young fellow! One can't believe one's eyes! Mr. Chaliapine, how young you are, on my word!"

It was amusing to hear people discussing whether my Adam's apple projected, or whether it projected as much as it ought to do. Many people believe that the power and volume of the voice depend upon the extent to which one's Adam's apple projects.

Altogether, there is always something to laugh at in a café, and something to hear that is worth listening to.

The expression of one kind of affection for artists which I often encountered in Russia, was very trying.

I would be sitting with friends in a café. Suddenly some fellow, obviously drunk, smelling of wine and with dripping moustaches would come up to our table:

"Great artist! Magnificent Chaliapine! How I love you! How I adore and respect you! Permit me to embrace you with all my heart!"

Affected by the fellow's repulsive appearance, I would answer:

"Many thinks for your kind feelings, but I cannot embrace you. I dislike embracing anyone!"

Then the man would be certain to look at me silently for a moment and turn away. In a second his feelings changed.

"Conceited, *canaille!*" he would throw at me as he rejoined his friends.

I have often had such experiences, but I am still at a loss to understand this kind of affection for an artist.

So there were some individuals who were not above talking against me, if only for the sake of satisfying their mediocre self-esteem which had been wounded.

*   *   *   *   *

I had learned to speak Italian fairly well, and began to dream of possibly appearing on the stage in Paris and London; although I had doubts whether I should ever realise my ambition in that direction.

In the year 1900 I went to visit the World's Fair at Paris with very pleasurable, though by no means definite, anticipations. I knew that my friend V. V. Andreiev would be there with his Balalaika orchestra, as well as many other Russians.

As formerly at Petrograd, Andreiev introduced me to various Parisian circles of music lovers. I sang at a number of afternoon teas, and achieved very definite success. I was also invited by the editor of *Figaro* to a soirée given by that newspaper. "The Two Grenadiers" was received by the Frenchmen with enthusiasm when I sang it on that occasion.

This journey to Paris and my appearances at soirées led to an event which I had not anticipated but which was of very great importance for me. In the spring of the following year I received a telegram from the theatre La Scala in

Milan proposing that I should sing Boito's "Mefistofele" there, and enquiring what would be my terms for an engagement. I was so surprised that at first I took the telegram for an ill-natured practical joke, but my wife persuaded me in the end to treat it seriously. I wired to Milan a request that the text of the telegram should be repeated, as I found it difficult to believe that the proposal was made in all seriousness. When I received a confirmatory reply and understood that no jest was intended, I yielded to an access of timidity. I could not sing in Italian, did not know Boito's opera, and could not make up my mind to reply in the affirmative to Milan. I passed two days in a highly nervous frame of mind and unable to sleep or eat. When I had recovered my equilibrium to some extent, however, I looked through the score of Boito's opera, and found that the rôle of Mefistofele was suited to my voice. As this alone was not sufficient to restore my self-confidence, I telegraphed to Milan a request for 15,000 francs for ten performances, secretly hoping that the management of the theatre would not agree to such a figure. But my terms were accepted!

Joy alternated with fear in my breast. I began to study the opera at once, and resolved to go to Italy for the summer. Rachmaninov was the first to whom I imparted the news and my state of mind. He expressed a wish to go with me, saying:

"Excellent! I will study music there, and in my spare time will help you to study the opera."

Like myself, he understood the profound importance of my forthcoming appearance in Italy. It was to both of us a very significant occurrence that a Russian should be invited to Italy, the land of celebrated singers.

We went to Varezze, a little spot near Genoa, on the road to San Remo, and settled down there to a very quiet existence, getting up and going to bed early, and giving up tobacco. Work was a pleasure to me, and I very quickly mastered the language, a task which was rendered easier for me to accomplish by the simple, kindly, and hospitable manners of the Italians by whom we were surrounded.

The wonderful smiling land of sunshine and its merry inhabitants enchanted me. The keeper of the little wine cellar which I used to frequent learned that I was about to sing "Mefistofele" in Milan, and forthwith I became his best friend. He did his utmost to encourage me, and was full of information about Milan and its celebrated theatre, saying that, whenever he went to the city, he as a matter of course attended a performance at La Scala. Listening to him, the hope involuntarily came into being in my mind that the innkeepers of Milan might turn out to be as great lovers of music as he was!

I was in a very nervous frame of mind throughout the autumn season at the Imperial Theatres during which my time was divided between the two great cities, Petrograd and Moscow, between the Mariensky and the Balshoi Theatre, as I was very much occupied with thoughts of "Mefistofele" and Milan. During the summer I learned the whole of Boito's opera, in the manner to which I had accustomed myself, and knew not only my own part, but all the others as well.

I had long had in my mind the idea of playing "Mefistofele" in a seminude state, as I considered that so abstract a figure called for its own special plastic representation. The devil in stage costume is not a genuine devil. I wanted to attain outlines which would do justice to the personality I had to express. The problem was, how to appear nude on the stage without shocking my audience.

I told my painter friends of my idea, and they approved of it. Golovin made several sketches for me, although he did not give me one of a nude Mephistopheles. I got something from his sketches, and resolved to play the Prologue, at all events, nude to the waist, although this was but little in comparison with what I had in mind. The chief portion of the rôle, however, was not the Prologue, but the Witches' Sabbath on the Brocken. I was in a quandary. The figure I dreamed of presenting was, as it were, of iron, metallic, mighty. In fact, I have special ideas about many rôles, but these ideas could be realised only in my own theatre, never in one in which I am an employee. In this case I was obliged to yield to necessity and be satisfied to represent Mephistopheles on the Brocken almost as everyone else did. Still, I managed an original touch by draping myself in a bit of flesh-coloured material. Naturally, I was not satisfied.

Having got my costumes made, I set out for Milan. I no longer had any eyes for Italy, being entirely taken up with thoughts of the theatre. The director of La Scala, no other than my dear friend Giulio Gatti-Casazza, received me kindly and told me that rehearsals had already commenced, and that he would be pleased to see me at the rehearsal next day.

I went next day to the theatre, in a very nervous state of mind and suffering for want of sleep, for I had not been able to sleep for some nights previously. La Scala gave me an impression of majestic size. I was astonished to see how far back the stage extended. Some one clapped hands to demonstrate its resonance, and the sound seemed to spread in a broad dense wave, and yet lightly and harmoniously.

The conductor, Arturo Toscanini, told me that the place had formerly been a church dedicated to the "Madonna della Scala," and that it had afterwards been converted into a theatre. I was much surprised at this, as such a conversion would have been an impossibility in Russia.

What I saw quite alarmed me at the idea of having to sing in this colossal theatre, in a foreign tongue, and with

MEFISTOFELE IN BOITO'S OPERA OF THE SAME NAME

strangers. All the artists, including Caruso, who was then a young man, began the rehearsal, using only *mezza-voce* (half-voice). I did the same, partly owing to fatigue and partly because it embarrassed me to sing loudly when no one else did so. The young conductor appeared to me to be rather a forbidding person. He was a man of very few words, and did not smile as everyone else did. His manner, when correcting the artists, was very brief and rather harsh. One felt that he knew his business and would not be argued with. In the middle of the rehearsal he suddenly turned to me and said hoarsely:

"Listen, signor! Do you intend to sing the opera as you are singing it now?"

"No, of course not," I said in confusion.

"But, my dear sir, I have not had the honour of being in Russia and hearing you there. I don't know your voice. Please be good enough, therefore, to sing as you will do at a public performance!"

I felt that he was right, and began to sing with the full power of my voice. Toscanini frequently stopped one or other of the other singers, for the purpose of commenting or advising them, but said nothing more to me. I did not know what to think, and went home after the rehearsal in an uneasy frame of mind.

"If he did not stop me," I thought, "he must disapprove of me."

Next day there was again a rehearsal in the foyer, where the walls were adorned with old portraits and photographs. Everything there inspired respect. What artists it had seen!

The rehearsal began with the Prologue. I sang the opening with my full voice. When I had finished Toscanini stopped for a moment, and with his hands still resting on the keys of the piano, his head a little inclined on one shoulder, said in his hoarse tones:

"Bravo!"

The unexpected comment resounded in my ears like a shot. At first I did not even understand that it referred to me, but as I was the only person who had been singing, I was obliged to assume that his approval was intended for me. Greatly rejoiced, I went on singing with enthusiasm, but Toscanini did not say another word to me.

The rehearsal over, I was summoned by Signor Gatti, who spoke very kindly to me and said:

"I am glad to tell you that you have pleased Toscanini very much. We shall shortly proceed to the rehearsals on the stage, with the chorus and orchestra; but you must first of all be measured for your costume."

"I have brought my costumes with me!" said I. He seemed surprised.

"Is that so? But have you ever seen this opera?"

"No, I have not seen it!"

"What costumes have you? We have certain traditions, you see. I should like to see, first of all, how you will be dressed."

"In the Prologue I propose to represent Mephistopheles seminude. . . ."

"What?"

I saw that the director was dreadfully alarmed. He was probably thinking:

"What a barbarian! He will create a scandal!"

"But listen," he said in persuasive tones; "that is hardly possible."

I began to explain to him the figure of Mephistopheles as I proposed to represent it. He listened, twisting his moustaches and interjecting from time to time in incredulous tones:

"Mm. . . . Aha. . . ."

At the subsequent rehearsals I observed that I was the

object of the uneasy attention both of the director and of the other artists. The director's secretary, with whom I had rapidly become good friends, told me plainly that I had frightened everyone by my intention of playing Mephistopheles nude.

I felt that I should have difficulty in depicting Mephistopheles in coat and breeches. Toscanini, who was also stage manager, came up to me and said that he would like me to stand and sit in such and such a way and walk in such and such a manner, first twining one leg round the other corkscrew fashion, then folding his arms on his breast in the manner of Napoleon and altogether showing me all the attitudes of provincial tragedians as I had seen them on the stage in Russia. When I asked him why he considered this or the other attitude to be necessary, he answered with conviction:

"Perche questa é una vera posa diabolica."

"Maestro," said I, "I have committed all your instructions to memory. Do not be uneasy. But at the dress rehearsal permit me to play the rôle as it seems to me it should be played."

He looked at me attentively and said:

"Va bene!"

When I came on the stage at the rehearsal wearing my costume and make-up, quite a sensation was created, which I felt to be very flattering to me. The artists and chorus singers, and even the workmen surrounded me, exclaiming in their delight and astonishment like so many children, touching me with their finger tips and feeling here and there; and when they noticed that my muscles were emphasised with paint their delight was extreme.

I was, of course, pleased by their delight and very much touched.

When I had finished the Prologue, I went up to Toscanini and asked whether I could count upon his approval. For the first time he smiled candidly and with all the grace of a child, clapped me on the shoulder, and said hoarsely:

"*Non e parliamo piu!*"

The date of the first public performance drew nearer, and those theatrical parasites known as the "claque" were already at work. In Milan they were known as *ladre nel guanti gialli,* or "thieves in yellow gloves." All artists, especially those unknown to the public, were then expected to pay tribute to the "claque," the amount of remuneration depending upon the artist's fee. I was, of course, unacquainted with the institution and had never even heard that it existed. Suddenly I was informed that some people had come to see me who would undertake to "assure my success," and accordingly requested me to present them with some dozens of tickets, and also to pay them 4,000 francs for applauding me at the first performance.

I ordered them sent away, but this mean proposal upset me; it was unpleasant to become aware of the presence of a drop of foul poison in the goblet of sacred wine which was my love for my art. Nevertheless, next day the same people came again and said:

"We will take only four thousand francs from Signor Chaliapine, as we like him personally. We have seen him out of doors and like his looks. We should want more from anyone else. . . ."

When they were again requested to leave, they went away, saying that Signor Chaliapine would be sorry for having dismissed them.

Indignant and angry, I went to the director of the theatre and told him:

"I came here to you with the same feelings with which a believer goes to communion. These people are a burden to me. Even without them I cannot sleep at nights, owing to my fear of failure. It would be better for me to go back to Russia. They don't do such things there!"

The director took my remarks very much to heart, calmed me, and promised to protect me from the impertinent pestering of the "claque." The method he adopted for my protection, however, occasioned me some embarrassment. Next morning, while I was still asleep, some men in civilian attire came to me from the police commissioner and informed my mother-in-law that they were members of the police force, with instructions to arrest any of the "claque" as soon as they should come to me. My mother-in-law and other relatives cautioned me that it would be far better if I were to ask the police to go away. In Italy people do not like to call in the police to their aid. I dressed and spoke to the policemen, begging them to go away. I told them that I was willing to sit and talk with them or to drink wine with them, but that it would be very disagreeable to me if they were to arrest anyone in my house, and that I could not permit it. The police evidently understood my position, and very politely explained to me:

"You are right, Signor Chaliapine, but you cannot alter the orders given by our commissioner. We must fulfil his instructions, although we quite understand that it will be unpleasant for you!"

I hastened once more to the director and begged him to have the policemen taken away. He telephoned to the police commissioner, and in the end the men were recalled. I recovered my peace of mind, but the incident became known in the theatrical world and in the town.

On the day of the first performance I went to the theatre with a feeling as though I were about to appear before a dread court of justice at which I should inevitably be condemned. I had a feeling that nothing good could come of the performance and that I should be sure to come a majestic cropper!

I was at the theatre before anyone else had arrived. Two doorkeepers met me, people who for some reason or other had taken a great affection for me. They were forever behind the scenes during rehearsals and looked after me like nursemaids. Everyone in the theatre was very kind and friendly towards me, but these two fairly overwhelmed me with their thoughtfulness. One of them was an old man with greying hair, but with black moustaches. The other, called Pisone, was also a man of respectable years, stout and paunchy. They were both as gay as children, both loved drinking wine, and both were very amusing.

They knew all the artists who had sung at La Scala in the preceding two decades, criticised their singing, imitated their manners and attitudes, sang and danced themselves, and were as full of jests and laughter as though they were two amusing good genii of the theatre.

"Don't be uneasy, Signor Chaliapino," said they on seeing me. "There will be a great success, we know! Oh yes, you will be successful. We have worked here for the last two decades, have seen various artists and been present at famous performances. If we tell you that you will be successful, then you may be sure of it! We know!"

These jolly fellows greatly encouraged me.

The performance began. I trembled as I had done at my first début in "Galka" at Ufa, and, as then, was unconscious of the boards beneath my feet, and my legs seemed made of cotton wool. Through a mist I beheld the vast hall densely packed with people.

I was drawn on a wheeled contrivance amongst clouds, and stood on this at an opening covered with gauze, whence I sang:

"Ave, Signor!"

I sang almost unconsciously, simply singing from memory all I knew, with all the power of voice I had at command. My heart thumped; my breath seemed difficult to draw; my eyes grew dim, and I felt dizzy.

I had just finished my last words, after which the chorus had to sing, when I heard a strange loud cracking noise. I thought that the wheeled conveyance on which I stood must have broken down, or some of the scenery fallen. I bent my head instinctively, but comprehended in the same instant that the dull booming sound proceeded from the auditorium.

What went on there was something I could never have imagined. Only those who have been in an Italian theatre can conceive what Italian applause or protest is like. The audience seemed to have taken leave of its senses, and the Prologue was interrupted in the very middle. I felt weak and overcome, almost unable to stand. My knees were knocking together; a wave of fear and delight invaded my bosom. The director of the theatre appeared beside me, in evening dress.

"Come, come!" he cried. "Thank them! Bow! Come on!"

The stout doorkeeper showed himself, dancing about and saying:

"Aha! Now do you see? What did I tell you? I knew! Bravo!"

He clapped his hands and applauded just as though he were the audience, then retired whence he had appeared, still dancing.

I stood before the footlights and bowed my acknowledgment. I could distinguish nothing in the vast auditorium but a sea of white faces, the bare shoulders of ladies in evening dress, and the sparkle of precious stones, while the thousands of pairs of clapping hands seemed like the fluttering wings of birds.

It was easier for me to sing after that; although after my efforts in the Prologue I felt weaker and seemed to have spent much of my nervous force. The entire performance, however, was a great success.

I had fully anticipated some manifestation of hostility on the part of the members of the "claque" whom I had driven away, but nothing of the kind occurred, not so much as a single whistle or hiss. I learned afterwards that in Italy even the "claque" loves art as everyone else does. It seemed that I had pleased even them.

The director, my fellow artists, and even the stage hands, were most charming to me. They congratulated me so joyfully and in so friendly a manner that I was profoundly touched.

In Italy the entire staff of the theatre, from the director to the carpenters, is always ardently interested, with true Italian vivacity, in what is doing on the stage. During performances the workmen collect behind the scenes, listen attentively, and discuss during the *entr'actes* the singing and acting of the performers, with a justness of criticism and a detailed knowledge of the opera which often surprised me. One would think that they must be bored with seeing performances every day and listening to the same opera several times in succession. But every day behind the scenes I heard workmen engaged in lively arguments as to whether such and such an artist had sung better or worse than on previous occasions, and so forth and so on. If an artist was not singing well or something or other had not been well done, they silently spread out their hands, but one could see from their faces the vexation they all felt at the failure.

Later on I sang in England, France, Germany, America, Monte Carlo, and elsewhere, and I noticed everywhere that if there were Italian workmen in the theatre they were always much more deeply affected than any others by the stage.

On the evenings when I was not singing I used to go to La Scala to listen to operas as a member of the audience. The administration kindly provided me with a seat in the stalls, and I was able to observe the Italian audiences from their midst instead of from the stage. I remember very vividly a production of the opera "L'Elisir d'Amore," in which Caruso sang wonderfully. He was then a young man, full of energy, a jolly companion and an excellent friend. He had the breadth of character on which we Russians pride ourselves, and was good-hearted and sympathetic to a very uncommon degree. He always willingly and generously assisted fellow artists who happened to be in difficulties.

Well, Caruso, who was already the favourite of the public in Milan, sang an aria in surpassing fashion. The audience called for an encore, and by some miracle he sang it again still better than before. In the wildest enthusiasm the audience again demanded unanimously:

"Encore, dear Caruso, encore!"

Next to me was sitting a man in eyeglasses and with a short grey beard. He appeared to be greatly moved, but did not applaud loudly, contenting himself with repeating in subdued tones:

"Bravo!"

To judge by externals, he was a small shopkeeper, perhaps the proprietor or senior clerk of a clothing store; a man who understood how to sell a necktie. When Caruso sang his aria the first time, this individual also cried "Encore!" but when the encore was given he confined himself to applauding, and when the audience began to demand the aria for the third time, he sprang to his feet and cried in a thin, high voice:

"Why are you all shouting for him to sing a third time? Do you think he can go on singing time after time, like a cannon loading and firing? Enough!"

This attitude towards an artist surprised me very much. I could see that the man would have been pleased to listen even ten times to Caruso, but that he understood that it was difficult for an artist to sing the same aria three times in succession.

In every way the Italians took the opera and singers very seriously. They listened to every performance very attentively right from the overture, and showed the keenest comprehension. It often happened that, at moments when an artist was more than usually successful in a rendition, the audience unanimously exclaimed in a half whisper:

"Bravo!"

and the artists valued such restrained approbation more than many a noisy outburst of applause.

During the *entr'actes* regular debates went on in the foyer. People collected in groups, buttonholing one another to discuss the merits of an artist's performance of a rôle, and I used to feel astonished at the knowledge of the history of opera and of the Milan theatre which was frequently displayed.

People I did not know in the least lifted their hats to me. I used to raise my hat again in embarrassment, thinking that they must have mistaken me for an acquaintance. The director's secretary told me, however, that they were holders of subscription seats in the theatre who wished to show their esteem for an artist whom they liked.

I had occasion to see an Italian audience express its indignation. It was really dreadful! I had heard some time previously that it was proposed to stage a new opera at La Scala, in which Tamagno was to participate, and I was very much surprised that not a word was said by anybody about the composer as a musician and that people confined themselves to relating his life story.   He was said to be a remarkably handsome young man who sang little *chansons* to his own accompaniment, not at all badly, and that a certain *principessa* had fallen in love with him, abandoning her husband in order to make the poor musician a wealthy man.   He was the composer of the new opera.   On his own account and at his own expense he invited Tamagno and a then well-known French prima donna to take the leading rôles.   The public interest in the performance was so great that I found it impossible to get a ticket at any price for the first performance, and was obliged to avail myself of the kindness of Signor Riccordi, a well-known man in the Italian musical world, who offered me a seat in his box. There I met also his father and mother, the latter an old lady of seventy or so, as well as the composers Puccini, Mascagni, and other celebrities of the day.

The orchestra played a rather weak overture, and then began to applaud itself in a somewhat undecided manner. In our box we exchanged silent glances of surprise, while some one in the audience said very loudly, as though with the object of tranquillising the public:

"The musicians are applauding to welcome their conductor, Toscanini!"

The curtain rose, and the opening scene of the opera, the action of which took place in ancient Rome, commenced with some one in a toga singing tediously to very tedious music.   The audience appeared to me to be paying absolutely no attention to the opera; almost perfect silence reigned, and in the neighbouring box I could hear people discussing which was the best steamer to take from Genoa to Naples and from Genoa to Marseilles, and where one got the best food and had the best time.

The first act ended.   The audience refrained altogether

from expressing itself in any way on the merits of the opera. Everyone simply got up and went into the foyer. It was as though the opera had not yet commenced, and nobody had as yet either seen or heard anything.

The French prima donna sang a great deal in the second act. She had a very ringing contralto voice, but she had a disagreeable *portamento*. I could see that the audience was displeased. Some frowned; others drew their nostrils in queerly; others narrowed their eyes as though offended. They looked as though they were all sucking lemons.

At length Tamagno came on the stage. The composer had prepared a very effective phrase for his entry, which called forth a unanimous outburst of delight from the audience.

Tamagno's voice was of an altogether exclusive quality; I might call it the voice of a century. Such singers are born only once in a hundred years. Tall and well built, he was as fine an actor as he was a singer. His diction was irreproachable. I have never met another singer who pronounced all the words of his part so distinctly and precisely as Tamagno always did.

After him, the Frenchwoman again sang for a long time. Tamagno broke in with short, angry replies. Then they embraced. After that neither the prima donna nor the orchestra was to be heard. Tamagno sang alone, and nothing else was necessary. The act closed. A genuine storm of applause burst forth. Riccordi's old mother, grown young as though by a miracle, cried "Bravo!" endlessly.

Tamagno came before the curtain with the prima donna and a very handsome man in evening dress, whom I at once guessed to be the composer of the opera. The audience, however, refused to understand who he was, and there were loud enquiries:

"Who is that?"

Some said it was the *régisseur*, others that it was Tamagno's secretary, others again asserted that it was the director of a cheese factory, a friend of Tamagno's.

At length some one cried, "It's the composer of the opera!" and the entire audience shouted forthwith:

"Tamagno alone!"

There was a tremendous uproar. It was evident that Tamagno had not heard that the audience called for him to appear alone, and he again appeared with the composer. Such a tempest broke forth as I had never heard, and could not even have imagined. Mature, respectable, well-dressed people in the stalls and boxes seemed to have gone mad, like everybody else in the theatre; everyone whistled, squealed, and howled so much that I was intimidated into wishing to leave the theatre. Riccordi's mother leaned over the rail of the box and cried out shrilly in frightful accents, as though she had been personally insulted to the very depths of her being:

"Begone, swindler! Begone, *mascalzone, ladro!*"

The third act proceeded after a very original fashion. The entire audience took part in it, as well as the orchestra and the singers. The goings-on were indescribable. First of all, people began to tease the prima donna, chiming in as she sang and imitating her, mewing and barking, or singing similar arias from well-known operas. From one side of the gallery people enquired of the other what was the best restaurant to go to for supper. Some one asked whether it would not be better to go at once, as otherwise it would be too late after this remarkable performance. People exchanged greetings and asked after the health of mutual acquaintancs. I ought to mention that all this went on without a sign of ill temper. Anger was observable only at the moment Tamagno brought the composer of the opera before the curtain for the third time. Now the audience was simply fooling. Everyone amused himself as pleased him best, revenging himself for the boredom of the unsuccessful performance. Some elegantly dressed officers in a box over the orchestra actually put out their tongues at the musicians. The latter replied with gestures comically expressive of regret. Afterwards I learned that the officers insulted the orchestra in this way for having applauded the overture.

"Well, this performance will never come to an end," said some one in our box. Riccordi asked me:

"Shall we wait for the end or shall we go away now? Perhaps you would like to wait? The finale will probably be quite out of the ordinary!"

"What could be more original than this?"

"It sometimes happens that a number of the audience pick up the conductor in his chair and carry him into the foyer."

"Surely that is rather an insult for him?"

"No! Why should he feel insulted? It is all done in a friendly way, as a joke. The conductor understands that the opera cannot be continued. Why should he be vexed?"

On this occasion, however, the conductor was not carried out. The performance terminated in an absolutely empty theatre, the entire audience having departed before the finale. As we left the theatre I heard some of the attendants saying:

"To the deuce with a management which stages such operas! The audience has smashed up the seats, and now we shall have to mend them."

I gathered that the attendants acted as carpenters for the theatre.

"Good Heavens!" was my reflection after the performance. "What if anything like that were to happen to me! I should never live through such a drama!"

During my stay in Milan I met several famous Italians. The first was Arrigo Boito. It was at one of the "Mefistofele" rehearsals that a doorkeeper told me Signor Boito was coming. I had not been aware that the author of "Mefistofele" was in Milan, and I was naturally full of curiosity to see him. He turned out to be an elegantly dressed man of about fifty, carefully shaven with well-trimmed beard and beautiful moustaches. He wore *pince-nez*. With his ultrarefined manners and a certain aristocratic simplicity which characterised him, he reminded me of a Polish magnate. I was introduced to him, and all through the rehearsal I kept my eyes on him, endeavouring to find out what he himself thought of his opera. He was as calm and apparently indifferent, however, as though it were not his own composition which was being rehearsed. He listened for a little while, said a few elegantly turned words of compliment to us, and took his leave.

During an interval in the rehearsal, when everyone went into a neighbouring room to smoke and relax a little, the doorkeeper, Giovanino Pisone, told us that "Mefistofele" had been staged twenty years before and had then been a complete failure.

Dear old Giovanino was an impassioned admirer of Boito, and had not a good word to say for the audience which had failed to understand the opera. He particularly liked the Prologue, the conversation of Satan with the Almighty, the trumpets included in the orchestral score, and the concluding words, "He can be polite even to the Devil."

While commenting thus in praise of the opera, Giovanino asserted that Boito had not been present at the first performance, as he was frightfully nervous.

"But he was perfectly composed during the rehearsal," said I. Giovanino laughed:

"Of course he would not let anyone see what a state he

was in. He is as good an actor as any of us, and knows how to conceal his feelings!"

When the performance was over Giovanino already had news that Boito was delighted, and told me:

"You will see how grateful he will be to you! We long ago determined to stage the opera again, but could never get a suitable Mefistofele. We have plenty of fine singers, but the opera requires a singer who is also an actor, as you are! The worst of it is that our singers eat so much macaroni that they get fat!"

Giovanino was stout himself, and therefore at once added a word in defence of embonpoint:

"One cannot be otherwise in Italy. It is such a splendid country. People work very hard here and they all have very good appetites, and there is plenty of good wine. One cannot very well be thin if one eats maraconi and drinks good wine! It would not be logical. Of course there are thin people here, too, but then they are ill!"

Boito only attended one performance, and even then did not show himself in the auditorium, but sat in a box in the wings.

I was told shortly afterwards that he would like to see me, and went to his house, which was situated near the town wall. There were aromatic pastils burning on the table in his study. He was a bachelor, and evidently loved little refinements.

He turned out to be a very jolly man, full of jests. Having heard that he was engaged on the composition of the opera "Nero," I asked him how it was progressing. With a look of horror, he pulled out a drawer of his desk and took from it an enormous pistol, which he placed on my knee, saying in comically gloomy tones:

"Shoot me!"

"What on earth do you mean?"

"Yes, shoot me for wasting my time! Shoot me on the spot," he said, jestingly.

Although he spoke in jest, one could see that he took his work very much in earnest. On several occasions afterwards, when in Milan, I called on him, but could never learn anything about "Nero." When I began once to look at a score, he shut it up, saying jestingly that it was "secret" music. He asked me many questions about the theatre and music in Russia, saying that he was very fond of Russian music, especially the works of Borodin.

I was aware that Boito had written libretti for Verdi's operas, and was told that in Italy he was regarded as an even greater poet than musician. The libretto of "Mefistofele" was written by him after studying the works of Goethe, Marlowe, and others.

I was told a very striking fact with regard to the attitude of the Italian public to Verdi. The composer arrived once at a railway station and entered the buffet. When those present recognised him they all rose and took off their hats, and no one sat down until the celebrated old man did so. No one cried "Bravo!" nor applauded. Everyone continued to eat and drink and converse, but when Verdi rose from his seat to go to the train, those present also rose and took off their cloaks, which they spread before the feet of the composer, and so he went to his train, bowing his acknowledgments to his fellow citizens as he passed over their garments.

After the first performance of "Mefistofele" I received a note on a scrap of paper: "Bravo, bravissimo, signor Chaliapine," and a variety of complimentary remarks. The signature was undecipherable, something like "Amasini." My wife told me that the writer was Angelo Mazzini. In high delight, I went at once to thank him. I have already told of the enchanting impression his wonderful voice made upon me.

This splendid man and divine singer received me kindly and heartily. The man I saw was no archangel, but the most everyday mortal, attired like an Italian workingman in well-worn trousers, a torn shirt, and a very odd-looking necktie. On his feet were a worn old pair of slippers. Looking me over with his little penetrating eyes, he said elegantly that he was pleased to witness the success of a Russian artist in Italy, that he loved Russia like a second motherland where he had won a success which had materially benefited him and where he had experienced that profound spiritual satisfaction which he looked on as the best thing in life.

"In Russia," said Mazzini, "they love me so much that I feel like a king when I go there! You can imagine how pleased I am to see your well-merited success! In applauding you, I did so with all my heart, as it were thanking Russia through you for what she has done for me!"

I was touched by his words, and expressed my regret at not having known of his presence in the theatre, and said that if I had been aware of it I should have come to his box during the *entr'acte*.

"My box?" said he, laughing. "You would not have found me in any one of the boxes. I always sit in the gallery!"

Mazzini insisted on my taking coffee and liqueur with him, which he himself brought on a tray, although I saw that he had a servant. When I took my leave he seemed to wish to help me on with my overcoat. I was much embarrassed, and did all I could to prevent him, but my kind, perhaps too kind, host said rather theatrically:

"Signor Chaliapine, I wish to give myself a pleasure!" laying emphasis on the word "myself."

A fortnight later I read a letter from Mazzini in the Petrograd newspaper *Novoye Vremya*, in which he gave particulars of my success at La Scala. It seemed to me a most wonderful and touching act of kindness!

As my acquaintance with this unusual man progressed, I observed that he led a very solitary life. He did not appear to have any friends, nor even acquaintances, although everybody in Milan knew him, as well as many other people in various parts of the world. Whenever he walked in the Galleria Vittorio Emanuele, everyone used to say respectfully:

"There is Mazzini!"

People laughed good-naturedly at his democratic garb and the plain hempen cord which he used in place of a watch chain. There were people who asserted that Mazzini was excessively mean, but I knew that it was not so and that the truth was very different. Mazzini knew how difficult it is to get money, but he did not stint spending it when necessary. He was a true democrat in his habits and character.

I told him of my emotion during the rehearsals, and also at my first performance before the public in Italy, and of how the "claque" had endeavoured to exploit me.

He said that it would be better if I did not spend much time in the Galleria Vittorio Emanuele, where I should only meet people who were likely to be a hindrance to me in my artistic work, and that only inferior artists frequented the gallery.

When the series of performances for which my services had been engaged was concluded, I went to a restaurant with some artist friends. People approached our table and congratulated me, expressing regret that the performances were over. It was all done in the simplest, most pleasant way in the world, without a trace of any desire to scrape acquaintance unnecessarily. When nearly everyone had gone home, I invited some young men who still remained to join us, and ordered a couple of dozen bottles of champagne, in the desire to give expression to my feelings. The waiters and the remaining diners looked at me as though they feared I had lost my mind, but my invitation was accepted, which gave me pleasure.

Amongst those present was Gabriele d'Annunzio, then a powerful-looking blond young man with a short pointed beard. He proposed a toast, which I think must have been very clever and literary, for I understood not a word of it. Afterwards I became very well acquainted with him, and not so very long ago, in fact just before the war, we were meditating together on the possibility of composing an opera which should harmoniously unite the drama with music, song, and dialogue.

I returned to Russia *via* Paris in a very good humour, with myself and the world, feeling that I had accomplished something which had not merely been of benefit to myself alone.

CHAPTER EIGHT

I Return to Russia—New Year's Eve at Yar's—Working Under Difficulties—Monte Carlo and Raoul Gunsbourg.

WITH my return to my native country my usual daily round began once more, with the usual endless little disagreeablenesses which so soon extinguish, as with a grey pall of ashes, the fire of enthusiasm.

I wished to stage Boito's "Mefistofele" at Moscow for my benefit performance, and looked forward to being able to accomplish there all that I had wished to do but had not been able to carry out when the opera was performed in Milan. "Mefistofele" was but little known in Russia, and it was a natural consequence that at rehearsals I had to act as a sort of stage manager for my fellow artists. It was necessary for me to explain and demonstrate various matters pertaining to the production, even to the ballet. The complicated scene on the Brocken, in particular, called for many explanations. I soon began to realise that my fellow artists received my explanations with displeasure.

"What is he trying to teach us for?" they grumbled. "What right has he to teach us?"

I did not give a thought to whether I had a right to teach or not, for, after all, I only wished to recommend that certain things should be done; but I found that I must beg pardon even for offering my advice in a manner quite free from offence. It was only natural that, with my habitual freedom of speech, I should sometimes "put my foot in it." Once, for instance, I remarked jestingly that my friend the *régisseur* V. was "behaving like a Turk's horse." V.

239

himself was in no way offended, but next day a paragraph appeared in the papers saying that I had called the ladies of the chorus "cows." When I read this I asked the chorus ladies whether I had said anything of the kind. They said, "No," but never thought of denying the assertion through the press, and for me to have done so personally would have been a departure from my usual reserve, which I did not think becoming.

There were other little incidents too numerous to mention. Every actor in the theatre went about in an offended frame of mind, and gave up doing even what he had hitherto done in passable fashion. The public performance of the opera gave me little satisfaction, although it was well received by the audience.

How much the fear of wounding some one's self-love can hinder one's work and interfere with one's life, by depriving one of the consciousness of being a free man and a friend to everybody!

The benefit performance gave rise to an unfriendly attitude towards me amongst my fellow artists, and was the source of a rumour among the public that I was a money-grubber. This rumour increased when, wishing to free the public from the speculative activities of ticket traders, I arranged for the subscription at my own home of tickets for my benefit night. After that I got called a "shopkeeper" outright!

It was all very unjust and wounded me deeply. I felt that I was changing from a cheerful man into an irritable fellow who suspected everyone of ill will. I began to realise that the stories of heroes who defeat thousands of foes with their single arm are indeed but stories. My growing disinclination to make fresh acquaintances in the theatrical world led to my being called conceited.

I am taking the trouble to relate all this, not out of a desire for self-justification, but because everyone has the right to imagine that he has, somewhere or other, an unknown friend who is nevertheless sincerely attached to him. Well, let me tell my story to the best of my ability to that unknown and unseen friend. However severe his judgment, though friendly, may be, I will accept it with gratitude.

Outside of the artistic world, amongst the members of the wealthy Russian merchant class, who are, or used to be, perpetually consuming salmon, sturgeon, caviar, and other dainties, and drinking champagne, in which latter occupation they apparently found the chief joy of life, I had many acquaintances. Let me try to describe to you briefly the kind of scene I sometimes witnessed when in their company.

Imagine, for instance, the following picture: It is New Year's Eve at Yar's famous restaurant in Moscow. There is a truly barbaric display of luxury; everywhere there are mountains of exquisite fruit, every possible and impossible dainty, champagne of every known brand. The diners are all of them in evening dress, and many of them are already intoxicated, although it is not yet midnight. When twelve o'clock strikes every one of them is drunk. People embrace, assuring one another with truly Russian bonhomie:

"I am very fond of you, swindler though you are!"

"You ought long ago to have been in gaol yourself, my dear chap!" says the other; and then they kiss each other on both cheeks most affectionately.

That kind of thing is no doubt very touching, but one is apt to become somewhat disgusted. It is noteworthy that, although everybody is very, very drunk, no one is too tipsy to miss an opportunity of saying something bitterly unpleasant to his friend. And yet you never see those people lose their tempers!

The night wears on. At four o'clock in the morning the tired waiter is leaning, half asleep, against the wall, with his napkin on his arm like a flag of truce. A man of respectable age and girth is lying under a couch, whence his beautifully shod feet project. His boots are stained with wine, and his dress coat is torn. Two other worthy gentlemen are still at table and on very affectionate terms. Weeping in sympathy, they complain of the unbearable hardness of their lot. To keep up their spirits they sing gipsy songs and swear that there is no place for an honest man to live in, except it be a gipsy caravan.

Reviving somewhat all at once, one of them says to the other:

"I'll show you a trick! Waiter, bring a bottle of champagne!"

The waiter brings the bottle and opens it.

"Keep your eyes on me," says the conjurer, all damp and sticky. His companion does his best to look steadily in front of him, which seems to cost him great efforts. The conjurer places a full glass of wine on his own head, which he shakes, endeavouring to catch the glass in his teeth and drink the wine "in full flight." He is not successful. The wine pours down over his shoulders, chest, and knees, and the glass falls on the floor.

"I've missed it," he truthfully remarks. "Wait a moment! I'll do it again. . . ."

His friend waves a languid hand and sighs:

"Never mind," and sings tearfully:

"*Ekh, raspashól, raspashól!*" (A gipsy song.)

It is all very ludicrous, but very sad, too.

These good-hearted drunken people, with something as it were crushed in their souls, were very fond of me. Often people said to me, with ardent embraces:

"You are ours! Moscow made you! We made you!"

On one occasion I felt impelled to say in reply to one of these importunate people:

"Listen! I am not yours! I am as God made me!"

People cried out at me that I had grown conceited, and next day the rumour spread that Chaliapine despised Moscow and its inhabitants.

Sometimes I had the feeling, when in the company of half-tipsy people like that, that what they really wanted was to bring me down, just as in the Sukonnaya Sloboda successful people used to get beaten for being successful. I felt that people were looking after me with their fists clenched and enquiring in malicious tones:

"How much are you getting, eh? Conceited, stuck-up fellow!"

However, when they found I was not above joining in a row, people usually thought better of it. By degrees I learned how to keep out of the company of people like those I have described.

In the theatre I was oppressed by the official attitude of everybody towards the work. Everyone was cold and mechanical in regard to the public performances. If ever I wanted to propose that some phrase or other should be sung differently, diverging somewhat from tradition, or in a more lively manner, I had to feel my ground, always trembling for fear of wounding someone's too tender self-love. If I said to the conductor of the orchestra that it would be better to sing such and such a phrase more slowly and expressively, very likely the answer would be that the violins and 'cellos could not draw out the passage. Maybe he was right. My musical education was not sufficient to enable me to dispute with him; but it has always seemed to me that the orchestra of the Imperial Theatres was simply wonderful and that there was nothing it could not do. Every one of the musicians numbered in it was a finished artist, having been selected for his post by competition.

By the way, with respect to almost all the orchestral conductors with whom I have sung, with the exception of Rachmaninov and a few Italians, I have always observed a lack of feeling for rhythm. There is too often an effect of looseness and shakiness.

I have been reproached for not founding my own school of dramatic art; but I think people overlook the fact that no one can be compelled to learn. In Russia people don't even trouble a very great deal about teaching reading and writing properly. It follows that it would be looking too far ahead to think of introducing the compulsory teaching of the art of the stage. Moreover, would the exaggerated self-esteem of most stage aspirants permit them to learn anything from Chaliapine, who never attended the Conservatory? Undoubtedly, no. I don't deny that everyone must learn, but my opinion is that people go on learning only until they attain their first success, until they are dazzled by the footlights and deafened by the roar of applause. That thunder but rarely proves to be like "the first thunder in springtime" for an artist, presaging a fruitful season. In most instances, it is the thunder of approaching autumn, presaging the fading season and the falling leaf. People ask me, sometimes, to open my own theatre. Well, if I did —and I have often reflected over the idea—I should certainly work zealously in it myself, and I should require others to put their hearts into their work, too. Not to mention the fact that by the end of the first season my collaborators would be calling me an "exploiter"; being better-educated and more cultured than I, they would inevitably let me know it. Some stage manager with a taste for innovations would enquire what was the colour of the hose worn by Italian courtiers at the court of Charles V, and I should not be able to tell him! Stage managers are such wonderfully well-educated people! I remember once hear-

HOLOFERNES IN SEROV'S "JUDITH"

ing a stage manager say to the person in charge of the scenery, with sincere vexation:

"Whatever is the meaning of these candelabra? Was there anything of the kind at that time? Poushkin says in 'Boris Godounov'. . . ."

Or, for instance, some tenor who had to play the part of a prince, would walk about the stage looking more like a barber. I would say to him:

"You need to adopt rather different gestures and movements. You approach your sweetheart as though you meant to shave her!"

He would ask me not to try to teach him; I should lose my temper and he would probably leave the stage in the middle of a performance. Then I should have to go before the curtain, bow to the audience, and say:

"Ladies and gentlemen, owing to the tenor having suddenly fallen a victim to cholera, we cannot finish the performance. Please be good enough to go home and amuse yourselves in any way you like!"

The audience would leave, after breaking up the furniture, and next day there would be a letter from the tenor in all the best papers:

"I am not suffering from cholera at all. That is a calumny invented by Chaliapine, who is so well known for his love of making trouble, and I have been driven from the stage by the necessity of protecting my own dignity. The vexation he has occasioned me has made me entirely lose my voice, and, consequently, my sole means of livelihood. I am therefore bringing an action against him for 600,000 rubles damages, and shall summon all who were present at the performance to bear witness on my behalf."

Such would be the probable outcome of setting up my own theatre.

I am joking, of course, but the reality of things in

Russia produces occurrences not so very unlike that, and much more malicious than any satirical anecdote.

To speak seriously, I don't find in theatrical folk that ardent love for their profession which it so insistently calls for and without which it is dead. There is naturally no reason why an artist should sweep the floor boards, assist in putting up the scenery, and clean the lamps, as I have done in my time, owing to my youth and excess of energy. But if, for instance, one were to ask a "well-known" artist to take a minor part, do you think he would not be indignant? He would, and very much so!

And he would be sure to write a letter to the editor of the most liberal paper, one that makes a specialty of defending various oppressed people, but which does not always clearly discern how much harm some of these oppressed persons do to their profession.

It must be pleasant to be a sculptor, composer, painter, or author! Their stage is their study or their atelier. They work in solitude, behind closed doors, unseen by anyone. They are hindered by no one from giving expression to their ideas as they wish. But try to give life to your ideas on the stage in the presence of three hundred people, more or less, some ten of whom are pulling in every direction away from you, while the others, being as indifferent as the dead to everything on earth, are altogether immovable!

Collective artistic work is possible only if all those who collaborate in it recognise that their aim is one and indivisible, and that co-operation is necessary to attain it. Where is there such a consciousness? In its absence every artist who loves his art sincerely and ardently is condemned to live and work "in a wilderness," which, alas, is not a solitude.

Very likely I am frequently in a very nervous state at rehearsals. Maybe I am inclined to be despotic and rude, and even to insult those around me, both great and small. People talk so much about it that I am inclined to believe it myself. I won't attempt to justify myself, on the pretext that each of us has his failing, but for another reason about which I am not perfectly clear in my own mind.

My view is this, that while of course the man is the creator of every work, still the work is more important than the man, and he must give up his self-love for its sake! Yes, I know it is not kind to be harsh to the little people; everyone knows that, although everyone is guilty of it. But what is to be done if a person shows no inclination to work and does not attempt to understand the importance of his part? In most instances I let myself go, I admit. Not that I don't respect the dignity of others. I do respect people, and, indeed, it would be monstrous if I, of all men, did not respect them; I who have gone through all the stages of a working career from the bottom upwards. I am harsh, and shall continue to be so when necessary, because I love the work my fellow artists have to do, and know that they are at their best when they are earnest in it, when they themselves understand the beauty and the value of what they are doing!

Abroad too, amongst foreigners, I have not hesitated to express my mind freely.

However, enough of all this, or else it will seem as though I were complaining. I do not wish to do that. There is a great deal that I should like to say, but lack the art of presenting as I would wish.

Perhaps people would have a better opinion of me if I were more politic, more tactful and diplomatic; or, to put it plainly, less frank; but I have been badly brought up and dislike hypocrisy, cannot bear deceit, and am consequently like a goose which comes to the kitchen of its own accord and begs to be cooked. Naturally, the cooks are pleased to see me and begin forthwith to pluck out my feathers, without even stopping to wring my neck.

*   *   *   *   *

My success in Italy had excellent consequences for me; very soon afterwards I received an invitation to sing in the theatre of Raoul Gunsburg at Monte Carlo.

Monte Carlo is one of the most beautiful places in the world. It is held in ill repute, owing to the existence of the Casino. At that time the theatre was a good one and its artists serious in their work. All the artists, members of the chorus, and musicians were thoroughly conscientious and devoted to their profession; they were all punctual and earnest, and the work went forward rapidly, cheerfully, and without friction.

In engaging to sing at Monte Carlo I undertook a task of no small magnitude, as it was necessary for me to study several operas in both the Italian and French languages.

A little man with an enormous nose and the shrewd eyes of a business man, met me on my arrival with a cheery, noisy welcome. This was Raoul Gunsburg. "How pleased I am to see you!" he cried in his broken Russian, and, twisting about continually as though he were in a frying pan, began pouring forth a veritable flood of words at the rate of some six hundred a minute, telling me that he loved Russia and had served in the Russian army during the Turkish campaign of the 'seventies, that he had been amongst the first to enter Nicopol, and had received a bayonet thrust. In proof of his assertion he showed me the wound, which was in the groin. I was very much amused at him.

He did not look more than about thirty-five, so that at the taking of Nicopol he could not have been more than ten years old. I learned later on, however, that he was older than he looked, and might have been fourteen when Nicopol was taken. Of course, in war some one must always take something. Otherwise it would not be war.

He informed me that he had a château of his own, with a museum and a collection of noteworthy pictures, that he was well-to-do and engaged in theatrical business entirely out of a love for music and not for the sake of any material advantage. I was rather nonplussed when he informed me that he intended writing an opera himself.

With him was Renaud, a very fine artist, who, I was informed, played the part of Mephistopheles in the "Damnation de Faust" very well indeed. Naturally, I was interested, and when the "Damnation de Faust" was staged I saw for myself that Renaud really made a lifelike and vigorous personality of Mephistopheles. He acted with a subtle feeling for artistic restraint. I went behind the scenes and told him of the delight I had felt in his performance. Later on, at home, I carefully considered and compared my Mephistopheles and that of Renaud. It appeared to me that our conceptions of the figure were by no means identical, any more than were those of the composers, Berlioz and Boito.

The series of performances in which I took part also commenced with "Mefistofele." Gunsburg's theatre and stage were small; there was hardly room to turn round in the dressing rooms. The place, however, as a whole was agreeable, comfortable, and even elegant. But the best thing in it was Raoul Gunsburg himself. He was always in good humour, and quite unjustifiably delighted with everything.

"What a wonderful performance today!" he used to cry, although the performance had not yet even begun. Just as in Milan, everyone, from the stage hands to the artists, took a keen interest in the performances. One felt that all of them took that lively interest in the work which redoubles

an artist's powers.   The audience received the Prologue
very sympathetically.   The reception given to it warmed me
up, and I played the scene on the Brocken as I have rarely
been able to do it.   The theatre helped me, too, as the dis-
tances in it were not so great as in the Moscow and Milan
opera houses.   Every word reached the audience, which was
also able to distinguish clearly every gesture and shade of
meaning in the acting.   I got an ovation, and later on my
colleague and rival, Renaud, came to me and said, pressing
my hand with sincere emotion:

"Well done, my friend!"

Raoul Gunsburg danced about, beaming with pleasure, and
overwhelmed me with noisy compliments. I have never
known another impresario like him.   Even if an artist was
not in good voice, or was not feeling very fit, a thing which
quite often happened with me, Gunsburg beamed with delight.   If he noticed that an artist was downcast owing to
lack of success, he immediately said:

"You are singing better than ever before, today.   You
are singing as no one has ever sung!"

Whatever he may have thought, he never spoke otherwise
than encouragingly.   He was a man born for the theatre,
and had a peculiar talent of his own.   He thoroughly understood the theatre and knew what would turn out well,
having a keen feeling for what would be effective or the
contrary.

I quarrelled with him more than once.   Sometimes we
did not speak to one another for a fortnight at a time; but
I never felt any dislike for him, and was never conscious
of a lessening of his esteem for me.   At bottom I respected
him, for I could see that he loved the work.   I am very
fond of this extraordinary man and will continue to be so
all my life.

We once had so serious a quarrel that we almost fought

a duel over it.   The incident was, however, more of a nature to provoke mirth than alarm.

Gunsburg, "with God's help," as he expressed it, had written an opera entitled "Ivan the Terrible." Heaven only knows what was not included in it.   There was a conflagration, a hunting scene, a Bacchanalian orgy in a church, dances, battles; Ivan the Terrible rang church bells, played chess, danced, and died.   All the Russian words which are more or less well known to foreigners, such as *izba, boyarin, batoushka, barinya, zakouska, izvoschick, samovar, steppe, vodka,* and so on, were made use of.   It was a truly colossal production of ignorance and audacity, but Gunsburg sincerely believed that he had written a fine work, and used to say:

"It's a very extraordinary opera!   I don't think there is a better one.   All other composers will be forgotten, and only Mozart and I who stand before you will be remembered.   Oh yes!   If the public doesn't understand the work at once, it will do so in a thousand years' time!"

I lost my temper and told the genius, Raoul, that in my humble opinion he had not written his opera "with God's help," but with the assistance of a certain fallen angel!   He got red in the face and said:

"Chaliapine, for words like those people have recourse to the sword in France!"

I assented to the appeal to arms, and advised Gunsburg to be sure to provide himself with a weapon of sufficient length—his stature was low and his arms were short— and suggested that the duel should take place after the first public performance of his opera, as, if he were to kill me, there would be no one to take the rôle of Ivan the Terrible.

Naturally, Raoul lost his temper still more at my jokes, and went off to hunt up his seconds.   I waited a long time for the latter, but they never came to me.   The end of it all was that we did not speak to one another for a fortnight, and then were reconciled once more after the first performance of "Ivan the Terrible." Although the opera was full of stupidities, and most of the music was imitated from other composers, it went very well on the stage. It was a true theatrical production, the fullest freedom being given to the actors for the exercise of their talents, with the result that out of a trifling work they were able to create a serious and even an instructive performance.

* * * * *

When I got back again to Russia, where everything was enmeshed in a network of prohibitions, and where those in power were so fond of giving orders, I got into hot water almost immediately. Preparations were on foot for the staging of "Russalka." The orchestra was under the direction of a former choirmaster, who had been appointed to the post of conductor probably because he was always able to compromise with his artistic conscience and conducted works whether he knew them or not merely because he was asked to do so. I knew the whole of "Russalka" by heart from beginning to end, and therefore did not pay much attention to the rehearsals. When the first public performance of the opera took place I was horrified to find that the conductor had altered the rhythm in the first act in an extraordinary manner. The effect was really so bad that I thought it must have been done out of sheer ill will. I felt as though I were bound hand and foot. The conductor kept his eyes glued to his score as thought he had never seen it before. The audience was evidently conscious that something was wrong somewhere, but bore the performance with the patient indifference of those who are accustomed to put up with everything, being convinced that stopping at home would be still more tedious than the theatre. For my part, I was furious, and at the end of the first act asked the conductor what he was doing.

He replied, raising his voice, that he had no wish to enter into a discussion with me, and that if I wanted to make any protest I might address myself to the management. My indignation was such that I took off my costume, dressed, and went home, resolved to have nothing more to do with the government theatre. On the way, however, I cooled down a little, and I had hardly entered my flat when an official arrived from the theatre and I was persuaded to return and finish the performance. It was fortunate that the Prince's feast and the scene with the Princess intervene between the first and third acts, and as I had not to appear in either of them the opera was not delayed by my absence. The audience knew nothing of what had occurred. I understood, of course, that the quarrels in our theatrical household were not to be made public property, but the incident became known somehow or other, and a day or two later I read a newspaper paragraph under the heading "Chaliapine's Latest Scandal."

"Yes," was my reflection, "I shall have to cause many more such scandals yet, though they won't do any good."

CHAPTER NINE

*My First Visit to America—Diaghilev's
Seasons of Russian Music in Paris—"Boris
Godounov" at La Scala—"Khovanstchina"
at the Imperial Theatres.*

BY THIS time my artistic reputation had increased to
the extent of receiving an offer to appear in America.
This came in the shape of an engagement to sing at the
Metropolitan Opera House, New York City, during the
season 1907-08. I signed a contract which called for appearances in "Mefistofele," "Faust," "The Barber of
Seville," and "Don Giovanni."

I was much excited at the thought of singing for the
first time in "the land of big business," about which I had
heard repeatedly from fellow artists. Consequently, I set
out on the trip across the Atlantic with the keenest anticipation.

The first object to claim my attention as we neared New
York was the statue of Liberty. Next, on the dock, I was
greeted by a small army of newspaper reporters. They
seemed to me amiable, clean-cut people, who lost no time in
coming to the point of their business. They plied me with
questions as to how I had endured the voyage; where I was
born; whether I was married or single; if married, whether
I was happy with my wife; whether or not I had ever been
in prison for some political crime; what I thought about the
condition of Russia at the time; what I believed to be my
country's future; and what I thought about America.

I was somewhat bewildered, much astonished, and even
rather touched by the interest in me displayed by these

people, and answered all their questions to the best of my ability.

My next ordeal consisted in rehearsals at the Opera House, closely followed by my first appearance there, which took place on November 20, 1907, in Boito's "Mefistofele." On that occasion, as in many subsequent performances, my companions in the cast included Riccardo Martin and Geraldine Farrar. I remember that the performances of "Don Giovanni" were conducted by the late Gustav Mahler and that the manager of the Metropolitan Opera Company at that time was the late Heinrich Conrad.

My stay in America was short and far from happy. My artistic ideals were misunderstood, my performances were adversely criticised, and, in general, it seemed that I was looked upon, artistically, as a barbarian. Complete ignorance of the English language prevented me from establishing sympathetic contact, to any extent, with natives of the great country, America.

For these reasons and also to avoid repetitions that might bore the readers of these pages, I will postpone discussing matters American until a later chapter, beginning with my return to New York in the autumn of 1921.

*   *   *   *   *

It was a lucky day for me when S. P. Diaghilev came with a proposition that I should go to Paris, where he was anxious to arrange a series of symphonic concerts, intended to acquaint Parisians with the historical development of Russian music. I was delighted to give my assent, as I knew the interest Russian music was exciting in western Europe and how little of it was really known there.

On arrival in Paris I put up at the same hotel where Diaghilev was staying. I saw at once that serious work was afoot and was being prosecuted with enthusiasm. There seemed to be almost as much movement and activity going on around Diaghilev as in all Paris besides. He told me that the Parisians were taking a great deal of interest in his enterprise, and that, although the concerts were to take place at the Opéra, it was going to be quite impossible to seat all who wished to listen to Russian music. He said that Rimsky-Korsakov would take part in the concerts besides Rachmaninov, Scriabine, and several other Russian composers who were then in Paris. Rimsky-Korsakov, Blumenfeld and Nikisch were to conduct. We commenced with the first act of "Russlan and Lludmilla," which the public liked very much indeed. After that I sang with success the song of the Viking Guest from "Sadko," Prince Galitzky's aria from "Prince Igor," Varlaam's song from "Boris Godounov," and also several ballads with piano accompaniment.

But it was not my modest success that mattered in these concerts, but the success of Russian symphonic music. It was a real joy to me to see the so-called "frivolous" French take the greatest delight in these profoundly original compositions.

Perhaps, being Russian myself, it is not nice or modest for me to be so enthusiastic about Russian music, and people will think that I am screaming with the hoarse voice of patriotism; but in reality I am expressing myself as an artist, not as a citizen of any country.

The concerts were a real success, and in consequence we thought of showing Paris a Russian opera—for instance, "Boris Godounov"—during the forthcoming season. When it was announced that Diaghilev's company would play "Boris," the Parisian press and the public began to speak of the Russian season as a gala one. I shall never forget the zeal and love displayed by the members of the chorus

and orchestra of the Paris Opéra in their work at our rehearsals!   It was a real holiday for me.

We staged the opera coronation scene in its entirety, which
was impossible in Russia, owing to the censorship.   This
scene loses much of its grandeur and solemnity in Russia
because it cannot be played there in full; but in Paris the
procession of ecclesiastical dignitaries with the ikons, church
banners, and censers, was staged.   The effect was very fine.
During all my years on the stage I have never seen a more
magnificent or carefully arranged performance.

We held first of all a general rehearsal, to which the
élite of Parisian society, artists, literary men, and journalists
were invited.   Unfortunately, the costumes and the scenery,
on which the painters Korovin and Golovin had been working, were not ready in time for the dress rehearsal, and the
latter could not be postponed.   We all feared that the proper
impression would not be produced if we sang in our ordinary
clothes and without making up.   My own costumes were
ready, but I refrained from using them and from making
up, in order not to spoil the general effect.

The opera began, and I sang my first phrase.   The chorus
sang magnificently.   I don't think the French had ever
heard such a chorus, for it seems to me there are no such
choruses abroad as we have in Russia, which I think is due
to the fact that in Russia chorus singers begin as children
in the churches, and learn to sing with the unusual shades
of intonation which our church music requires.

Personally I regretted very much that we had not the
scenery and that I was not in costume; but I knew that the
impression which an artist can and must produce is not
wholly dependent on these externals, and I was successful
in producing the impression I wished for on my audience
when I pronounced the words:

"What is that rising and stirring in the corner? . . ."

I observed that some of the audience turned their heads in alarm in the direction towards which I was looking, and one or two even rose from their seats. . . .

I was rewarded with a storm of applause. The success of the performance was assured. We all felt triumphant. My comrades congratulated me sincerely; some of them pressed my hand, with tears in their eyes. I was as happy as a child.

The first public performance of the opera went off every bit as well as the general rehearsal. The artists, the chorus, the orchestra, and the scenery were all such as befitted the music of Moussorgsky. I venture to say so, for the entire press of Paris bore witness to it. The scene of the death of Boris created an overwhelming impression. The opinion of the public coincided with that expressed in the press— that it was a work "worthy of Shakespeare." The audience behaved as only the emotional French can—people shouted and embraced us, expressing their gratitude to the artists, the chorus, the conductor, and the management.

I speak all the time of our success with the Parisian public, but what to me was even much more important and touching was that great actors and actresses like Sarah Bernhardt, Gabrielle Rejane, Mounet Sully, and Lucien Guitry closed their own theatres to come to see me in "Boris Godounov." I was so praised and petted by these great artists that I considered myself the proudest man on earth. To have had this experience remains an indescribable and unforgettable happiness.

When I remember that night I cannot but admit that, although my life has been hard, it has had its rewards. I have experienced moments of the greatest happiness, which I owe to the art I so dearly love. Love always brings us happiness, whatever may be its object; but the love we give to art is the greatest happiness in life!

PARIS—MAY, 1908

LEFT TO RIGHT, STANDING: 1. HAROLD BAUER; 2. RACHMANINOV; 3. KROUGLIKOV, MUSIC CRITIC; SEATED: 4. CHALIAPINE; 5. MME. FÉLIA LITVINE; 6. SAINT-SAENS; 7. BLUMENFELD, CONDUCTOR, MARIENSKY THEATRE; 8. RIMSKY-KORSAKOV.

Much to our regret, we were obliged to omit from our performance the splendid scene in the tavern, as it requires artists of a calibre such as we were unable to procure, rich as Russia is in persons of artistic gifts. In my youth I have more than once played the rôles of both Boris and Varlaam in one evening, but did not venture to do so in Paris. I looked on this first operatic performance in Paris as a test of our Russian capacity and originality in the field of art, a test which we were to undergo before the eyes of all Europe. We had come through the ordeal with flying colours.

Altogether, we staged "Boris" some ten times in Paris, but did not present any other operas there at that time.

* * * * *

A new director of the Milan theatre, Signor Mingardi, a charming man, approached me with a proposal to stage "Boris Godounov" at La Scala. As I knew fairly well what were the tastes of the Italian public, I thought that an Italian audience would not care for Moussorgsky, and told the director of my opinion; but he appeared to have weighed the matter well, and said:

"I am an Italian and the opera has produced a profound impression upon me, so why should you think that other Italians will not like it?"

I liked Milan and its sensitive, critical audiences, and was therefore very willing to sing again at La Scala. At Paris, however, we had sung the opera entirely in Russian, while the director of La Scala wished to make use of his own Italian artists and chorus. That meant that I should have to sing in Italian also. No translation of the opera in Italian existed, but the director told me that if I would consent to sing he would at once arrange for a translation to be made by some one who knew both Russian and Italian well and who had already declared his willingness to undertake the work. I consented, though I was doubtful whether it could all be arranged, and fully anticipated that the Milanese would very shortly inform me that they could not present such a "barbarous" opera!

On my return to Russia, I found that the administration of La Scala had already requested Golovin to supply designs for the scenery; and I speedily received a score with a translation into Italian, which, however, was very badly done: certain rhythms in the music had been altered; notes had been added, and other notes removed. This was inadmissible.

I requested Drigo, the conductor of the Petersburg Imperial Ballet, to assist me in correcting the translation. He consented, and between us we succeeded in making a new and fairly satisfactory translation.

Almost the first person to meet me on arrival in Milan was the good old porter Giovanni. He greeted me very warmly, and poured forth a torrent of congratulations on my success in Paris, saying that he had taken an interest in "Boris Godounov" ever since the summer.

The rehearsals began. The orchestral conductor was Vitali, a man about thirty years of age, an excellent musician and conductor. He took me to the hall where the rehearsals were to take place, and asked me to show him about the tempo in certain parts of the score. When he began to play the score of the opera on the piano I was surprised at his insight and correct understanding of Moussorgsky's music. He expressed his delight at the beauty of the opera and the originality of its harmonies. It made me happy to perceive how deeply he was impressed with the great creation of our Russian genius.

During the rehearsals I had to act as stage manager and demonstrate and explain to the Italian artists and chorus much that was foreign and not easily comprehensible to them. They all paid the utmost attention to what I said. I felt, with triumph in my heart, that Russian art was conquering and charming these impressionable people.

There were many quaint incidents; for instance, the costumes of the police officials were made in accordance with the drawings which had been supplied from Russia, but their subordinates were attired like policemen of the present day; the *boyars* (nobles) looked like the highway robbers in Russian popular pictures; while the painting of the scenery was poor and reminded me of a Chromo, as is generally the case abroad. The orchestra, however, played divinely; it was like wax in the hands of the talented conductor and he made it do all that he wanted of it, as though it were inspired. I was astonished at the responsiveness of the musicions to the movements of his magical bâton.

The chorus also sang splendidly; but one cannot demand of an Italian chorus all that Russian choruses are expected to do, most of whose members, as I have said before, have been brought up from childhood on our church music. Almost all Italian chorus singers have other occupations in life as well; they are working people, sometimes small shopkeepers. They all love singing and are gifted by nature with good voices and an excellent ear for music. Many of them have aspirations towards an artistic career. Their voices are, so to say, brilliant; when it is necessary to sing with the full power of the voice, the effect is splendid; but it is difficult to get them to sing well in a minor key or with a piano or pianissimo effect. In order to obtain the proper effect of the prayer in Pimen's cell, it became necessary to place the chorus a long distance away behind the scenes and to conduct it by means of signals with an electric lamp, the switch of which was under the hand of the conductor in the orchestra. The result was very good. The voices of Pimen and Dimitry stood out clearly and distinctly, and the chorus was only just audible.

I cannot describe all that I went through on the day of the performance; I felt as though I were on hot coals. I feared what might be the behaviour of the fiery Italian audience if the opera did not please it. Certainly, I should have been sorry for my own sake if I had failed; but at this performance my own destinies were inseparably bound up with the début of Russian music and Russian opera in Italy, and I trembled when I thought of the significance of the occasion.

The orchestra began playing. More dead than alive, I listened from behind the scenes, unconscious of myself.

When the first scene ended there was a friendly outburst of applause and I grew easier in my mind. After that the opera went on more and more successfully. The dramatic qualities of the work held the keen interest of the Italians, and they listened to the end with the greatest attention, following the action closely.

I was ready to cry with happiness, and could not refrain from embracing several of the artists who had played with me. We were all as merry as children, and everyone, from the chorus and the musicians down to the carpenters, had a share in our triumph.

"How the all-conquering power of art unites us all!" was my reflection.

The doorkeeper Giovanni was as proud as though he had written "Boris Godounov" himself.

I played the opera eight times, and then went to Monte Carlo, whence I had to return on two separate occasions to Milan to satisfy the insistent demands of the public, who had become very much enamoured of Moussorgsky's opera.

*　　*　　*　　*　　*

The simpler the manner of one's acting is, the easier it appears to the spectator. Sometimes this apparent facility occasioned queer misunderstandings and amusing questions. Italian actors and singers said to me more than once:

"How simple and easy you appear on the stage, yet you use no gestures and poses prepared beforehand. On every occasion your acting is new and fresh. . . ."

A certain basso, C., who had a beautiful voice, and who took the part of Pimen, paid more attention than others to the methods of my acting. He was greatly taken with "Boris Godounov," and considered my acting of the title rôle to be very fine, but said:

"What a pity it is that Chaliapine has not as good a voice as I have! I can take not only upper G, but even A flat. If I were to take the part of Boris, I think I should do better with it than Chaliapine does. The acting is really not so very difficult, and I should certainly sing better!"

C. made no attempt to conceal his opinion even from me. He requested in very diplomatic fashion to be permitted to watch me when making up for "Boris," as he looked on that as the most difficult portion of the task. I made myself up in his presence and explained to him my method.

"Yes," said he, "it is not at all complicated, but one cannot get such paints in Italy, nor any good wigs, beards, or moustaches!"

After my last performance I took off my wig and beard, and moustache for the part of Boris, and handed them to him, also giving him my make-up box and telling him that I should gladly take off and give him my head, too, if I could!

He thanked me sincerely and was evidently much touched by my action. He seemed very much surprised that I would part with my wig, beard, and moustache so easily.

A year later I was again in Milan, and when walking one day along the Corso Vittorio Emanuele whom should

I see but C. running across the street towards me, regardless of the passing traffic.

"*Bon giorno, amico Chaliapine!*" he cried, kissing my hand so that he attracted the attention of the passers-by.

"Why the excitement?" I enquired when he had somewhat calmed down.

"Why?" cried he. "But because I understand now what an artist you are! I have played 'Boris' and made a hash of it! I am quite aware of how badly I acted the part. Everything which seemed so easy when you did it turned out to be appallingly difficult to put in practice. Make-up and wigs are only trifles, after all! It gives me pleasure to tell you, and I feel it my duty to let you know, what an artist I have found you to be!"

"Don't make so much noise," said I. "People are looking at us."

But he cried: "Never mind that! I must make confession that I did not know how to appreciate you! I love my art, and feel that I ought to kiss your hand!"

This was too much. But Italians are unrestrained when expressing their delight with anything. I was very much touched by C.'s praise.

In general I found the Italians wonderfully warmhearted and friendly.

I recollect another incident in Milan. When rehearsing Gounod's "Faust" I observed that the very fine prima donna who took the part of Margarita did not appear to have any idea of how she ought to behave on the stage. She was a very good singer but a poor actress. Choosing a convenient opportunity, I went to her and told her of this as gently as I could.

"Yes," she admitted regretfully, "I feel that I don't know how to act. What a pity it is that I am not better acquainted with you, or I would ask you to show me the rôle!"

I was very pleased, and stayed behind with her after the rehearsal and sang some numbers, demonstrating some of the scenes to her.

She took my advice to heart and the audience gave her a good reception at the performance, while the newspapers next day said unanimously that she acted her part in a new and original manner and with great success. She came to me next morning with a big bunch of flowers and wanted to thank me; but I told her that her excellent acting had more than sufficiently rewarded me for the little assistance I had rendered her.

I can say without boasting that many artists abroad asked me for my advice about their parts, and were even taught to some small extent by me. I was always sincerely pleased to help them to learn.

Things are rather different in Russia, unfortunately.

When "Boris Godounov" was staged at the Imperial Theatres, as I said before, I noticed at once that the artists were very cold and indifferent about their rôles. The part of Shouisky was sung by a fairly well-known tenor. He was young and had a good voice. He sang well, but his tonal colouring was not suited to the rôle and not characteristic of the personality he had to portray.

I ventured to remark to him that his singing was not suited to the personality of the cunning Prince Shouisky.

"I never thought of that," he confessed. Then I asked him to look on and listen to my interpretation of Prince Shouisky, and sang the part. He listened attentively, thanked me, and then repeated the phrases he had to sing, in considerably better style than before.

Other actors, however, had been watching us, and the result was that they at once gathered together in the foyer and began protesting that Chaliapine was not a stage manager, but only an artist like themselves, and that I had no right to demonstrate and to teach them. They came to the conclusion, finally, that I ought to be told about it, in order to teach me not to take upon myself the rights and duties of the stage manager. However, for some reason or other nothing was ever said to me, in spite of all the talk.

The attitude taken by the artists tied my hands. When I told the management of my objections to the manner in which the operas were staged and performed, I was told that I might try to put my ideas into practice myself.

When I asked, however, that I might be given absolute authority on the stage, the management put an end to the discussion, knowing very well that if such authority were granted me I would never permit the curtain to be raised until I was quite sure that whatever opera it happened to be would be performed in a really artistic manner.

It was determined to present the opera "Khovanstchina." At rehearsals I noticed that the artists sang the opera exactly as they would have done "Rigoletto" or "Madame Butterfly," or any other in which the dramatic action is of very little importance and the libretto insignificant, and which might, indeed, be sung without any words at all. That sort of performance may give an effect of gaiety, or tragedy, or may be merely tedious; but it will not do for an opera the text and the music of which are like Moussorgsky's.

I was unable to conceal my vexation, and told my fellow artists that if we sang the opera like that it would inevitably be a failure and would be so tedious that the audience would probably go to sleep. I then sang all the parts over as I considered they ought to be sung. This time I was believed and a friendly attention was paid to my words; even the chorus admitted that I was right. I was greatly encouraged. Heartening to my work, I carried through the rehearsal vigorously, giving particular relief to the finely delineated figure of Martha. Everything went well, and at the general rehearsal the opera not merely pleased the audience, but was a huge success. I was in a state of bliss, and recollect making a speech to the chorus with tears of joy in my eyes. I wound up by asking them to come with me to the Kasansky Cathedral to sing a memorial service for Moussorgsky. The chorus willingly consented to go, and sang splendidly when they got there; after which I carried wreaths to the cemetery for the graves of Moussorgsky and Stassov.

Having presented "Khovanstchina" so successfully in Petrograd, I was desirous of producing it in Moscow, but when I arrived in the old capital I found that the artists were alarmed by anticipations that I would demand the impossible of them. I requested the conductor to go over the score with me, which he agreed to do. It appeared to me that in order to secure a better dramatic effect, and a higher relief, it was desirable to make certain changes in the tempo. The conductor protested against any deviation from the composer's indications of time, but in the end fell in with my views. I should like to remark that I am, as a rule, very rigid in adhering to a composer's indications; but in this one instance I resolved on certain variations. When the orchestral rehearsal commenced, however, I noticed that the conductor was flourishing his bâton with a magnificent carelessness, and the dawn music was coarse and lacking in distinction. I drew the attention of the head of one of the higher musical schools, who happened to be sitting near me, to this, and he agreed with me that matters were going badly.

The chorus came on the stage and began singing all at sixes and sevens, in an indifferent, uninspired way. I said to them:

"Gentlemen, don't sing in that dispersed way; pay attention to the orchestra!"

From a remark made by the conductor I saw that he did not see eye to eye with me in my desire to make the mass scenes more alive. I said to him that the discord between the chorus and the orchestra was due to his not paying sufficient attention to the former.

"Oh, so you don't like the way I conduct," said he, put down his bâton, and walked off, leaving the orchestra with no one to lead it. Some of the artists applauded him, and I was hissed. The rehearsal came to a full stop.

I could have gone home, of course, as did the conductor, but the public performance of the opera would have been a fiasco. I knew the opera. What if I were to take up the conductor's bâton and attempt to continue the rehearsal? Perhaps, out of sympathy for the conductor, the musicians would begin to play false or would not play at all. There would only be more talk about Chaliapine making scenes, but there would be nothing gained for the work I had at heart.

This incident was immediately reported to Teliakovsky at Petrograd. He at once understood the situation and replied that he would send a very talented young conductor, whom I knew, to Moscow. One seldom finds anyone so noble and understanding as my dear director, Teliakovsky.

The conductor arrived next morning, and we began the dress rehearsal at noon. The public performance was to take place that evening. The rehearsal went well. Everyone was attentive; the singing was rhythmical. Somehow or other things went unusually smoothly. The newspapers were full of paragraphs about my despotic ways, my rudeness and ill breeding. It was not a very happy omen for the performance, which would call for great efforts, for of course it roused public sentiment against me.

In the evening, when I came on the stage, the audience seemed ominously silent. I had to conquer their ill will, which is not included in the aims of art as I understand them. However, when I sang the concluding phrase:

"Father, my heart is open to Thee,"

to the sound of the great church bell, the audience honoured me with a thunderous burst of applause. My latest "scandal" was forgotten.

To me singing is not a trifling business or a pastime, but the sacred work of my lifetime. But the majority of the public regards an artist in much the same way as that *izvoschick* with whom I once drove along an endless Moscow street. Our *izvoschicks*, like barbers, love talking to their patrons, particularly if these patrons are alone.

"What do you do, sir?" this man asked me.

"I sing, brother," I replied.

The *izvoschick* clucked to the horse and, grinning, went on:

"I'm not asking you that. We all sing sometimes. So do I, especially when I am drunk. But you don't understand. I asked you what you do."

I understood that to him singing was not work, so to satisfy him I told him that I had a lumber business, dealt in firewood and made coffins.

"Oh, well," he answered, "that I understand."

In my opinion, this wise and serious-minded cab driver expressed the views of a very large proportion of the public, to whom art is not work, but an amusement, which helps one to drive away boredom and kill time.

"You surely wouldn't mind singing four or five songs at our benefit for dead cats," a lady patroness for a charity concert once said to me. "It would only take you a quarter of an hour, besides the going and coming!"

"Excuse me, madame, but I need a holiday!"

"How silly! If I could sing, I would do so day and night without any holiday!"

So thought the lady patroness, who could speak five languages, and so thought the simple *izvoschick*.

CHAPTER TEN

*South America—I sing in a London Drawing-
Room — "Mefistofele" at Orange — My
Operatic Debut in London—English Hospitality—A Meeting With the King—Freedom in England—"Don Quixote"—Berlin
and Ex-Kaiser Wilhelm—August, 1914.*

IT WAS shortly after my return to Russia that I received an invitation to appear in South America. I was
far from wishing to undertake the voyage, but old Cecci, my
impresario, insisted that I go, refusing to abandon the idea,
although I intentionally imposed very severe conditions.
In May, therefore, I was on my way to Buenos Aires. The
voyage was remarkably quiet and pleasant. For eighteen
days the sea was as smooth as glass and we seemed to be
sailing over a mirror. When we crossed the equator, a *fête*
in honor of Neptune was held on board, and those who were
crossing the line for the first time got a ducking in the
ship's swimming pool. The proceedings were funny enough
to bring tears of laughter to one's eyes.

I was utterly enchanted by the wonderful port of Rio de
Janeiro, full as it was of such a vivid life, such variegated
beauty and brilliant holiday atmosphere.

When I arrived in Buenos Aires I noticed that work
seemed to be a pastime there and that life was easy and
gay. Everything reminded me of Europe; the numbers of
people of Latin race, Italians and Portuguese, Frenchmen
and Spaniards; also the architecture of the town, including
the fine newly built theatre. The staging and the performances were excellent, and the theatre was very popular.

271

On the 14th July, the great national holiday of France, a deputation came to me from the French colony with a proposal that I should sing the "Marseillaise" at the theatre. I was, naturally, very pleased to do so, and sang the splendid French patriotic song together with the chorus of the theatre. There was a soul-shaking tumult of applause, in which the representatives of all nations joined.

The French colony of Buenos Aires caused a medal to be struck in commemoration of the day and in my honour, and presented it to me.

I voyaged homewards on an English steamer. An old French actor friend of mine, who was accompanying me as companion and secretary, met with a misfortune just as we were leaving. Our vessel was casting off from the dock at Buenos Aires and he was waving farewells to his friends ashore, when all at once he turned pale and cried:

"*Ça y est!* I have been robbed!"

The poor fellow had been in the habit of carrying his lifetime's savings in his hip pocket. They amounted to about 14,000 francs. As he had been paying all my expenses and disbursements out of this pocket, thieves had evidently observed that he kept his money there, and they probably expected to get all my earnings, too. The unfortunate Frenchman was so much upset at his loss that I feared he would lose his reason or jump overboard. I reimbursed him his 14,000 francs, and thus restored the poor fellow to his normal equilibrium.

Our steamer stopped at St. Vincent in the Madeira Isles —I think it was for coal. The sun was setting and the air was still as we approached this island, which rises treeless and bare from the sea like a gigantic meteor fallen from the clouds. I had been told that the whole place boasted of but one single living tree, which the natives worshipped as a sacred object. My curiosity was sufficiently aroused to wish to see it, and so pushed off from our steamer in a small boat.

I found the tree, which was grey, stone-coloured, and of poor growth. Looking over the bleak island, I remembered my own country as something far away. I sighed and softly began to sing a sad song, which was popular in Russia. It seemed strange, but after a few moments, natives, coal black and absolutely nude, gathered around to listen to my singing. Such an attention touched me and I purposely repeated the last verse of the song, to make it longer. When I finished, these black people opened their black mouths, ornamented with rows of dazzlingly white teeth, and began gargling words that, according to intonation and expression of face, sounded much more like "Bravo!" than "Go to h——l!"

"What power lies in the human voice!" I thought. "Even these black people feel it!"

As if to prolong their expressions of admiration, they escorted me back to the little boat.

Some of them came out to our steamer in their own primitive crafts, loudly appealing to us to throw coins into the water, as the boys do in the Bay of Naples. Then they plunged into the blue waves, catching the coins as they sank, with the same adroitness with which I have seen Neapolitans perform the same feat.

At Madeira, we of course tasted the famous wine of the country and also drove about the stony streets of the town on sledges, which are used there instead of wheeled conveyances. This reminded me of some parts of the province of Viatka, where people use sledges both in winter and in summer, owing to the marshy character of the land.

* * * * *

At length England began to take an interest in my successes. I received repeated offers to sing at Covent Garden opera house, but for various reasons always put off going to London.

I was spending the summer in the country, fishing, swimming, and hunting, in expectation of going in about a fortnight's time to Orange in the south of France, where Raoul Gunsburg intended arranging a series of performances in the open air, in the ruins of the ancient Roman theatre. Quite unexpectedly, a telegram came to me from London. It was from an enormously wealthy American lady, who wished me to come to London for one evening to sing a few ballads in her drawing-room! As she did not know where I was, she had telegraphed to me at several different addresses, and I received one copy after another of the telegram, sent on first of all by the management of the Imperial Theatres, then by two different acquaintances.

The idea of going to London for a single evening was too eccentric for me, and I therefore wired in reply, asking for terms which seemed to me to be incredible that the lady could accept; but the result was not what I hoped for: she replied immediately, accepting my terms, and thus I was obliged to go to London.

On my arrival I engaged a small room with an oval window, on one of the upper floors of a many-storeyed hotel. From my window I was able to see Westminster Abbey, the Tower, a bridge over the Thames, and rows of stone-fronted buildings. Many of the buildings had an air of having been built to endure for ages. The city gave me an impression of being fast-rooted in the soil, and seemed to frown a little with a sullen strength, while yet inspiring the newcomer with courage to meet the future.

Next day I went to see the American lady at a very fine house in the midst of a beautiful park. Young in face, although grey-haired, my hostess reminded me very strongly of the portraits of Catherine the Great. There were two

MEPHISTO IN GOUNOD'S "FAUST"

or three other ladies in the drawing-room. I was offered tea, and we began to converse in French. It soon became evident to me that the fair American was very anxious to ascertain whether I was capable of justifying the fee I had demanded. She hinted repeatedly that she would like to hear me immediately. To set her mind at ease, I sat down at the piano and sang to my own accompaniment. She was evidently well pleased. The next day I came again with my accompanist. We were received by a resplendent major-domo, who ushered us into a small room which looked on to the garden in which the trees were abundantly orna-mented with Japanese lanterns of various hues. We could hear a hum of many voices and the trilling of a nightingale. It was strange to hear the nightingale singing undeterred by the large gathering and in spite of the inappropriateness of the midsummer season.

The butler brought us tea, and I asked him if the nightin-gale was caged. He told us, however, in atrocious French, that as a matter of fact the supposed nightingale was an artist, who sat on a branch of one of the trees and imitated the "immortal bird," for which he would receive ten pounds at the end of the evening.

I most fervently hoped that I should not be asked to sit in a tree and sing! Fortunately, nothing of the kind was requested of me. I sang a number of Russian ballads in my native tongue and was encored many times. Afterwards, my hostess invited me to stay for a buffet supper, a most informal affair, during which some stood and others sat. Everyone chatted gaily and I felt myself an honoured guest.

At the American lady's house I met again Lady de Grey, later the Marchioness of Ripon. I had first seen this sweet, beautiful, and charming creature at Monte Carlo. Now, on our meeting a second time, she was delightful to me and asked me with the greatest cordiality to come and see her. When I called upon her she urged me to sing at Covent Garden, and also told me that the Queen wished to hear me and had already spoken to her of her desire to summon me to Windsor. Contrary to all rules of etiquette, although a date was set, I was regretfully forced to decline this honour, for a telegram came from Orange informing me that rehearsals were being delayed by my protracted absence. I made my excuses to Lady de Grey and set out for Paris, whence I travelled to Orange in the company of Monsieur Colonne.

At Orange I met Paul Mounet, whose truly French wit and gaiety at once awoke my sympathies. At his suggestion we went to lunch at a restaurant.

When Mounet was terminating his university career he distinguished himself by an excellent oration on the harmful effects of alcohol. During lunch, however, he ordered one wine after another, till I felt that their abundance was beginning to overwhelm me. Mounet drank more than I did, and appeared to feel no ill effects from his potations. In reply to my protests he said:

"You must grow accustomed to wine. It is a necessity of life, and to an artist it is the nectar which awakens his inspiration."

"What about your oration on the harmfulness of alcohol?" I reminded him.

"I was young then, and, after all, an oration only advocates a theory, but life swallows up theories as Saturn did his children. I assure you that I would not undertake now to pronounce a dissertation on the harmfulness of wine, but should be very willing to speak in its favour."

Mounet impressed me by his acting when on the stage quite as favourably as he did in real life.

The performance at Orange has remained in my memory

as one of the profoundest impressions of my artistic career. It was a wonderful southern evening; the stars burned brightly in the dark blue sky, while the stone steps of the ancient amphitheatre were occupied by a numerous audience, glimmering like rows of bright-coloured spots in the light of the electric lamps. I stood high up, in a niche of the ruined walls, clad in the costume of Mephistopheles. I had climbed up to my perch, not without some risk of a fall, by means of hastily built and very shaky ladders and ropes. Now and again I could hear nocturnal birds calling and fluttering about.

The orchestra struck up; a cold beam of light fell upon me from a reflector.

"*Ave Signor!*" I sang. . . .

A strong wind was blowing, which carried my voice away from the audience. Changing my position, I went on singing, feeling the influence of my unusual surroundings.

Even though not very artistic, the performance had in it an element of the fantastic which pleased the audience a good deal. There was enthusiastic applause after the Prologue. I descended by the ladders and ropes into the arena, and bowed my acknowledgments, feeling the atmosphere of the stage about me once more.

* * * *

The time came at length for my appearance on the stage in London.

I went thither feeling that very much depended upon me; for I imagined that Russian music and opera would not be very comprehensible to English people. Although I had already visited London and had some knowledge of the town and its inhabitants, still, I had heard much about the hauteur of the English and their indifference to everything foreign. I was told that they looked on Russians as bar-

barians. Small wonder that I entertained fears as to the outcome of a series of Russian performances; but at the same time, what I had heard aroused in me the ambition to conquer the scepticism of the English about everything that was not English. Though doubtful of myself and my own powers, I believed unshakably in the greatness of Russian art and never lost my faith in it.

I came to London with a company formed by Diaghilev. Apart from rehearsals, my days were spent in viewing the metropolis, and I came to the conclusion that it would certainly require at the least three years to see all it contained. The British Museum, with its treasures gathered from all ages and climes, in particular aroused my admiration and astonishment. London as a whole, from the docks to Westminster Abbey, overwhelmed me with its greatness and solidity and a sense of the calm self-confidence of its populace.

I began once more to fear that the Londoners would not accept at its true worth our Russian music and our conception of the ethical meaning of life, which differs so much from that of the Briton!

I was wildly happy when thunderous applause and cries of "Bravo!" broke out after the first scene of "Boris Godounov." During the last act the performance became a veritable triumph for Russian art.

The last of our performances was even more triumphant. The audience unanimously called for and thanked everybody, beginning with the Beechams, and proceeding seriatim with the actors, the orchestra conductor, the stage manager, and the chorus. None were forgotten. A member of the audience made a splendid speech, to which my fellow actors asked me to reply for them, and in doing so I thanked London sincerely for the touching reception we had received.

It was a memorable evening, and there was a sincerity about the proceedings which warmed my heart.

"So much for the cold English," I reflected as I looked on the enthusiastic audience.

From the very first performance, the London public seemed to like me, and I am proud to say that charming society ladies and simple working people were equally good to me. I have been in a Prime Minister's drawing-room, and in the homes of orchestral musicians have drunk champagne in embassies and porter with theatrical carpenters; and I feel positive of what I say.

*   *   *   *   *

While in London I received many letters which I was unable to read owing to my ignorance of the English language. I recollect requesting a friend to translate for me such a letter, which had been lying about in my rooms for some time, and being much embarrassed to learn that it was from Mrs. Asquith, the wife of the Minister, and that it contained an invitation to lunch. I was just five days too late to accept the invitation. Courtesy required that I should apologise to Mrs. Asquith, which I did through the intermediation of some ladies who were acquainted with her. Their kind offices were successful, and she insisted on my lunching with her at a later opportunity.

I was much struck by the excellence of English domestic arrangements, and the comfort and simplicity which appeared to prevail everywhere. The more aristocratic the household, the more one is made to feel at one's ease. The English appear to have a peculiar inward conviction of the essential worthiness of every man, no matter who he may be. I dined and lunched so frequently at other people's houses that I felt myself under an obligation to give a dinner in return. After discussing my intention with some of my English friends, and obtaining their promise to assist me in carrying it out, I engaged an entire floor of a well-known restaurant. A lady of my acquaintance declared that she would undertake all the arrangements in connection with the dinner, so that I need only organise the dances, music, singing, and general entertainment of my guests.

The dinner was a formal function. Among my guests were many English people of high rank, besides many distinguished foreigners. A number of toasts were proposed in honour of art. As host of the evening, I had, of course, to reply. I overcame my diffidence somehow or other, and managed to say, although in the tones of one condemned to penal servitude for life, that art was beautiful, and so was England, too. Indeed, there were many beautiful things in the world, but the best of them all was the ladies, and that if there were no women there would be no art and no life, and very likely the universe would never have existed at all.

My remarks appeared to meet with approval.

After dinner Chuprinnikov's quartet sang, and my friend Arthur Rubinstein played. The quartet was very much liked by my guests. A young English lady of very high birth danced a Cossack dance, and did it very well, too.

I left London in a really happy frame of mind. The impression left upon me by the islanders was that, in spite of their businesslike seriousness and their high esteem for work, there is something wonderfully pleasant, childlike, and inexhaustibly cheerful in their character.

In the following year Diaghilev again assembled a company to appear in London, this time including "Khovanstchina," "Prince Igor," and "Pskovitianka," in the list of operas to be presented during the season. In the second opera I took two different rôles, those, namely, of Vladimir Galitzky and Konchak. His Majesty the King became interested in our performances, and came to hear "Boris

Godounov," which he applauded quite as warmly as did the rest of the audience. After the scene of the Vision, Beecham came in haste to my dressing room to tell me that the King wished to see me. I had to pass through the body of the theatre amongst the audience in order to reach the royal box. As I passed them, still wearing the costume and make-up of Tsar Boris as I had appeared in the scene of his madness, many of the audience rose from their seats to get a better view of me.

When I entered the royal box, the King rose, and there was a moment or so of silence, which made me feel very embarrassed. It appeared to me that His Majesty was shy of speaking, and I therefore made up my mind to be the first to open my lips, although to do so is prohibited by strict etiquette. I said that I was inexpressibly happy to have appeared on the stage in the presence of the ruler of so great a nation as the English. His Majesty told me very kindly what pleasure he had derived from the beautiful opera, and expressed surprise at the simplicity of my manner of acting the rôle. He smiled good-naturedly when telling me that he hoped it would not be the last time that he should see a Russian opera in London.

I afterwards heard from Beecham and others that His Majesty left the theatre very well pleased with the performance, and that he had requested that his thanks should be conveyed to all who had taken part in it.

On the occasion of my second visit to London, when I went to the orchestral rehearsal, the entire orchestra, including the conductor, were already in their places. I went on to the stage and came close to the footlights, and the conductor introduced me to the musicians, who welcomed me with applause.

As in other theatres, the musicians worked a fixed number

of hours per day. "The Maid of Pskov" was being rehearsed. I don't recollect whether we were delayed on account of some scenery or whether there was not a dispute
about something or other, but anyhow the rehearsal lasted
longer than it should have done. Four o'clock struck, and
the musicians were due to go home. Mr. Cooper, the conductor, told me that he intended to let the musicians go, and
proposed that I should sing without the orchestral accompaniment. This did not upset me at all. I knew my part,
and in reality was rehearsing only for the benefit of others.
I answered him from the stage, where I was standing, that
I was willing to do as he suggested. We spoke in Russian,
and none of the orchestra knew what we were saying, but the
musicians observed us, and when the conductor told the
orchestra that they might go, a grey-headed old violinist
rose and said something to him. The conductor explained to
me that the orchestra had guessed what was the matter and
had offered to finish the rehearsal. I was sincerely touched
by this conduct. We Russians are not used, in our own country, to such kindness, such a loving attitude to work, and
comprehension of its importance.

These pleasant, unassuming, jolly people gradually won
my sympathy and liking in ever-increasing measure. I grew
to be on very friendly terms indeed with many of them.
In my hours of leisure I used to invite one or the other of
them to take tea with me, and on one occasion I in my turn
was invited to the home of one of them. I went thither with
Mr. Cooper. The musician who was to be our host lived in
a comfortable little house in an unpretentious street. His
home, though poorly furnished, was yet very comfortable
and conveniently arranged, and was even not without a
certain elegance. Several other musicians came in, and they
played a quartet of Tschaikowsky's for us, and also one of

Borodin's compositions, executing both works very well indeed, and with great enthusiasm and love. Afterwards we drank tea and ate sandwiches, smoked and chatted, as far as we were able, all on a footing of the most friendly equality.

I have been all over Europe and have visited both North and South America. Everywhere I have seen liberty, but nowhere greater freedom than exists in England. The meetings in Hyde Park surprised me especially. One hears socialists and anarchists speechifying almost side by side. The crowd listens with equal attentiveness and respect to both of them. A Catholic defends religion with fiery zeal, and, not far away, an atheist deprecates all faith no less ardently. I was very much astonished at some of the speeches that were translated for me by my friends, and my Russian habits of thought made me involuntarily wonder what the police would have to say about it. At times I even felt like asking the park policeman how he could listen to such things unmoved!

The guardian of the law, however, listened to everything in majestic immobility. Before his very eyes orators consigned the British Empire to destruction while he twisted his moustaches and gazed with indulgent approval on pretty girls passing by. What an incredible phenomenon it seemed, that a policeman should be the free servant of a free democracy!

An English friend told me once, indicating a particularly fiery speaker:

"He is running down the police in general, and the English police in particular."

"But what will the police do?" said I.

"There they are."

Two policemen were listening to the orator, with their arms behind their backs, in the calmest way, as though the matter did not concern them in the least. It seemed as though they were weighing with due deliberation how much truth or falsehood there might be in what the speaker said.

When the meetings broke up, some of the audience would go away singing revolutionary songs, and others chanting church hymns. It made not the slightest difference. Old England will never be shaken down by the one or the other!

In Hyde Park people sit about on the grass, sometimes they even have their lunch there, although there are pathways and benches everywhere.

There were notices everywhere which said that the park was entrusted to the care of the public, and I could see for myself that no one touched the flowers in the beds.

I was walking in the street once when I heard a band playing the "Marseillaise." An enormous crowd of women approached, wearing ribbons over their shoulders and round their waists, and carrying baskets of flowers in their hands. Policemen walked at the sides of the procession, looking absurdly self-important, and some of them smoking their pipes. From time to time a woman would shout something or other, which I did not understand, and the whole crowd would take up her cry, completely drowning the music. Flags and banners of varied hues waved in a dense forest above the women's heads, and there were also a number of placards with inscriptions. The spectacle was very colourful and gay. A handsome girl went in front, beating a kettledrum. I stopped open-mouthed at the sight of all this. The young lady with the drum ran up to me and made as if to close my mouth with her drumstick, but instead of doing so, laughingly placed a flower in my buttonhole. I found out that this was a procession of suffragettes.

By night, when the streets grow empty and well-to-do people are in their homes, human wretchedness and misery show themselves in London, as they do in all cities. Silent, drink-sodden women with children in their arms make their appearance. Give such a woman a shilling, and she will go straight to the nearest bar with it. There are a great many drunken people in London; although one does not notice them except at nighttime, when they creep out of their lurking places.

The British Museum is a great and marvellous book of the world's culture, a book which is written in wonderfully plain and comprehensible characters.

When I left London I felt myself to be stronger and younger than when I came there, for the great city had inspired me with a new courage to face life.

*   *   *   *   *

It was during my next season at Monte Carlo that Henri Cain, the celebrated librettist and my very good friend, came to see me at the theatre in a state of the utmost excitement.

"Chaliapine," he said enthusiastically, "how would you like to play the part of Don Quixote? Massenet has an idea for an opera on the subject and he sent me to ask you what you think about it and if you would like to create the rôle. He says to tell you that he already has an ideal Dulcinea in Mlle. Lucy Arbell, and I would write the libretto. What do you say? *Cette idée te sourit?* See, my friend, I have even made a sketch of you in the part for your approval."

The idea fairly took my breath away. The thought that Massenet should have chosen a big Siberian bear like me to play Cervantes' immortal hero was an overwhelming honour. In a word, I was thrilled to the utmost.

"Nothing would delight me more," I said to Cain. "Particularly if you are to do the libretto."

Cain then showed me the sketch he had made. I looked at it a long time and then told him that while I liked it, indeed thought it very fine, I had still another idea for a sketch. Cain was very nice about this.

"All right," he said. "I don't want to hold you down to anything. The principal thing is that you consent to create the part. We will call the matter settled."

He went off to Massenet, leaving me the sketch and all the pleasures of keen anticipation.

Some two years later, in Paris, I received a letter from Massenet asking me to come to his home.

"I am not sure," he wrote, "but I think things have turned out well. At any rate, Henri Cain will call for you tomorrow at three. Come and listen and tell me your opinion."

At that time Massenet lived on one of the boulevards on the left bank of the Seine. He was already full of honours, an elderly man with grey hair and such eyes as I have never seen, before or since. It always seemed to me that when he went to bed he must take his eyes out and leave them all night standing in a bowl of oil, they were so lustrous and shining.

When Cain and I arrived, we first sat over tea and sandwiches for some time. Massenet showed me the proofs of his score fresh from the presses and still smelling of printer's ink, which he had just been correcting. Then he sat down at the piano and began to play.

From the very beginning the music touched me very deeply. Soon tears came to my eyes. By the time he reached the beginning of the last act I was sobbing so hard that Massenet stopped playing for a minute, looked at me, and exclaimed:

"Chaliapine, please, please! *Calme-toi!* Control yourself! Let me finish! Wait until the end and then you can have your cry!"

I did my best to keep down my feelings, but when he had played the last bars of the opera, in order to be as little of a nuisance as possible and at the same time in order to pull myself together, I asked permission to retire to another room, where I could be alone for a few minutes.

By degrees I grew calmer. When I came out, however, I was still too much under the spell of this work, so touchingly, so immortally beautiful, played by Massenet himself, in the sanctity of his own home, to be able to talk very much. Sometimes when the heart is full one simple gesture, a hand-clasp, an embrace, means more than the most elaborate flow of language. And just then my heart was too full for words.

"*Maître*," I said huskily, "permit me to embrace you!" Massenet understood.

There are many composers, of course, that I could mention who have written more profound music than Jules Massenet. Yet I must confess that I never remember being more intensely moved than by his interpretation of the score as he played it to me that day for the first time.

* * * * *

While at Monte Carlo, Raoul Gunsburg told us artists that we were invited to give a few performances in Berlin, and that I was to play "Mefistofele," "Don Carlos," and "Barbiere di Siviglia" there. I was nothing loath, as I had hitherto never sung in Germany, and I consequently went to Berlin with considerable curiosity to see that city. For some reason or other we travelled in a special train ordered by the magnificent Raoul. We could have done without it, of course, but Raoul Gunsburg had a certain tendency to throw money about in true Muscovite style, in which I am proud to trace the influence of Russian culture on a cosmopolitan! We travelled in great style, stopping at stations where luncheon and dinner had been ordered for us in advance by telegraph, and where the people from the neighbouring villages gathered to watch us eat, drink, sing, and even dance. There was a branch of the Monte Carlo casino in every coach of our train; we played cards, but the losers only had the cards rapped on their noses instead of paying up!

Germany seemed to me also a very interesting and cultured country, although it is true that one was conscious of a certain restraint and oppression there, which I have never observed in France or England. One too frequently saw the laconic announcement, *"Verboten,"* in the fatherland. From the very first day I was conscious that, unlike the neighbouring cultured countries, in Germany the conception of liberty is a purely philosophical one and is entirely subordinated to the conception of order. On our arrival in Berlin we undertook a series of rapid rehearsals of all the operas we were going to present in the Royal Theatre. Prohibitions of every kind hampered us, and our Italian and French comrades as well, but by putting our shoulders to the wheel all together we overcame the hindrances represented by the dread word, *"Verboten."*

The first opera to be presented was "Mefistofele." As usual, I was very nervous prior to appearing before an audience, and lighted a cigarette in my dressing room to tranquillise my nerves a little. A bearded, stony-looking fireman appeared, and said to me:

"Verboten."

I tried to convey to him by means of every sort of gesture that I *must* smoke. He declined to be convinced and made a long speech, of all of which I understood but the one word *"Straf."* "Well, let them fine me," I thought. "I shall smoke, all the same." The fireman went away frowning, and I got the idea, from what I could overhear going on outside the door of my room, that I should probably be arrested very shortly. Happily, Gunsburg made his appearance, and I asked him to petition the proper authorities for permission for me to smoke. The all-powerful Gunsburg arranged the matter for me. The fireman came again, this time carrying two pails of water which he placed one on each side of me, explaining that water possessed the remarkable property of extinguishing fire.

"*Ja wohl,*" said I.

He went out of my dressing room, evidently much relieved, but I could see him standing outside my door the whole of the evening, whenever I was not actually before the audience. I very much wanted to ask him to hold a fire extinguisher in his hand, but had not sufficient command of German to tell him so.

The public appeared to like everything we presented very much indeed, and the elegant and comfortable little Royal Theatre was quite full. The Ex-Kaiser, Wilhelm, was present, and it seemed as though he were the honoured guest of the audience.

"Mefistofele" very much surprised the German actors. Besides Barnai, whom I knew already as the stage manager of the Royal Dramatic Theatre, many other artists came to my dressing room and expressed their surprise at my acting opera as though it were drama. I received many wordy and ponderous compliments.

The Kaiser came to all our performances. He laughed so loudly during "The Barber of Seville" that he could be heard all over the theatre, hung over the edge of his box, and altogether behaved in a very free and easy manner, quite like a typical German university student. On our last evening we acted portions of various operas. I appeared in "Il Barbiere di Siviglia." The Kaiser sat in a box next to the stage, and during an *entr'acte* the Frenchman Renaud, who had played Mephistopheles in the "Damnation de Faust," Cooper, myself, and the stage manager, were all summoned to the Imperial presence.

Wilhelm was standing, resting his weight on his right foot and with one hand on the hilt of his sword. His features showed the traces of advancing years; there were deep wrinkles behind the fiercely twisted-up moustaches, and there was a good deal of grey in his hair. The whole aspect of the man and in particular his keen, grey-blue eyes spoke eloquently of an energetic and persevering nature.

"You are a Russian artist?" he said in French, turning to me.

"Yes," I said, "I am an artist of the Imperial Theatres."

"I am very pleased to see you here, and have been delighted by your unique talent. . . . I wish to give you something which will be a souvenir of our country and of our theatre. . . . Do you sing Wagner?"

"Only at concerts. I have not hitherto ventured on singing in his operas."

"What do you Russians think of him?"

I replied that he was greatly esteemed and beloved.

The Kaiser took from the hands of a tall man in evening dress a case containing the golden cross of the Prussian Eagle. He wanted to pin the order on my breast with his own hands, but not one of those present had a pin, although the Kaiserin and other ladies were in the box. With a smile, he therefore placed the order in my hands.

I felt embarrassed, standing there in the costume of Don Basilio. I was wearing a greasy cassock. My face was frightfully made up and I was adorned with a monstrous false nose. The serious tone of our conversation was absurdly ill suited to my costume and appearance. I felt it the more as I could see that everybody, including the Kaiser himself, could not refrain from smiling at sight of me. I was very glad when the interview was over.

Renaud, Cooper, and the orchestral conductor were also decorated with orders, and were naturally very much flattered by the distinction conferred on them, as was I. We resolved to celebrate the occasion fittingly, and a large party of us went to the Hotel Bristol, where I was staying. We pinned our orders on our dress coats, and went into the restaurant. The waiters, who hitherto had not paid any marked attention to us, now seemed to incline themselves before us with unusual humility, scraping their heels on the floor and gazing with respectful awe on our crosses. The *maître d'hôtel* informed us that there were excellent wines in the cellar, such as were only ordered on exceptional occasions. Perhaps we would like to try them? We hastened to state that we were always ready to drink good wine in all the circumstances of life. We drank, and congratulated one another in absurd speeches, some of which were so amusing that even the staid Germans in the restaurant could not forbear to smile.

The restaurant was empty and most of the lights were out by the time we made up our minds to separate and go to our beds. The wine had affected my legs, and I found myself under the necessity of hanging on to the door before I could get out of the room. But I clearly recall that the hour hand of the restaurant clock was pointing to four. I had totally forgotten the number of my room. Feeling incapable of going downstairs to the hotel porter and climbing up again, I resolved to open a door which appeared to be at least very like that of my room. I did so, and went in. . . .

Some unseen person in the darkness said something or other hoarsely in German. I asked, in surprise, what he was doing there, and requested him to go away, as I wished to sleep and did not require anything. The electric light came on suddenly and a baldish man with curls on his temples sprang out of bed. Stamping his bare feet on the floor, in nocturnal *déshabillé* and with eyes swollen with sleep, he shouted at me and clenched his fists; but when he noticed the cross on my breast he calmed down considerably and explained that I had made a mistake and that this was not my room.

He obligingly assisted me to reach the door again, and left me in the corridor, in which all the doors were exactly like my own. But I knew now that I should never find the right one. Accordingly, I went and sat on the staircase, where I speedily fell asleep, but was awakened before long by some men in green aprons who were manipulating various machines of diabolical aspect. I begged them to leave me in peace. They did not understand me, but appeared to regard with awe the gold cross on the facing of my dress coat. Recollecting that I had lost my way, I summoned up my entire German vocabulary, and at length succeeded in making them understand my position. They found my room and put me in it, and I slept the whole of the following day.

That is what comes of being presented with decorations!

I have received others, amongst them the cross of the French Legion of Honour, a star from the Emir of Bokhara, and also the fourteenth or sixteenth degree of the order of St. Stanislas from the Russian government.

* * * * *

In the summer of 1914, after a delightful visit to London, I went to Paris, with the intention of going on to Carlsbad for rest and a cure. I arrived in the "Ville Lumière" on July 25, 1914. Crowds of people were promenading the streets, eagerly devouring the telegrams posted up in the windows of the newspaper offices. At dinner that evening, at the house of a well-known banker, I asked my host whether there were any serious foundations for the rumours of war. He said confidently:

"There will not be war!"

This decisively expressed opinion set my mind at ease. I

felt no hesitation in leaving for Germany. But after two or three hours of travel our train stopped and we were told to get out, as it would go no farther. War had been declared. There were no trains returning to Paris. All horses were immediately requisitioned by the military authorities, and I was stranded with all my baggage at a little wayside station. The French people around me were all completely engrossed in their own affairs and were very serious. To facilitate my return to Paris, as I could get no train or carriage, I began to lighten my baggage. Opening my trunks, I gave away to the poor all my clothes and small articles, retaining only what was absolutely necessary. Small change disappeared from circulation in a moment. I had only banknotes of fifty and one hundred francs in my pocket, and no one would change them. When I went into a restaurant to get something to eat, the waiters refused to give any change for a fifty-franc note, so that I had perforce to leave it in payment for my meal. The same thing occurred more than once on my slow journey by road, afoot and sometimes in wheeled vehicles, back to Paris. It seemed to me rather stupid to throw away money in that fashion, and I more than once invited hungry-looking ill-dressed people, whom I happened to see in the street, to share my lunches and dinners. I used to pick up acquaintance with people like that and chat for a few minutes about the war, inviting them eventually to enter a restaurant with me. In the small provincial towns of France a dozen people can have dinner in a restaurant for one hundred francs, and so I used to ask my new friend to invite his acquaintances to join us. This was the only way in which I could entirely consume my one-hundred-franc notes.

I soon began to see that the French, whom so many people regarded as peculiarly boastful and frivolous, were fully conscious of the horror of war, although those I met discussed it with entire tranquillity. No one ever spoke of an easy victory over the Germans; all admitted that the war would be long and would call for the utmost efforts of the entire country. Paris was preoccupied and nervous. The streets were filled with crowds of noisy gesticulating folk; but when a German airplane passed over and dropped bombs and proclamations calling on Paris to surrender, the incident called forth nothing but witticisms and loud laughter.

"The German army is at the gates of Paris!" said the proclamations.

"Enter," said the Parisians, laughing.

When a motor-car tyre burst in the street and two ladies promptly went into hysterics, the crowd made fun of them. The merry Gallic spirit never faltered, though every hour threatened an attack of Zeppelins and a hail of bombs.

There was nothing for me to do in Paris, and for the first time in my life I was longing to get home to my native country. I went to Labolle in Brittany, and thence to Calais, with the object of crossing over to England. At the English office, however, where the steamer tickets were sold in Calais, I was asked what was my nationality, and when I said that I was a Russian I was told that they could not sell me a ticket, as that route was reserved exclusively for British subjects. It was impossible to go back to Paris, and there was no other route open except that *via* Dieppe, with which town communications might be stopped at any moment. I applied to the British consul for a permit to go to Dieppe, but my request was again refused. The consul told me that he had first of all to facilitate the transit of British subjects, and those of allied nations must come after.

It was only after representations from the British ambassador that the consul at Calais consented to give me a permit to travel to Dieppe *via* Paris. I accordingly returned to Paris, and travelled thence to Dieppe with the last train that went through; before the train started the railway officials entered the cars and advised the passengers to lie down on the floors in the event of German patrols coming in sight.

My Chinese servant, who had served as an interpreter in the Russo-Japanese war, took a tremendous interest in everything, bustling about and going on to the platform of the car, and keeping a sharp lookout on the sky and the countryside in the hope of seeing a German 'plane or patrol. I had two revolvers with me, of one of which he possessed himself, telling me in his broken Russian that the muzzle of a revolver was very effective!

When we reached Dieppe the town was as full of people as it would hold; there were people lying in the streets, on the ground, on piles of goods—in fact, everywhere. I saw a Belgian soldier at the railway station. Some Frenchmen were treating him to wine. He got rather drunk and was trying to talk gaily and make his auditors laugh. It must have cost him a great effort of will, for, in spite of his jests, I could see that his eyes were full of an expression of mingled awe and sorrow. Ragged and dirty as he was, just as he had come from the battlefield, his laughter, which seemed to conceal unshed tears, shook me entirely out of my composure. Looking on him, I began to understand what a tragedy was going on in the world, and realised the bitterness which must be felt by a man whose country had been seized on and violated.

No one was allowed to go on board the steamer by night, at Dieppe. In the morning the English sailors formed in two lines on the quay, and the passengers had to go between them, showing their passports. An official called out continually:

"British subjects first!"

If any foreigner attempted to pass before a British subject, he was stopped and sent back to the end of the queue, thus losing his turn.

In the same way, when the steamer reached the English port, the British subjects were the first to be allowed to go ashore.

I must say that I admired this attitude of Great Britain towards her own subjects. I dare say many Europeans found it very disagreeable to see thick-lipped coal-black negroes given the preference before themselves, but the negroes were British subjects, and that made all the difference.

My reception in England was very hospitable. My arrival happened to coincide with the Russian retirement from eastern Prussia. Everyone asked me who Samsonov was, and expressed much sympathy and concern. I knew nothing of him, however, and was equally ignorant of our defeat, as I had had no time recently to read the papers. I was conscious of the alarm which lay behind the questions that were addressed to me, although I but half comprehended them; and the uneasiness they induced in me made me long to get back to Russia as quickly as possible.

I was advised by my English friends to stop in England, in view of the dangers of the journey; but I resolved to go, and accordingly telegraphed to Russia for money.

When I received the remittance, an official of the English bank at which it was payable asked me if I wanted it in gold. I was surprised, for in France gold, and even silver, had long since disappeared from circulation. When I answered him in the affirmative, the official took a scoop and excavated from a drawer a quantity of gold coins, which he weighed on his scales, and then offered them to me. I wanted to count the coins, but he assured me with a smile that the amount, which was £250, would be sure to be correct.

I was very much struck by the good work done by the Boy

Scouts at Newhaven, London, and Glasgow. The boys came to every car of the trains to offer their assistance to foreign travellers. The attention they paid to one Jewish family was quite touching. They amused the children, who were in tears, reassured the distracted parents, joked and laughed, looked after their luggage, and did it all so adroitly and with so much humanity that it drew tears of admiration to my eyes. I felt again how many varied misfortunes war brings with it, and reflected once more what a wonderful nation the English were!

We reached Glasgow in the early hours of the morning, and went straight to the port, where we intended to take passage by an old Norwegian vessel, the *Sirius*, of only 1,000 tons, and built long and narrow, like a yacht. There was such a crowd on the wharf that it was clear the *Sirius* could not accommodate one half of the would-be passengers. Some one began to say that the old hulk would be sure to capsize and drown the lot of us, which caused the crowd to diminish appreciably, and in consequence I not only got on to the steamer, but even secured a berth in a very dirty and smelly cabin.

We started. It was the end of September and there was a good deal of fog. Owing to the small size of our vessel, everyone was very sick, especially as the weather was very rough during all the three days it took us to reach Bergen. Even some of the crew were seasick. The cabin was so disgustingly dirty, and the motion of the ship so unpleasant, that I felt I should be better up on deck. Masses of grey water rose and fell all around the little *Sirius*, and there was a continuous drizzle of rain. I went to the bow of the boat, over which waves broke every now and again, drenching me with spray in spite of my waterproof.

We reached Bergen, lying at the foot of great dreamy cliffs, early one morning. Stocky, powerful-looking Norwegians were at work in the harbour in the pouring rain, with their sleeves rolled up to their shoulders, showing their great sinewy arms. They worked as calmly, with unhurrying speed, as though there were no alarms anywhere in the world.

Next day I was in Christiania, which is a handsomer and more stirring town than Bergen. I inspected the beautiful theatre which was built in honour of Ibsen and Björnson, whose statues are in the neighbouring gardens. I reflected how many of our great Russians—Turgeniev, Dostoievsky, and Nekrassov, for instance, are still without their monuments. I visited the industrial exhibition which was then being held. The buildings were plain and uninteresting, but the arrangement of the exhibits was very good. Although I did not understand the inscriptions, I was able to comprehend every detail of the fishing and timber industries, not only as they are conducted at the present day, but also their gradual development from age to age. It was obvious to me from the very first that little Norway was a very advanced country.

Stockholm is livelier than Christiania. The people are more animated, and there is more colour in the town. There was a band playing in the gardens, and young people were walking about singing. At the railway station and on the quays there was a wonderfully good system in existence for aiding Russians returning to their country. Girls and women walked about with placards on which was written in Russian information as to the whereabouts of the Russian consulate and embassy, as to which steamers were going to Finland, and from which station one went to Torneo, the Russian border station at the head of the Gulf of Bothnia. It seemed as though the principal part of everybody's day's work, both of the general public and of the soldiers, was to assist Russians;

and everyone was very hearty and obliging in rendering us this help.

When I reached Torneo, the frontier, it was early morning. The sky wore grey trousers. There was no rain, but the dampness was oppressive. The weather was so cold and sad that—if I may be pardoned the expression—it was as though God, Himself, had a cold.

I went into a restaurant near the customhouse. It was so pleasant to enter a warm room.

"Coffee, please," I said to a blond Finnish girl who bounced about the room like a ball. In spite of the fact that everything outside was dark and dreary, this girl was singing something to herself. I noticed a word often repeated in her song. It sounded like "Aurrinka." I was longing to ask her the meaning of this "Aurrinka." At last I shyly said:

"Mademoiselle, what is the meaning of that ardent word 'Aurrinka?' "

"THE SUN," she answered.

CHAPTER ELEVEN

Russia in Wartime and Revolution—I Leave Home After Seven Years—En Route to England—London Once More!

BEFORE returning to Russia I had signed a contract to sing in America during 1915. The outbreak of the war put an end to this plan, and when I arrived in my country fate decreed that I was to remain there continuously for seven years.

In the early days of the war my heart was torn by what was going on at the front. When war is declared it is not the people who want it, but the leaders. I am for the people, always the people, regardless of religion or nationality, and —the people were being butchered.

What could I do to help? Little enough, alas! Bring what cheer and comfort I could with my singing to those who remained at home suffering the tortures of cruel anxiety, and help to raise funds to care for the sick and wounded that soon filled our hospitals to overflowing.

With the generous assistance of doctor friends I had the opportunity of establishing two tiny hospitals with about seventy beds. But the unfortunate seventy who occupied them were but as a drop of water in the ocean of victims, beyond the power of human reckoning, whose numbers increased as the dreadful carnage continued.

During one winter of the war I read in the papers about terrible attacks made by the Germans on the city of Warsaw in Poland. Shortly afterwards I went to Warsaw to give a concert for the sufferers in Poland. When I arrived I was asked if I would care to visit the trenches, and I was taken to the Forest of Sakontiansky, where the most horrible attack had been made. What I saw distressed me terribly and brought the horrors of war very near. Everywhere were evidences of destruction—trees torn up by the roots or shattered by flying shells, poor nature wrecked by the angry passions of men. Most tragic of all were the rows of newly made graves, hastily dug and, in some cases, marked only by rudely carved wooden crosses. On some of these crosses hung the caps of the dead who slept beneath.

Walking among them, I noticed a small object lying on the ground near one of these pitiful graves. When I stooped down and picked it up I found that it was a torn and blood-stained military service book. Opening it, I found these words: "His service completed with honour." Looking over this field of death, it' seemed to me that more than one of those whose lives had been sacrificed were entitled to such commendation.

* * * * *

During the war, we simple citizens imagined that communication between Russia and France, as well as between the other countries, was cut off by the battle line at the front. What was my surprise and pleasure to read one day in the newspapers that a visitor from France had arrived in Petrograd. This was Thomas, a French socialist, who had come with Viviani to address a political meeting. Although I have never been attached to any political party, I was glad to see representatives of the French nation in my country. A banquet for the two visitors was given at one of the smartest restaurants in the city, the French restaurant, Constant. The best that the times could afford in the way of food and wine was set before the guests. About two hundred people were present and there were many speeches. When Viviani, a highly gifted orator, had finished speaking, I was so thrilled by his eloquence that I went immediately to the platform and started to sing the "Marseillaise," accompanied by my dear friend Glazounov. Those present were so stirred by the French National Anthem that they began singing wildly with me, and the banquet hall rang with an overpowering volume of sound. I, myself, was almost in tears, so great was the excitement of the occasion and so moved was I by thoughts of my beloved France.

Yes, I love France. I love the French people, and all the more because this dear country has shown me hospitality and kindness during nearly twenty-five years. My heart is filled with pride and gratitude when I think of one among a thousand other gracious gestures made to me by France, when I remember that shortly after this banquet I was presented with the gold cross which made me an officer of the French Legion of Honor.

During the revolution this was one of the treasures in my house that I strove with all my might to preserve. From sheer necessity I was forced to sell all the gold I possessed for flour, sugar, and other indispensable commodities. All the other gold decorations and presents, one by one, were thus sacrificed. But still I kept the cross, and have it in my possession to this day!

It was long after midnight when the speeches were over, the singing voices were silent, and everyone started to go home. Some one offered me a carriage, but I refused, preferring to walk. In the street an icy wind wrapped me in a powerful embrace. Under my feet the glistening snow, tinged with the bluish light of dawn, crunched crisply. With every step it whispered more and more insistently the words —"Serrrvice. . . . Serrrvice. . . . Serrrvice. . . ." I remembered Warsaw; I remembered the Forest of Sakontiansky, the torn and bloodstained service book. And all the events of that evening faded into heavy mist through which appeared a vision of newly made graves with wooden crosses, crowned with soldiers' caps! "His service completed with honour!" Sighing wearily, I entered my own door.

* * * * *

In the spring of 1915, I arranged a performance for workers at the theatre in the Narodny Dom (People's House) at Petrograd. I wanted to bring a little colour and gaiety into the hard lives of the labouring masses in a difficult year, when public events were creating so much sadness.

Friends helped me to distribute tickets for the performance through the Sick Fund Offices at various factories and work centers. Everything was going smoothly, when a few days before the performance was to take place a catastrophe occurred on the Okhta, where part of a powder factory was blown up. There were many victims. The official account of the disaster was delayed, which increased the public alarm and consternation. The administration of People's House began to say that perhaps the performance was ill-timed. For my part, I considered that the unfortunate occurrence on the Okhta, by increasing the gloom felt by everyone because of the World War, made it all the more desirable that I should do whatever lay in my power to brighten the feelings of the masses.

On the day before the performance, the Gradonachalnik, or Governor of Petrograd, telephoned to me and suggested that I cancel the performance, as he had been informed that a disturbance had been planned to take place during the matinée.

In spite of a wholesome respect for his official position, I could not bring myself to believe that his information was accurate. I therefore asked for permission to go on with our schedule, assuring him that I had not the slightest fear of any unpleasant interruption. The official reiterated that the performance would certainly be broken up, and that the leaders of the disturbance would so contrive that all the blame would rest on my shoulders.

When I suggested that the performance be officially forbidden, since he was so positive that there would be disastrous results, he hinted that on top of the accident at the powder factory such an act would be received with very bad grace by the workers. Finally, after long-winded arguments, the Gradonachalnik decided to assume the responsibility of officially forbidding the performance.

Two hours later he sent me an official letter to this effect but couched in such terms that it actually appeared as if I and not the authorities had cancelled the matinée.

Our conversation had taken place at night and it was already two o'clock in the morning. Everyone in my household was greatly upset, particularly my secretary, Isai, who shook his head mournfully and said to me:

"When you die, Feodor Ivanovitch, the authorities will certainly be sincerely grateful to you."

This young man, by the way, Isai Grigorievitch Dvorischin, I had long known as a member of the chorus. Both at rehearsals and during performances he amused everyone whenever the spectre of boredom stalked behind the scenes. He was a genius at sensing the moods of those about him and, being a born jester, lost no opportunity of making the most of his talent for creating a cheerful atmosphere. I was often charmed by his jokes and anecdotes, and our friendship resulted in his becoming my private secretary.

But to return to our muttons. I respectfully informed the Gradonachalnik that my actual feelings did not coincide with the tone of his official letter, and that if he would not assume the blame for cancelling the matinée I certainly wished to carry out my original plan. Here the matter ended. It was by this time six o'clock in the morning and I was worn out with all this discussion and loss of sleep. I was convinced that my first appearance in opera before an audience of workers would be far less successful than I had hoped.

Before the performance, I noticed that most of my friends, including Isai, wore very brave faces but were secretly trembling as to what might occur. My own nerves were numb. I could think of nothing except how to play "Boris Godounov" as well as possible.

Everything went well. When I came on the stage, the audience of four thousand people greeted me in stony silence, but as soon as I had sung the opening phrases of the opera there was a burst of friendly applause. The audience applauded as one man, and I was much impressed by the single-heartedness of these simple working people.

During the *entr'acte* I experienced a reaction which was the natural result of the commotion I had undergone for the past twenty-four hours. In my dressing room I burst into tears from sheer nervousness. Afterwards I went on with the opera, singing easily and with a feeling of great exaltation. The workers were not stingy with applause and made me feel that their enthusiasm was whole-hearted and sincere. After the performance, Isai told me that the audience wished to see me without my make-up. I removed my wig, wiped the grease paint from my face, and appeared before the curtain to be greeted with cheers and cries of gratitude.

When I left the theatre two long lines of working people were at the stage door to escort me to the waiting motor, with more applause and expressions of appreciation.

* * * * *

As time went on, work in the theatres became more and more difficult. This can readily be understood. People's minds were not on the theatre. On every side rumours were rife and gossip rampant. For the most part one heard the names of Rasputin and of the Tsarina. People whispered of new and mystic ecclesiastical rites and of courtiers suspected of being spies.

On top of everything else, the throng in food lines, which had been established, grew in alarming numbers as provisions dwindled in proportion. Growing public discontent was fanned by exaggerated reports from the Douma. Soon public sentiment against the government ran so high that the food lines were broken up and men, women, and children stormed the provision shops. Any attempt to preserve order was met by the overturning of tramcars and the building of barricades. At the front a big victory was sorely needed to restore public confidence, but none came, and there were only small personal triumphs.

Then, one day, a bomb burst—the announcement was made that at a station called Dno, the Tsar had received a delegation from the Douma and signed a treaty of abdication.

The result was that everyone seemed happy. It was said that a bloodless revolution had taken place. I, too, was happy that since, as it seemed, a revolution had indeed taken place, no guillotine had been erected, no deputies had been carried through the streets in cages, there had been no slaughter and carnage—none of those things which made the French Revolution, according to historians, both hideous and picturesque. In fact, it was to me a rather pleasing sight to see everyone, men, women young and old, and children decked out with red ribbons.

But this state of affairs did not last long. One fine day the Palais de Justice was burned. Then the people began to war against the police. The army had no desire to put down the general disorder and soldiers marched to the Douma to declare themselves revolutionists.

It was not long before people came to me and asked me to give up my automobile. Soon general requisitions were in order. Some people lost their cars, others carriages and horses, silver, furniture, houses, everything conceivable in the way of personal property. Among those who suffered losses was Madame Kshessinska, a famous ballet dancer and one of the Tsar's favourite artists. Her beautiful house was taken for the purpose of holding meetings, and soon the fiery breath of revolution was blowing through every opening in its stately walls.

Finally the tempest of revolution, which was sweeping the river Neva, blew across to the Bay of Finland, and one fine day the armoured cruiser *Aurora* steamed into Petrograd.

On that very evening I was singing at the Narodny Dom, just across the river from the Tsar's palace. The opera was Verdi's "Don Carlos" and I was just singing the rôle of King Philip II of Spain. At the very moment in the opera when the prisoners condemned by the Inquisition were passing before the King and Queen, the walls of the theatre and my "prop" crown were shaken by the booming of a cannon. We knew something extraordinary had happened but were not sure just what was the nature of the disturbance.

I think that my poor subjects' first thought, in the panic that seized them, was to run away from me, from the stage, and from the theatre, and I was obliged to make use of a great deal of kingly power and authority to calm them.

"Subjects, my dear subjects," I exclaimed *sotto voce*, nervously taking off my crown, "surely you are not going to desert me in this horrible moment of kingly existence! Besides, what would be the use of running away? You could not escape from cannon shots in the dark."

And in spite of the cannon shots and great public disturbance, my subjects obeyed and remained with their king to finish the performance.

At last the opera was over, and with a companion, a lady, I left the theatre. We tried in vain to find a cab.

"Let us walk home," I suggested.

When we came out into the Kamennoi Ostrovsky Prospekt, we felt more than uncomfortable, for bullets were actually whistling around us. Then, certainly, I was frightened. In fact, I am such a brave man that I started running to save myself, while my companion, who was wearing a narrow skirt, became nauseated with fear. But I soon felt ashamed of displaying fear before a lady and slowed down to a normal pace. When we reached home I was whistling "La Donna e mobile!"

Little by little life became more and more difficult. It was as hard for me to get milk and bread—the bare necessities—as for the humblest workingman to provide food for his family. I was glad to sing for the reward of a bag of flour, a ham, some sugar. Sometimes, even, I received a little money, which had already become of very little value.

The health of our little Marina, always a delicate child, became seriously threatened from undernourishment, and I was grateful for the permission granted to send her out of the country in charge of an old friend.

As there was not sufficient fuel to heat the theatres, the musicians in the orchestra were often obliged to play in their overcoats, while we singers shivered on the stage, for performances of opera still went on, although certain works, such as "A Life for the Tsar" were discarded from the *répertoire*. The management of the period was kind enough to offer me an electric stove for my dressing room and, although I felt rather ashamed at the thought of others, not similarly provided for, who were suffering around me, I must confess that I did not refuse this opportunity for keeping warm.

Not being a great hunter of bullets, I stayed at home, in

KING PHILIP SECOND IN VERDI'S "DON CARLOS"

those days, more than I went out. However, it was of course necessary for me to go to the theatre for rehearsals and other matters as well as for performances. To do so I was obliged to walk the distance between my house and the Mariensky theatre, which amounted to five or six miles. I say walk because Freedom had no other means of transportation!

Sometimes one saw amusing sights in the streets. Freedom was advertised everywhere. The people had been told that everything belonged to them, and so the people of this free nation began to break into the wine cellars. In the larger ones, like the royal cellars, it was not uncommon to find a crowd literally drowning in wine.

Those in power, frightened by this people's holiday, sent patrols to break the bottles and throw the wine into the streets. Then the mob did not hesitate to stoop down and drink from the gutters! Seeing this, the patrols opened fire.

On one of my walks to the theatre I saw two men staggering towards me around a corner. They were hopelessly drunk, utterly care-free, and bawling revolutionary songs at the tops of their voices. Suddenly there was a shot. One fell. I immediately noticed blood on the snow.

"Petia, are you hurt?" mumbled the other man, staggering about in his efforts to stoop over his companion.

"No, I-I-I'm k-i-lled!" came the incoherent reply in a hoarse voice.

"Well, then, if that's the case," suggested the other, "le's go to the cemetery. Tha's the on'y place to find real life, nowadays!"

* * * * *

At the time when the Bolshevists took possession of Kronstadt, a deputation of soldiers and sailors came and asked me to give a concert for them. I consented immediately. Certain friends tried to influence me against it.

"This is dangerous," they said. "Perhaps even a trick. You will be killed for a bourgeois!"

But I was not at all afraid.

"Why should they kill me?" I argued. "I have not offended them. Perhaps my songs will calm their hatred."

I sang in a huge military riding school, crammed to suffocation with nearly fifteen thousand sailors, soldiers, engineers, stokers, and some women. Most of the men were grimy and unwashed. Among them sat my faithful Isaika. On one side of him sat an engineer who had either undergone an operation or been wounded in the revolution, for his throat was tightly bandaged and he could scarcely raise his voice. However, he had evidently attended concerts before, for he greeted the conclusion of every song with muffled cries of *"Bis! Bis!"*

The word in its French meaning was new to one of his neighbours, and there happens to be one in Russian closely resembling it but with a most uncomplimentary meaning. On the other side of this music lover was a toil-stained stoker, who grew visibly irritated. Presently he rolled up his sleeves in a belligerent manner and exclaimed in a loud voice:

"What the h——l do you mean by calling Chaliapine names? If you dare open your face again I'll break your jaw!"

With these words he proceeded to exhibit a fist more than equal to the task.

Now the word *"Bes"* in Ukrainian means "devil," and it was the idea that this term was being applied to me that so enraged this good friend. Some one near by, having overheard the rebuke and seeing trouble imminent, explained the mistake. The good stoker scratched his head and said to his neighbour:

"Excuse me, Tovaristch! That's what comes of being ignorant!"

When I left the place I was touched by the gratitude expressed by the crowd waiting outside the door. One old woman, in soiled and ragged clothing, came close up to me and looking at me intently, mumbled:

"Thank you! Thank you, darling Feodor Ivanovitch! How wonderful it is to see you, at last!"

* * * * *

So through all these seven years of horrible revolution the voice of music was never stilled. Perhaps this was because Russians cannot live without music. What had been art under the Tsars remained art under the Soviet. As for me, who had never played any part in politics but had consecrated my life to art, I was looked upon as a "*bayan*," our ancient Slavonic word for bard or singer.

Through it all, no threats of violence were ever directed against me nor against members of my household, although certain thrusts, figuratively speaking, were made at me by petty officials who suddenly found themselves in positions of authority, and certain requisitions were made upon my personal property.

For instance, one day soldiers came with an automobile truck and took away three hundred bottles of wine. Later on this wine turned up before my eyes in certain restaurants, marked, Specially sent for M. Chaliapine.

Some silver, which was at the bottom of a chest covered with hospital uniforms and bandages, shared the same fate as did quantities of packs of playing cards and—my revolver, a Webley-Scott. One of the communist soldiers held this weapon in his hands for a long time, turning it about in every direction and staring at the trade-mark. At last, scratching his head, he asked:

"What's that writing?"

"It's the trade-mark," I answered, "Webley-Scott."

"Biblia, Biblia—Biblia Scott," he mumbled. "Hey, you, over there, mark down that this revolver is a Bible make."

At one time during the revolution I was very ill with inflammatory rheumatism. For six weeks I suffered agonies of pain and was unable to leave my bed. Moreover, in addition to the physical torture I was undergoing, the thought of the hunger being endured by my family made me utterly wretched. At that time the slogan pasted everywhere was, "No work, no food!"

Can I look critically at life as I saw it during the years of the revolution? Certainly not. It is not for me to pronounce judgment as to who was right and who was wrong, for each day the revolution assumed broader proportions. Many parties developed. Soldiers, sailors, Menshevists, Bolshevists, strove against one another and shot at one another in the streets. In a word, there was civil war on a colossal scale.

* * * * *

As a result of these long years of war and revolution I had lost hope of ever getting out of Russia. Only in dreams, I saw, for example, the beauties of Switzerland. Sometimes I seemed to be standing on a balcony looking into the distance at delightful forest paths and the grandeur of the Alps. These visions were confusedly mingled with others that included tempting loaves of white bread!

The day came when it seemed to me an absolute necessity to get out of Russia and see if I had been forgotten. Of course, it was not so easy to procure a passport. I went to see the Soviet Commissioners, who were kind and gave me permission to go.

As is usually the case in every country, the big men were

kinder than the underlings. It was both amusing and disgusting when petty officials examined my stage costumes meticulously—for I intended taking them with me—feeling them all over to see if by chance I had not hidden some jewels in their folds.

I had a million rubles in my pocket on the evening of my departure, when I was informed that it would cost me several million rubles for the tickets. In despair, I went to see Lunacharsky, for whose help I shall always be grateful. He made it possible for me to travel in a special train with Litvinov and other Soviet Commissioners, who, it appeared, were on their way to Riga. And so, in August, 1921, I left my country in a coat, vest, and trousers that bore absolutely no relation to one another, taking with me only my theatrical costumes, my make-up, and my worn and patched dress suit for concerts.

When I got out of the train at Riga with Litvinov and the other Soviet officials, the newspaper correspondents and photographers who were on hand at once took me for a politician instead of an artist, a mistake, considering the circumstances of my arrival, which was easily understood.

But in Riga I very soon met artist friends, and almost immediately a manager asked me to give a concert. This proposition was very welcome because I was told by the Latvian bank that my rubles were worth only about seventeen or eighteen francs. The concert was a distinct success and I was given a great reception.

To be sure, there were some shouts from the gallery of: "Better go back to your blood suckers!"

But I had expected some sort of trouble or demonstration, and this disagreeable incident made very little impression.

As soon as the news of my singing got into the papers, telegrams and cables began to arrive from England and America, and even from China and Japan, offering me engagements. To fill some of them involved getting both English and America visas. I went first to the British consul, who said quite frankly:

"No. It is impossible."

"Why?" I asked.

"It is not my duty to tell you, sir," he replied.

I began to feel very much embarrassed about the matter. From the British consul I went to the American, expecting to receive the same answer. To my surprise and joy, the American consul said nothing, but merely cabled to Washington. Within five or six days, I had my visa for America.

I was much disappointed at the idea of not being able to go to London, for I was destitute of clothes and had been dreaming of ordering new suits, linen, and shoes. However, I resigned myself and began thinking about what boat I should sail on for America.

Suddenly, one day, I received word from a London manager that if I would sing at a reduced price for some charity league, he would arrange for my visa. I answered:

"All right, on condition that this charity shall be for the starving Russians."

My condition was accepted and I was happy at the thought of going back to that same London where just before the war I had been treated like a king!

And then, before going so far away—for from England I would continue across the Atlantic Ocean—I had a great longing to see my little daughter, who was resting and convalescing at the Huvenge Sanitarium at Helsingfors. The Finnish consul, to whom I applied, was a very kind man. He reminded me more of a Russian than a Finn and he spoke Russian perfectly. In fact, before the revolution he had been a lawyer in Moscow or Petrograd.

He explained to me that, as Russians were not allowed to land, it might be difficult for me to obtain a visa. He,

MOSCOW, 1921

however, promised to write to the proper department, and sent me away hoping for the best. I had seldom been in Finland and never farther than the Immatra waterfall, one of the principal sights of the country. At this time I not only wished to go there to see my little daughter towards whom the Finns had shown great kindness and hospitality, but to see at first hand how the country was thriving since its declaration of independence.

After several days the consul obtained permission for me to visit Helsingfors for one week. Then another complication arose. Since I was on my way to London, I of course wished to take my valet Nicolai with me. This the consul said might be impossible. There was nothing for me to do but start off alone, hoping for the best. Imagine my feelings of gratitude when, immediately upon my arrival at Helsingfors, I went to the Foreign Office, and there received the second kindness from the Finns—permission for Nicolai to join me!

In this world I have observed that everything goes according to convention. I was amused by the manner in which friends whose homes I had visited in Russia and who had been at my house greeted me hastily and then rushed off. It was as though they had said, "He is mixed up with the Bolshevists!"

All the same, I thought to myself:

"If already there is so much feeling shown here, what will happen to me when I go to England and America! No one will want to be seen speaking to me, but if anyone has anything to do with me at all I shall be asked to meet them in some *cabinet particulier*!"

No one asked me to give a concert in Finland, although I was available and would have been disposed to sing. And now, perhaps, fate will never again send me to that country.

I found my darling little Marina very happy and much

improved in health. We had great fun together playing at robbers in the woods and other exciting games invented on the spot. After a good visit with her I sailed for Hull.

On the way, the boat stopped at several ports, among others the delightful city of Copenhagen. We arrived about noon, and as we were not to leave until night I shaved, made myself as presentable as possible as to clothes, and, armed with my Soviet passport, started to go ashore. I had scarcely set foot on land when a very charming policeman stopped me with a gesture and said something in a language which was intelligible to me only by the intonation. When I showed him my passport he only made a face as though he had just swallowed a rotten oyster and gave me to understand that my presence on Danish soil was not desired. I felt most depressed, but pretended that I quite understood his attitude of: "No Bolshevists allowed!"

Retracing my steps, I went back on board our boat and sought consolation in the company of kind, good-natured Liza, who was in charge of the boat's bar and restaurant. Hoping to counteract the effects of this frosty reception, I asked her for a highball. Who knows how many times I might have repeated this request had not a man stepped on board at that moment asking for me.

"Here is M. Chaliapine, now," said Liza.

The man handed me an envelope which was marked, "Answer."

"Dear and great artist Chaliapine," said the letter, "we hear that you are passing through our city. Won't you give some of your profoundest admirers pleasure by dining with us?"

Many signatures followed. They were those of my eternal comrades, artists of every description—singers, actors, painters, sculptors, besides writers and critics.

"Many thanks, my dear friends," I wrote back. "I am

deeply touched by your invitation, but it is impossible for me to accept. I am not permitted to land because my official papers are not in sufficiently good standing. I have only a wolf's passport!"

To understand this joke, dear readers, you must know that the official paper given to convicts condemned to Siberia is known as "a wolf's passport."

It could not have been more than half an hour later when two gentlemen came on board, accompanied by two ladies. They were members of the Copenhagen Opera House and had come to carry me off! At six o'clock that evening we gathered for dinner in a large private room of a well-known restaurant. The table was beautifully decorated with flowers and fruit. Everyone was in evening dress and I had to excuse myself for my worn and mismated clothes. At the sight of those well-dressed people and in the presence of oysters and champagne—oh, noble wine!—which was immediately opened, I began to feel a little ashamed. I remembered many people in Russia who could not even afford to buy bread, and who were dying of starvation.

Still, surrounded by artist comrades and charmed by their cordial welcome, I forgot, for the moment, all the pain that lay behind me. Much time has passed since that evening, but expressions of true affection in tragic moments are so rare that when experienced they can never be forgotten. The memory of this occasion has been with me ever since, and my eternal thanks go out to my dear friends in Copenhagen.

It was not till one or two years later that I sang in concert at Copenhagen, and then it was not only my friends the artists, but the general public who gave me the heartiest of welcomes.

* * * * *

The morning after this marvellous dinner I said good-bye to my kind friends and started for Hull. When the boat arrived the first person I saw on the pier was my dear little Fred Gaisberg, one of the oldest officers of the London Gramophone Company and a real friend to artists.

I was happy as I stepped off the gangplank. What a joy to be on English soil once more! Dear country! Dear British oak! After I had been photographed for various newspapers and answered the reporters' many questions, Gaisberg and I got into the train and that very evening I was walking about the streets of London. The last time I had been in London was in 1914, before the war. Now it was 1921. How many years had passed! How much blood had been spilled!

"I have taken a small furnished flat for you on St. Jermyn Street, because I knew you could not stand very heavy expenses just now," said the ever-thoughtful Gaisberg.

When I reached my quarters I found them clean and comfortable. There was a huge tin bathtub in the bathroom. What a pleasure it was to splash about like a whale!

Having bathed and once more enjoyed the pleasure of English ham and English ale, I prepared to sleep in a clean, soft English bed. As I sat on its edge I thought of former days in London. I had made many friends in all classes of society. Among them were aristocrats, simple musicians, stage hands. All these people had met me more than half-way. Tomorrow I should see some of them again after seven years of absolute silence! They could not have forgotten me, but already they might feel differently about me! On my night table lay the same book which had caused the Copenhagen policeman to refuse me entrance to the city.

What if tomorrow I should go to see the Duchess N. N.,

send up my card, and the butler should bring me back this message:

"Madame says, sir, that she is not at home, sir. In fact, she is never at home, sir!"

Suddenly I felt cold and plunged deeply into the blankets.

"No!" I said to myself. "I will pay no visits. If my old friends remember me, they will come to my concert at Albert Hall."

Having made this decision, I shut my eyes and began to think of the lakes and rivers of Russia where I used to fish. I thought of the fish that had looked at me with friendly or offended eyes! With the consoling reflection that in general the fish all respected me, I fell into a sound sleep.

In the morning—I think it was only ten o'clock and I was barely awake—there was a knock on my door. What was my surprise and joy when this arrival proved to be the first of many messengers bringing me flowers, fruit, and even champagne from those friends whom I had so stupidly decided not to call upon the night before. With the gifts came kind greetings and words of welcome. My charming friends had heard that I had taken a modest flat and felt it needed brightening.

Naturally I dressed quickly, ate a delicious apple, and— remembering my dear Paul Mounet—drank several glasses of sparkling champagne, although it was morning. Then I rushed to call upon my friends. I will never forget those visits, although long ago in Russia this custom was considered a stupid, bourgeois convention.

When I was shown into Duchess N.'s drawing-room I realised that all my qualms had been in vain.

"Chaliapine," said this charming English lady, "you gave my soul such joy as an artist when you were here in Russian operas, that I am not at all interested in whether you are a Bolshevist or not! I know you only as an artist!"

"And that, dear lady, is exactly what I am—only an artist. No matter what people may say or do, still—I am an artist. It is not nice to talk about oneself, but sometimes it is necessary, and so, I again repeat, I am an artist, I am a real artist."

There was no doubt about the feelings of the London public towards me. On the evening of my first concert, the car which had been loaned me could scarcely get through the crowd of private motors and public conveyances about Albert Hall. My dear English bobbies looked furious and had all they could do to keep order.

Inside, the great hall was packed from top to bottom. Again I saw men and women of distinction in evening dress, a sight to which the past seven years had made me feel unaccustomed. I felt a tremendous emotion sweep over me when I stepped out on the platform and the whole audience rose to its feet and greeted me with an ovation which lasted several minutes.

And when I began to sing, my voice rang out confidently in the great hall. I no longer felt that I had a wolf's passport in my pocket. I felt that my wings were free and that my songs could soar above the clouds. I felt myself neither Russian, nor Chinese, neither Bolshevist nor Menshevist, but once again—an artist!

CHAPTER TWELVE

*Return to America—My First Concert in
New York—"Boris" at the Metropolitan—
American Womanhood—Impressions and
Experiences During Subsequent American
Seasons—California—Christmas at Sing-Sing.*

REMEMBERING my visit to America in 1907,
I thought, involuntarily, of the Russian saying, "A
crow once shot at dreads every bush." Indeed it was with
this saying in mind that I at last stepped on board the steamship *Adriatic* and found myself once more on the way to
brave those haunts where, many years before, the gun had
been aimed at the "white" crow—Chaliapine!

Again I must say that I was evidently born with bourgeois tendencies (even in starving youth I loved cleanliness, comfort, and beauty, while to this day I much prefer
a bath in a shining porcelain tub to a dip in the surf), for
I greatly appreciated and was delighted to make the most
of all the modern comforts of the *Adriatic*, in every sense of
the word a first-class steamer.

Scarcely had I come on board when, strolling along the
deck, I met the composer Richard Strauss and the no less
interesting and delightful writer H. G. Wells. Not so
very long before this, Wells had been a guest at my home
in Petrograd and had done me the honour to say that amid
the horrors of the revolutionary desert my house seemed an
oasis.

It was a great pleasure to meet these two men and in general the voyage proved to be a real pleasure trip. Everyone
felt gay and light-hearted. We passed the time playing
games on deck and cards in the smoking room. A concert

for the benefit of the seamen and their families was the climax of the voyage. For this worthy cause Wells drew caricatures and I ventured to do the same, besides singing several times. Richard Strauss played the piano and was also good enough to act as accompanist for a German soprano and myself. Altogether this evening was one of the pleasantest memories of the voyage.

On a beautiful autumn evening we finally sailed into New York harbour and tied up alongside the pier. A number of Russians had come down to meet me and gave me a hearty welcome. Many of them I did not know.

No sooner had I stepped on shore than the gentlemen of the press, as before in 1907, began plying me with questions. Unfortunately, their chief preoccupation seemed to be concerning a matter in which I could be of little assistance to them—politics, Russian politics.

"Politics—?" I said. "To ask me about politics is as though you were to ask an Eskimo to give his views about a Beethoven sonata. The art and beauty of every nation— that I sing well and give always of my best—these are my only politics."

Alas! Hardly had I settled down in a mid-town hotel than I realised that I had caught a heavy cold, and when the doctors examined my throat they said I was suffering from a severe attack of laryngitis. It would be utterly impossible for me to give a concert within a few days, as had been planned. It was necessary to postpone this and other concerts and my illness lasted about six weeks.

Three times I hoped to be able to get through my New York concert and three times I was forced to put it off.

Finally the managers said:

"Another postponement is impossible. Either we must cancel this concert altogether, or you must somehow manage to sing."

"Alas!" I exclaimed after a moment's silence.

My managers went on to explain that, knowing the kindly feelings of the public towards me, they felt sure that if I would only agree to show myself on the stage and sing as best I could, everyone would be pleased.

"The New York public realizes that you are not well and, even if you cannot sing your best, this will not count against you," they argued.

It is impossible for any audience to know or understand what terrible suffering an artist undergoes when he has promised to sing and is not well. How often an artist appears to be perfectly happy when in reality his eyes are filled with tears! But tears would not help matters. Sing I must!

They said it was amusing when, in answer to my valet's consoling assurance:

"Never mind, Feodor Ivanovitch. God will help you!"

I fairly shrieked:

"God is not interested in the concert business!"

Then I put on my evening clothes and went to the Manhattan Opera House. How grateful I shall always be to you, my dear old friend, Anna Pavlowa! Your sympathy and understanding helped me through the terrible ordeal of that evening!

I sang, but not with my real voice, for that organ was utterly ill. In spite of this, the audience was more than friendly. When I first walked on to the stage I was deeply moved by the ovation which greeted me from a theatre crowded from top to bottom. I was ill, yet the audience understood and applauded me!

* * * * *

Among people who were introduced to me after the concert was the American manager, Morris Gest. Further acquaintance with him made me realise one of the finest things about America—the richness of the soil that forms the basis for the country's social life and relations. This soil is so fertile that any plant, northern or tropical, may grow in it. Here was an example for, in this fertile soil, this man with the tired face, wide-brimmed soft hat, and La Vallière tie had grown from a gamin selling newspapers in the streets into a theatrical power capable of bringing across the ocean interesting Russian productions, not alone for money, but to show a special form of art.

*   *   *   *   *

The day after my first concert I went to the little village of Jamesburg for a change of air. Then, somewhat improved in health, I returned to the gay city of New York to appear at the Metropolitan, for the Opera House, hearing I was in America, had asked me to give several performances.

I spent most of my time looking about the city and observing the changes that had taken place during my absence. I found New York had grown. In fact, it seemed half as large again. The activity in the streets had so increased that, to one watching the throngs on Fifth Avenue from a distance, people seemed to be actually embracing one another!

"How beautiful to see such brotherly love!" I reflected.

But, unfortunately, when I came quite close to the crowd, I saw that what I had imagined sentiment was mere necessity, the enforced proximity that reigns in the well-known box of sardines!

I avoided the Metropolitan Opera House as much as possible, because every time I saw it I remembered how I had been misunderstood and how my artistic sensibilities had been hurt there in the past.

Still, the time came for me to go to rehearsals of "Boris

Godounov," in which I was to appear for the first time before an American audience.

My dear old friend, Giulio Gatti-Casazza, who, as I have already said, was my impresario when I sang for the first time at La Scala, Milan, welcomed me heartily and kindly.

I had been warned that it was customary to invite the critics to attend the dress rehearsal at the Opera House. At first this idea disturbed me, but when the morning of the final rehearsal actually came, I was too preoccupied with matters on the stage to be conscious of the character of those who largely comprised the picked audience in the darkened auditorium.

At the close of the rehearsal, applause from the musicians in the orchestra cheered me, as did friendly expressions of admiration from the chosen company before whom the rehearsal had taken place.

At last, came the day of the performance, and I trembled with twin fears—that of a first appearance and that of the "white" crow.

I lived through that day, as I live through all others upon which I sing, preparing myself for the ordeal like any Toreador. (No doubt everyone knows that the Toreador undergoes special religious preparation before entering into mortal combat with the bull.)

To me, of course, the theatre is a shrine. I enter its doors as I would those of a temple, with little or no interest as to who may be in the audience.

So on this day I drank the usual two cups of coffee, dressed about six-thirty, prayed after my own fashion, and went to the Opera House. Of course, my dear, thoughtful, and understanding Gatti-Casazza, who knows my habits well, met me at the door.

"Hello, Chaliapine!" he said. "Don't be nervous! A

great audience is waiting for you and everyone is almost too thrilled and excited about hearing and seeing you again. Come; I have had Caruso's dressing room prepared for you."

With a friendly hug, he took me to—Caruso's room! Still another emotion!

"Just a little while ago," I thought, "he was in this room, perhaps as nervous as I, at the thought of the coming performance—Caruso, with his sunny nature, so full of life and health and gaiety. Now he is in his grave! No one will ever see him again in this theatre or in this room!"

Remembering the friend, the artist, an overwhelming desire came over me to write a few lines in memory of him and in his honour. Although I do not pretend to be a poet, I snatched a black pencil from the make-up table and wrote these lines on the wall:

> Today, with throbbing heart,
> I entered thy art's shrine,
> Oh, friend of many years!
> But thou didst not reply to my greeting.
> Snatched by cold death from sunny climes,
> Thou liest in the earth!
> My tears fell and,
> Seeing my grief,
> Thy Muse wept,
> Sharing my sorrow.

The overture started. At last came the Coronation scene. . . . To this day I do not know who crowned me —the composer, my comrades the artists, the chorus, the musicians, or the public. I only realised this—that on that evening I had indeed been crowned as an artist, at the Metropolitan Opera House!

*   *   *   *   *

BORIS GODOUNOV IN MOUSSORGSKY'S OPERA

I intended to relate before this that one of the first things to claim my attention on my second visit to America was American womanhood.

During my illness of the first few weeks many reporters called on me continuously, seeking interviews, a difficult problem for me, since I spoke no English and was alone.

Among these journalists was a young lady who came to see me with a Russian acquaintance. She spoke French well, which made it easy for me to talk with her, and I asked them both to stay for tea. Conversation soon took on a friendly tone and I did not hide my complaint that I was ill, utterly alone, and overwhelmed with letters and telephone messages, all requiring answers. To be sure, my friend Gaisberg had come with me to America, but now business called him back to London. What was to become of me?

I was both surprised and touched when this young lady offered to come to me for a few hours every day, to act as secretary and look after my letters, telephone calls, and engagements. I was still more astonished and moved when she absolutely refused to take a single penny for these services. It made all the deeper impression upon me, because everyone had told me that in America no one did anything from sentiment, but that everything was reckoned in dollars. When I saw the great care and pains taken by this young lady about my artistic life in America, I felt more and more gratified.

During my travels in the United States within the past five years I have met many charming and helpful American women but, first among them all I place this same young lady, Katharine Wright, now editing this book, who, out of sympathy and admiration for Russian art, learned the Russian language in seven months. On my return the following autumn, for another season, what was my surprise to have her greet me in my own tongue!

Meeting such an American woman and having so magnificent a welcome at the Metropolitan made me feel full of courage and enthusiasm for my work in America.

"Nothing very terrible can happen to me," I reflected, "for in America I have found true womanhood!"

In fact, I believe that in America woman holds the most important place. It was not without reason that later I devoted the first part of an article in a woman's magazine to the American mother.

Travelling over America from coast to coast, I have noticed that the education and moral stability of the country seems to depend wholly upon woman. Man in America works with his whole brain and all his muscles, but it is woman who directs this brain and controls these muscles.

Finally, I must say that a real American woman is a treasure and that on the broad plains of this country, so richly sown with corn and wheat, woman is a flower that never fades!

*   *   *   *   *

After finishing my engagements in America, I returned to Russia, stopping in London for one or two concerts. In June I again left Russia, this time taking with me members of my family.

I spent the summer at Bad Homburg, where my happiest occupation was playing with my little daughter, Dassia. If I had any worries, I forgot them all in the presence of this laughing little girl.

Before sailing for America once more, I made a concert tour of the Scandinavian countries, Norway, Sweden, and Denmark. Then came a long tour in the United States, which included both concerts and operatic performances.

America began to interest me more and more. I visited many cities, seeing them more thoroughly than most foreigners. The more I observed the manners and customs of American life the more I realised that in the United States much is accomplished and little said. This caused me to think rather sadly of my mother country, where exactly the reverse is true—little is accomplished, but there is much talking!

In America, too, I noticed that work is considered not only a necessity, but a pleasure. The more I travelled, admiring the strength and power of this wonderful country, the more I was convinced that work, work in which there is the spirit of coöperation, can alone make people rich and—although I cannot define happiness—perhaps happy.

Among other observations I was impressed by the striving of the American people towards the beautiful. An example of this is the striking fact that nearly every large American city has its own symphony orchestra. Anyone unfamiliar with American symphonic concerts can have no idea of how wonderfully this feature of the country's artistic life is carried on. I have listened with greatest pleasure to the symphony orchestras of Boston, Philadelphia, Cleveland, Detroit, Cincinnati, and New York.

Another remarkable fact—in America symphonic music not only lives in the halls consecrated to its service, but also in certain motion-picture theatres.

During this season, greedily anxious to study every form of American life, I went often to the theatre. The theatres themselves impressed me by their dazzling interiors, but I nearly always felt it a matter for regret that their exteriors were smothered by towering office buildings. Indeed, were it not for the electric signs and posters it seemed often impossible to realise that these were theatres.

Undoubtedly the most striking feature of the American stage consists in entertainments called *revues*, in which music, singing, dancing, and cleverly designed costumes are

adroitly combined.   These entertainments are elaborately,
even magnificently presented.   I confess an admiration for
these *revues*, for in them delightful and clever eccentric
comedians provide continuous amusement.   I think that the
most gifted comedians in the world are to be found in England and America.

On the other hand, my explorations of theatres, other than
those which house revues, revealed excellent acting, which
gave me great pleasure.

The American vaudeville theatres, too, are astonishing.
Tired working people crave amusement and in every city a
hundred theatres are waiting with open doors.   It is true
that the entertainment in these houses is not of a very lofty
nature, yet it wholly satisfies a tired audience.

Negro musical shows are another extraordinary American
touch.   Seeing a number of these, I was charmed not only
by the singing and dancing, but by the spontaneous attitude
of those on the stage towards their work, an attitude I
believed possible only with happy children, an attitude I
myself possessed when I was fifteen years old.

*   *   *   *   *

Among other engagements that season was one with the
Chicago Opera Company.   I will not discuss it here because
such impressions require special attention and will perhaps
find a place in a future book I hope to write about art, music,
and the drama.

I will only relate one curious incident.   When I first
found myself on the stage of the Auditorium theatre as
guest artist with the Chicago Opera Company, I fell a
prey to a curious illness.   For the first time in my life I
had hallucinations!   During an *entr'acte*, I noticed several
gentlemen walking about the stage, chatting with this one
and that.   They wore immaculate evening clothes with

stiffly starched shirts, and carried high hats. Suddenly the tails of their dress coats seemed to move as though by their own volition. Horrors! Looking closer, I saw that these imposing personages actually had, not very big, but quite furry—tails! On their foreheads horns were plainly visible. Their footsteps made a special sound. Hooves—in their shoes! Gasping for breath, I asked a stage hand:

"W-h-o are those gentlemen over there?"

"Why Monsieur Chaliapine," he answered, "they are very important people in the theatre!"

I have sung in many theatres all over the world and had many strange illnesses, but never such a droll and original malady as this. Thank God, it did not last long!

$$* \quad * \quad * \quad * \quad *$$

While my headquarters were in Chicago I learned that I had been booked for a concert in Milwaukee. As this city was only a few hours distant, I determined to make the trip by motor, to the great disgust of both my manager and my accompanist, who were convinced that in this wintry weather the bad condition of the roads threatened an accident to the car. I would be late in arriving, they gloomily informed me, if, indeed, I arrived at all. However, I reminded them that I had often taken such risks, and that up to the present time travel by motor had never caused me to miss an engagement.

So a car was engaged and I started out for Milwaukee at two o'clock on the day of the concert, proposing to make the return trip in the same fashion, immediately after finishing the program. The day was clear, the country buried in a glistening blanket of snow, the air crisp and invigorating. I was warmly dressed and, further, weighed down with rugs, while my feet rested upon a heater mercifully provided by the motor company. I was in excellent spirits and happy at making the trip under such pleasant conditions instead of seated in a stuffy train.

We stopped at a grocery store in Racine to buy fruit and sandwiches, which with a thermos filled with hot coffee provided us with all the makings of a picnic. Although a hardy young native, my chauffeur appeared to think I had taken leave of my senses in planning this drive at such a season of the year. Still, he drove manfully ahead. The condition of the roads prevented much being accomplished in the way of speed, and the time calculated in which to accomplish the trip grew into twice the number of hours. My good spirits lasted until the early twilight deepened into utter darkness. The cold increased. There was no sign of Milwaukee. To my repeated enquiries as to when we would arrive the chauffeur gave evasive answers.

Six o'clock came, then seven, seven-thirty, and still no signs of the city. Finally at a quarter to eight the lights of Milwaukee came into view and better roads permitted increased speed. The car drove up to the hotel where I was to put on my evening clothes. Fortunately, the theatre was only a few blocks away. Tired and stiff from sitting so long in the intense cold, I ordered tea and that splendid American dish, apple pie! Then I dressed as quickly as possible. At this Milwaukee hotel I encountered unusual hospitality. The management absolutely refused to accept the slightest remuneration for the luxurious suite placed at my disposal!

After the concert, to save time and make the earliest possible start, I changed into travelling clothes in my dressing room at the theatre. When we started back I felt tired and pensive. It was bitterly cold as we sped along, past lakes and wooden houses that loomed dark and forbidding in the shadows of night. From these houses winked occasional lights. I thought perhaps that their fitful flames shone upon refugees or emigrants. This brought thoughts of Russia, its forests, its steppes and—its wolves!   I began telling my companions stories of how once, in the wilds of the steppes, my sleigh had been followed by wolves and my dogs torn to pieces!

What if we should be set upon by a pack of hungry wolves or—held up by bandits!   Only that week there had been accounts in the Chicago newspapers of hold-ups that had taken place on this very road!

I had barely reached the climax of my story and my companions still sat open-mouthed, when there was the sound of whirring wheels.   It was a motorcycle.

"Voilà!" I thought.   "This is most certainly a hold-up!"

All our money was hidden in one corner of the automobile, so that in case we were searched nothing would be found on us.

An electric torch flashed in the face of the chauffeur. He stopped at once.

After a few minutes' parleying the car sped on again. Mystery!

Not fifteen minutes later the same incident was repeated.

This time, furious at the delay, I got ready for action.

"Please do nothing," some one whispered.   "I beg of you, don't attempt to talk!"

A minute later the door of the car was opened and a figure, so muffled that it was impossible to guess whether the stranger was highwayman or police officer, flashed an electric torch in our faces.

"Are you the Racine chief of police?" the intruder asked me gruffly.

Since my fur cap and heavy winter overcoat gave me a rather military appearance, I decided to trust to luck.

"Yes," I answered in the same brusque manner.

"All right then, go ahead!" was the reply.

To this day the identity of the two motorcyclists remains an unsolved riddle. Bandits or policemen, we never knew. When we reached the hotel the chauffeur said that to the best of his belief, the two men were additions to the regular police force, specially engaged to guard the region where the recent hold-ups had occurred. If his surmise was correct, how fortunate that neither policeman had asked me to show a badge of office! Lengthy explanations might have been required!

* * * * *

It was in Chicago that I had certain significant encounters with the press. The first instance consisted in a flamboyant and utterly false article alleging my exaggerated attentions to a certain lady, a member of the cast of "Mefistofele." According to the newspaper report a friend of hers, a basso, also a fellow member of the Chicago Civic Opera Company, had succumbed to an attack of jealous rage.

The second incident was more amusing.

My manager took me to visit a certain Chicago newspaper office. The representative of the paper, who greeted us in shirt sleeves and trousers, appeared very much embarrassed.

"Pleased to meet you," he stammered. "Didn't you come from Czecho-Slovakia? What do you do, and how did you happen to come here?"

My manager appeared most upset, probably because he had informed me that this celebrated paper very much wished to make my acquaintance.

"Pardon me," I answered. "I am not from Czecho-Slovakia, but from Russia! And," I think I continued, in a soprano voice, "I sing."

"Oh!" was the reply. "In which operas?"

To save the situation my manager hurriedly stated that

M. Chaliapine was very much interested in American newspapers, whereupon the gentleman, becoming exceedingly
amiable, showed us through the building and revealed several secrets of the art of printing.

The third incident was less amusing. I had been showing
a certain member of the Chicago Opera Company my ideas
of how Shouisky should behave in his scene with Boris
Godounov in the Tsar's palace. Those who have seen the
opera will remember that Godounov is highly overwrought
in this scene and that his treatment of Shouisky is far from
gentle.

Well, as ill luck would have it, some one unversed in
matters operatic, not realising that all this manhandling
and cursing was mere play acting and part of a rehearsal,
spread the report that I had engaged in a quarrel in the
course of which a certain gentleman had broken my nose.
Newspapers throughout the country carried the incident
with flamboyant headlines. Armies of partisans sprang up
for each side. The incident was cabled to Europe. Even
my faithful Isai sent me a message asking for the truth.

I replied that if the report of a certain gentleman's having
broken my nose was not followed the next day by news of
a funeral he might rest assured that the story was untrue.

However, it is all very well to say that my spine is too
hard to break, but with such jokes as these one may be very
deeply buried, and I feel sure that among the printing
presses lies the possibility for deeper thinking. As such
things have happened to me only in Chicago, I am obliged
to conclude that the newspapers of that city have a special
psychology!

* * * * *

Amongst the cities that I visited that season was Cincinnati, where delightful hospitality was shown me by Mr.

Lucien Wulsin. This young man, an admirable example of what a cultivated American gentleman may be, spoke French as well as he did English and had travelled extensively abroad. He had even been in Russia. He is the son of an unusually good and sweet American mother, and you will remember, my dear readers, what I have already said concerning American women! He is also the husband of a beautiful and charming American lady and the father of several charming children. His household afforded me the opportunity of observing American family life at its best. Nothing was left undone by these kind friends that could possibly have contributed to my pleasure and entertainment, including a dinner at their home, luncheon at the country club, and an amusing stag party at a well-known man's club of the city. I only wish I could remember that song we sang in which the words, "Bulldog, bulldog, bulldog!" occurred so often.

It was in Cincinnati, too, that I first visited a cafeteria, where I greatly enjoyed carrying my own tray and making selections from the various eatables displayed on well-stocked counters.

* * * * *

My first trip to California was something of an ordeal to face, considering my restless nature, love of walking, and the discomforts I habitually suffer in overheated trains.

On this occasion, however, train life resolved itself into a pleasant enough routine. I had my morning coffee and grapefruit in my drawing-room and rose late, making my first appearance in the dining car about the time when other travellers were finishing their luncheon. There I sat for a long time after the car was empty, watching the scenery. The changing light, the rugged grandeur of the mountains, the adobe houses, now and then an Indian on horseback, a solitary figure against the horizon—everything interested me.

Finally, tired of peering out of the window, I used to return to my drawing-room to play solitaire for hours. This occupation would be interrupted by dinner. Then I would get rid of the long evening by another game, our Russian Preference, in which my accompanist and the young 'cellist travelling with us would join me. Sometimes Nicolai would make a fourth, when he was not himself consulting the cards to determine the state of his wife's health and whether she still loved him!

As the train crossed the desert, I remember that I fell to reciting poetry by the yard! Over and over again, my beloved Poushkin's verses about the steppes came into my mind.

So the time passed. As soon as the desert was left behind, the scenery again became interesting. I was enchanted with the orange groves, the luxurious vegetation and picturesque houses. Late on a warm, sunny afternoon we drew near to Los Angeles. The trip had been bearably cool, its only unpleasant feature, dust, which had sifted in through every crack, defying the paper bags provided by the railroad company for the protection of clothing. Of course, fur coats had been left aside, and no sooner had I stepped on to the platform at Los Angeles than I joyfully threw aside my overcoat.

A Russian friend, also a musician, for several years a resident of California, met us at the station with his open touring car. Soon we were whirling through the city on the way to a hotel on one of the suburban boulevards.

This hotel was the last word in modernity. Its accessories included shops, tennis courts, a golf course, swimming pool, and even a cafeteria. Its imposing foyer, decorated with flowers and palms, led on to a terrace, which in turn overlooked a charming garden. An exotic note was furnished, as we approached the office to register, by a young Chinese girl in native dress, who was rearranging disordered chairs and tables just vacated by various bridge parties.

A day or two after my arrival I accepted one of repeated invitations from one of the larger movie establishments to visit Hollywood. When I arrived at the studio, a ballroom scene was being "shot"—as they call it—and I spent some time watching the director's operations. Later, on a tour of inspection, I was fascinated by the elaborate "props." On one lot a circus tent had been reproduced. Camels, elephants, tightrope walkers, clowns, and jugglers were hanging about, waiting to be called into action. Only a few feet farther on, a Russian street with familiar-looking houses met my gaze. Only one more wish remained to be gratified— to pay a visit to that admirable artist, the immortal Charles.

I was told that this might easily be accomplished, and in a few minutes I was sending in my card by a bowing Japanese. Although busy on a set, Mr. Chaplin at once threw open the door of his studio. He did more. I told him of my desire to see him on the screen, which had hitherto been foiled. In every city on the tour, Chaplin pictures had either just closed prior to my arrival or were being announced for a date following my departure. What was my joy when Mr. Chaplin ordered "The Pilgrim" run off in his private theatre and sat beside me explaining through an interpreter the progress of the picture.

None of the disorder and confusion that necessarily reigned at the larger studio was in evidence at the Chaplin workshop. While Charlie completed a few directions on the set, Japanese servants bowed the way to his study, a delightful room, luxuriously furnished and filled with flowers, books, and photographs. Later we had some snapshots taken with members of his company.

Altogether this first visit to Hollywood was a delightful experience.

Soon after this I decided to look for an atmosphere less elaborate and more reposeful than that of the great hotel. Friends urged me to try Beverly Hills. There the hotel represented perfection in another form. Comfortable rooms looked out on a gorgeous natural setting, with noble mountains in the distance. If they wished, guests might occupy bungalows in the tropical garden, through which every morning, flitted soft-footed Japanese or Hawaiian waiters bearing breakfast trays. No bungalow was vacant when I arrived, so I found rooms in the hotel proper.

Beverly Hills was so beautiful that, many times each day, I exclaimed:

"This is Paradise!"

I felt that were I an American citizen this was the only spot in which I would choose to live!

One wish, however, remained unsatisfied—I wanted to see more Indians! Some one said there was an encampment not far from the hotel, and I immediately started off in that direction. I found, indeed, a wigwam or two in which crouched squaws with papooses, while several braves strolled about in full regalia of paint, blankets and feathers. I was almost thrilled, but romance fled when, upon my asking to take some photographs, a chief in gold spectacles replied in English much better than I could boast, that he would be pleased to permit this favour at so much per "shot!" It appeared that these particular descendants of the children of the plains were part of the "props" at a "movie" theatre in Hollywood, for the run of a Western picture! Looking at them, I remembered how I had lain awake, through long winter nights, far away in Russia, huddled on top of the stove, reading by the dim light of half-burned candles stuck in bottles, the adventures of the first American settlers with the Indians. I remembered with what pleasure and excitement I had pored over tales about the daring and terrible redskins, and it was a pleasure to see these savages without their enemies' scalps!

* * * * *

The nobility of California's scenery impressed me deeply. Again I felt the urge to express my feelings in verse. More than that, the beauties of California inspired me with an intense desire to compose a song! After working for days, I managed to write the following verses, which I later set to music. Here are the verses. I called them "Songs, My Songs!"

Songs, my songs. . . .
You are born in a heart that's o'erfilled—
You are sent me from Heav'n so high.
I'll sing till the day I die.
To all the world, birdlike, telling
Dreams that I would might come true . . .
Dreams of mine. . . .

Fly, fly, my songs, like birds of the air,
Bearing your message everywhere.
Fly far away like the nightingale.
I, too, would fly.

Songs there are that sadly sounding
Seem like sighs wrung from my heart.
Let them fly away like birds,
Like nightingales that trill so sweet,
Pouring forth with torrent power,
Yet bringing ease in saddest hour!
Songs, my songs.

Fly, fly, my songs, like birds of the air, etc.

Swift, aspiring, never tiring,
Wing your way unto my dearest,
There descending in her garden
On a bough of the laburnum,
On a spray of lilac hover,
Tell your message from her lover,
Songs, my songs.

Fly, fly, my songs, like birds of the air, etc.

Since I must die, I pray you then,
My songs, that you'll not leave me when
The churchyard bell for me shall sound;
Over fields and over valleys,
To and fro in forest alleys. . . .
Songs, my songs. . . .

*   *   *   *   *

I remember once singing at an afternoon concert in Boston
and, afterwards, being taken to see a Chinese theatre. Boston's Chinatown is unobtrusive. The theatre resembled an
ordinary dwelling house with darkened windows and a for-
bidding-looking door. Much ringing brought a responsive
clicking. Up one dark and narrow flight of stairs was a tiny
cubbyhole. This served as a box office. Another door, to
the left, led into the room where the play was going on.

Once inside its portals, the spectator was in Wonderland.
The room was large, with rows of chairs facing a stage.
On the left side sat the musicians, indulging at given intervals in the twanging of stringed instruments, the squeaking
of flutes, and the hollowness of thumped instruments of
percussion. These combined sounds represented the bedlam
recognised by Oriental ears as music.

On and off the stage, in various groupings, and in accordance with the action of the piece, wandered Chinese men and women. Their costumes were a wonder and delight. Gorgeous textures, rich colors, elaborate embroidery, the full panoply of fans, umbrellas, grotesque masks, and Oriental jewelry dazzled the eyes.

One or two of the girl actresses were beautiful and seductive in the extreme. Several of these were required to sing, which they did in a pinched, nasal manner. Others performed intricate dances. There were no programs, and no way of learning the portent of the tragedy on the stage was provided. Imagination was the only resource. But here, hidden away in an unfrequented street, was rare and exotic entertainment—a feast for the eye. The whole performance was so fascinating that I deeply regretted my ignorance of Chinese life and habits, and hence the utter inability to understand the psychology of the drama I was watching.

*   *   *   *   *

It is impossible, in so short a space, to do justice to so great and interesting a country as America. Some day I hope to devote an entire book to the United States. But as Christmas is here again, before taking leave of my readers for the present I will relate one more experience—my visit to Sing Sing prison on a certain Christmas Day.

I happened to be in New York as Christmas was approaching, and remembered that once in Moscow, during the revolution, I had sung for the inmates of a Russian prison. They were chiefly political offenders, not criminals. I remembered that my songs had seemed to bring them special joy. Having heard a great deal about the famous American prison at Ossining, I wondered if I might not be permitted to celebrate the day in a similar fashion. Learning of my desire, the warden offered me this opportunity.

As the motor sped up the Hudson, I felt myself facing a solemn occasion. It was bitterly cold. The skies were overcast and there were intermittent flurries of fine snow. I was reminded of those lines by the great French poet, Paul Verlaine:

Il pleur dans mon coeur
Comme il pleut sur la ville.

Why must human beings transgress the universal laws of human decency and mutual consideration, when such transgression means the loss of man's most precious possession— personal liberty? And is not that punishment the severest that could possibly be inflicted? Why should there exist in the world that form of premeditated murder, capital punishment?

So I mused sadly in my corner of the automobile.

Still greater oppression seized upon me as we came in sight of the grim, forbidding pile of stone beside the sullen river. As I stepped inside the outer office, I felt an ominous atmosphere. Suppose I myself were facing confinement? What if my own personal liberty were to be snatched from me? In those fifteen or twenty minutes before the concert began I went through in imagination all the feelings of one confronted with life imprisonment!

At last the heavy iron gateway at the entrance to the cell block was locked behind me and I was escorted to the great hall where I was to sing.

I looked at the sea of faces before me. Alas! that there should be so much evil in the world! How I pitied those who were paying the penalty for their own acts!

Never have I tried harder to give my best. My audience was wonderfully responsive and their applause touched me unspeakably. At the end of the program I spoke to the prisoners. I told them that Christ's ideal was forgiveness, that outside those huge dark walls were warm hearts beating for all those who had lost their liberty, and that I felt that all of us, good and bad, would one day find and embrace one another in green fields, beneath a shining sun!

When the prisoners had left the hall I was invited to make a tour of inspection.

Oh, my friends! No doubt all of you have seen and read that sign on the walls of universities, where accomplished professors give profound and clever lectures; in churches, where one is asked not to disturb the sacred ritual; or in theatres, where the audience is requested not to mar that special silence of actors—the pauses between lines of the dialogue—SILENCE! But do you appreciate the significance of this union of mute letters that form the word?

In the center of a small and humble room there is a common, well-worn armchair. It is here, in this room, that individuals, profoundly guilty of crime or perhaps the victims of tragic misjudgment, feel for the last time in their lives the solid comfort of such a chair—SILENCE!

I can well imagine how difficult it is for a strong, vigorous man, lately emerged the victor from a struggle with his peers in strength, to maintain this silence in the last moment before death. How hard to obey the sign posted at the entrance to this room—SILENCE.

I knew that several times during my stay in New York this silence had been broken by the crackling of an electric spark. I wished to hear this tiny sound defying the huge printed letters. But—I never dared. I think perhaps I was afraid to hear a superhuman cry of hatred against that word—SILENCE. I was afraid—and am still afraid to this day!

But I remember how an old man, with grey eyes and a gentle voice, no doubt the head of a patriarchal family, showed me that chair, that room, those benches for witnesses

—what a hard profession!—and the special refrigerator in the wall, with doors opening so easily on to metal shelves.

"Yes, sir," he said, in his gentle voice. "Sometimes we keep the body here until parents or friends come to claim it for burial, but more often we do the burying."

When I went from that room into the courtyard, for a second it seemed that I had lost my sense of direction!

"Straight ahead, sir! Straight ahead!" said our guide.

And I was so glad to follow this injunction, to go neither to the right nor to the left, but straight ahead to the door, to the gate, which locks in the living dead!

I cannot say what is right and what is wrong about all this, but one thing I may say:

"Brothers, people! Find a way so that it may always be possible to speak aloud, so that there may never be the need for that accursed sign—SILENCE!"

CHRISTMAS DAY, 1926.
NEW YORK CITY.

END